Laurie,

Thanks for your interest in this story. I'm proud to share it with a fellow teacher and a good friend.

Dan Bebah

The Animal Keepers

THE STORY OF AN UNLIKELY HERO AND AN UNFORGETTABLE SEASON

The Animal Keepers

The Story of an Unlikely Hero and an Unforgettable Season

By

Donn Behnke

ISBN: 978-1-940056-31-9

This book is available in quantity at special discounts for your group or organization. For further information, contact:

3340 Whiting Avenue, Suite 5
Stevens Point, WI 54481
(800) 697-3756
Fax: (715) 344-2668

Book Layout and Design: Nicky Brillowski

Photos courtesy of Donn Behnke, Glenn Behnke, Dale Hanson, Keith Hyland, Don Ceplina and Stevens Point Area Senior High

Printed in the United States

TABLE OF CONTENTS

To Scott: the mysterious, scruffy, misfit who crossed our path for a few short months in 1985. Your child-like joy, contagious enthusiasm, and never ending optimism pushed us to more fully appreciate the good things in our lives, no matter how small.

And to all of the runners I've coached at Stevens Point Area Senior High, from the guys that helped start the program back in the '70's to the young men on the team today. Together we built something to be proud of.

ACKNOWLEDGEMENTS

I have no particular skill for putting words on a page, no formal training in the art of writing, and until recently very little interest in becoming an author. However, *The Animal Keepers* is a story that demanded to be told; a book that needed to be written. For nearly 30 years I mulled it over in my mind, jotted down notes, and organized a couple of file folders but most of all I procrastinated as friends, family members, and co-workers asked, "When are you going to write that book?" Someday, was my standard answer, someday when I have the time, maybe when I retire.

There are a number of other people I'd like to thank for their support along the way as I worked on this project beginning with my friends and fellow teachers in the Social Studies Department at P.J. Jacobs Junior High for their years of encouragement and my retirement gift, a book titled *Write that book Already!* Thanks to the P.J.'s retired teachers breakfast club, our neighbors the Menzels, and my close friends Gloudemans and Rath for the many hours they spent listening to me and their endless, and best of all free, advice.

I'd like to thank authors Roy Benson, Hal Higdon, and Chris Lear for allowing me to contact them and for their frank, honest advice about the challenges of getting my work published.

To Pete Clark of KCI Publishing for taking the time to read the story, agreeing to publish it, and helping to produce a final product that I'm very proud of.

Writing, like running, is an individual effort but I can't imagine anyone becoming good at either without a fair amount of help and support from others along the way. In my case I have no doubt that the guidance provided by my teachers and coaches had a profound and lasting effect on me throughout my career as an educator. In particular, Leo Potochnik, my coach at Milwaukee Marshall High School, stands out as one of the most positive influences in my life and the best role model any young man could have hoped for.

I'd also like to thank my father Roger who seldom missed a meet, mother Jean who encouraged me to give college a try, brother Glenn who paved the way for me in running and coaching (and is still the NCAA DIII national record holder at 6 miles), and my sister Lynn who was always there for me, helpful, caring, and supportive no matter what. We may not have been a perfect family but I know that I am extremely fortunate to have grown up among such good, generous people and I can't imagine where I'd be without them.

And finally, I'd like to thank the only two people in the world who know and love this story as well as I do, my wife Cheryl and my daughter Beth. Together we share a life surrounded by runners, immersed in a sport that concludes with a state meet in early November and yet, somehow, never really seems to end. They are my biggest fans, my support system, my sounding board, and my compass when I stray off course. I can't begin to express how much I love them, how important they are to me, and how important they have been to this project.

Cheryl was the first to suggest I write this story and she never stopped believing that I would. Like the elementary school teacher she is she offered her assistance, constant encouragement, and best of all the positive feedback that helped me believe that I could actually become a writer. Beth, on the other hand, supplied me with the technical advice I so desperately needed. Her writing skills, attention to detail, and sound advice were invaluable to me along the way and I know that her influence is reflected on every page of this story. So thanks Cheryl and Beth, I know that I could never have done this without you. Ultimately this is not just my book, it's our book.

The Animal Keepers is a story I am happy to have published. I'm proud of the effort I put into it and thankful for all the people who played a part in it. It was, just like the '85 season, a team effort.

FOREWORD
BY CHRIS SOLINSKY

Chris Solinsky is a 2003 graduate of Stevens Point Area Senior High and an alumni of the SPASH cross country program. He was an eight time Wisconsin state champion in cross country and track as well as the 2002 Foot Locker national high school cross country champion. After high school Chris had a stellar college career at the University of Wisconsin where he was a 14 time NCAA Division I All-American and won five national titles in track. He went on to run professionally, competing at the 2009 World Championships where he finished 12th in the 5,000. Chris became the first non-African distance runner to break 27:00 for 10,000 meters and is a former American Record holder in that event with a time of 26:59.60. His 5,000 meter personal best is 12:55.53.

I grew up in Stevens Point, Wisconsin in a family with strong ties to the cross country and track programs at SPASH. My parents had a wide range of running stories to tell. My father told me about running with Keith Hanson, the freshman who was so small and wheezed so loud on runs that no one wanted to run next to him, who went on to become an NCAA champion athlete. My mother shared stories about running with Suzy Favor, the young talent who showed amazing gifts early in a career that lead to her making three U.S. Olympic teams. Not to mention their stories of the many state championship team titles won under the watchful eye of the tall, sometimes intimidating to middle-schoolers, but always tender hearted Donn Behnke.

I was reluctant to try cross country at first, even with the success of the team and my parents praise for Donn. I was one of the kids who played the "S-word" (soccer) and only ran as long as it took me to chase down the ball. The summer before my 8th grade year I got a letter in the mail from Donn asking if I had any interest in following in my parents' footsteps as a runner. I was flattered, but defiant. I ended up promising my parents that I would give cross country a two week try and if I still didn't like it after that I could go back to soccer.

The morning of my first day of practice I was in tears. It was raining and this man that I barely knew was going to make me go out and run in it. The *nerve*! I got to practice and sat against the wall alone, not really knowing anyone and not making much of an effort to try to meet people. I was determined to put in my time and get back to my friends on the soccer team. Then two things happened that, like dominos tipping over, made me slowly begin to let my walls down and maybe give this running thing a try. The first was when the captain of the team, Dave Cisewski, approached me to tell me how excited he and others were for me to come out for the team and how they looked forward to the year. The second was that Donn, as he often does, broke into one of his elaborate stories about teams and individuals of the past. That was it, I was hooked. The detail of the stories and how well he remembered every interaction as if it happened the moment before kept me hanging on every word. All the success that he was able to foster and encourage regardless of anyone's background, social hierarchy, or body type was inspiring. I knew I wanted to have that same success and be among the stories he told to his runners years later.

Through the years I have heard stories about "The Animal" many times and am always amazed by the things he went through, the success he was able to achieve, and the accomplishments of that 1985 team that went from a rebuilding year to something special. The first time I heard this story I knew I was a part of a group of people destined for great things led by one of the most unassuming yet caring, nurturing individuals a young man could ask for. I am proud to say Donn was not only my coach, but someone I consider a second father.

What unfolds in the pages to come will bring you on the roller coaster of emotions that the young men of that 1985 team rode all season long. You don't have to be from Stevens Point or have run for SPASH to relate to this story. If you like a story about a group of ragtag kids from all backgrounds that are united for a greater cause and empowered along the way by an unexpected strength you will love this book.

Reading the story you feel like you were on that team and can feel the emotion as Donn tells one of his greatest stories about our beloved SPASH cross country program. You can hear Donn's voice as you turn the pages with his dry humor and always present realism in lieu of optimism. Many legends have sat in the far corner of that field house, but Scott Longley remains one of the largest. What he did for the team and what the team did for him is a true testament to the town of Stevens Point, to the members of the SPASH cross country team, and especially to the man and mentor that is Donn Behnke. This story is a perfect representation of the tradition of SPASH cross country.

INTRODUCTION

I began my coaching career in the spring of 1977 when a friend suggested I apply for a job as an assistant track coach at Stevens Point Area Senior High School. Lured by the prospect of making an easy four hundred bucks I accepted the position and found myself suddenly surrounded by the oddest, most likeable group of young men I'd ever met. Right out of college, it was an ideal place to test my coaching philosophy and take on the challenge of molding young people into good runners, good teammates, and good people. Sure, I wanted to coach guys with great talent, but I was determined to coach the average and even below average runners with equal enthusiasm. I wanted to be the kind of coach who did his best to advise and encourage all of his athletes, regardless of ability. My runners would pound out lots of miles and they'd have to make a commitment to our sport, but anyone who ran, walked, or stumbled through the fieldhouse doors on the first day of practice would be welcomed onto our team without exception.

This philosophy of inclusion has been well tested. Early in my coaching career I watched a scrawny, anemic freshman, through sheer force of will, turn himself into an outstanding runner. On his first day of practice I'd run at his side as he wheezed, gasped, and staggered his way through a three mile run. Four years later he was a state champion, a Foot Locker finalist, and an 8:56 two-miler. At Marquette University he earned All-American honors and capped off a great collegiate career with a national title at 10,000 meters. The Keith Hanson story is the kind of "anyone can do it" tale every coach needs to have in his collection. It has a clear message, it's inspirational, and it's fun to tell. It was my favorite coaching story until the fall of 1985, when a young man named Scott Longley decided to become a cross country runner. He was a big, awkward kid from the special education classroom and I'll admit, I wasn't exactly thrilled to have him join us at first. I gave him a chance though, simply because on our team everyone was given a chance. Everyone.

The Animal Keepers is the story of a high school cross country team, their coach, and a special young man who forced his way onto the team and into the hearts of all who got to know him. Like a force of nature he unleashed his boundless enthusiasm and infectious optimism onto his unsuspecting teammates and together they somehow managed to turn a quiet "rebuilding year" into something truly memorable. For those of us lucky enough to have been along for the ride, it was a season filled with indelible memories and lessons none of us ever expected to learn at cross country practice. "Someday I'm going to write a book about this," I remember saying... and so, here it is, a mere 30 years later, my favorite coaching story.

ONE

TRACK PRACTICE

F ive minutes, guys! We start in five minutes!" I announced loudly, doing my best to be heard in a field house filled with noisy high school track athletes anxious to begin the first practice of a new season. Standing on the green tartan surface of our indoor twelve-lap track with clipboard in hand, I watched with interest as guys of all shapes and sizes filed in from the locker room. "Gotcha! You're it!" one of them screamed after firing a tennis ball squarely into the back of another at close range. Tennis ball tag was one of the many improvised games our track and cross country guys liked to play as they burned off a little excess energy before the start of practice. It kept them occupied and since none of them had, to this point, figured out a way to seriously hurt anyone with a tennis ball, I saw no need to ban the activity.

Surrounded by several small groups of upperclassmen engaged in calm, possibly even thoughtful, conversation, I did my best to take an approximate head-count as our younger guys raced about.

"Looks like we're gonna be well over a hundred," I said to several of those standing nearby.

"Really?" asked Jim, our star pole vaulter. "How can you tell?"

"Counted all the arms and legs and divided by four," I answered with a smile while raising my arm to check my watch. "One minute! Get ready guys!"

At my command 108 guys formed 10 wavy lines while team captains led a series of simple stretches. The first practice of the 1985 season had begun. Wading among the masses, I began the challenging job of taking attendance in our crowded, noisy field house. As a former high school and collegiate distance runner, personally, I considered stretching to be a waste of time, but the guys seemed to enjoy the process. It's not difficult and most of them knew that it afforded them an excellent opportunity to watch the girls' team stretching on the other side of the gym.

With attendance complete, I set my clipboard down and began to circulate among the nearly thirty distance runners in my charge. Happy and excited, they'd looked forward to this day since the end of our cross country season. After finishing one heartbreaking point short of a state title, they were anxious to put the disappointment of last fall behind them and move on to the challenge of track. As with most serious distance runners, motivation was not a problem for "my guys." Unlike most of the young men sprawled across the field house floor, they'd done their off season training. They were ready.

With a mop of tightly-curled hair piled atop his head, Mike Monk was hard to miss. Positioned front and center, he attacked each stretch with a level of focus and determination rare among high school athletes. Short and stocky, he made up for his physical limitations with intensity and strength of character. Mike was all about attitude. He expected to be good at everything and let nothing stand in his way as he pursued his goals. Already a great student and the best musician in our school, he had somehow, through sheer force of will, turned himself into one of the best distance runners in Wisconsin. After a 13th place finish at the state cross country meet as a junior, he had his sights set on an individual title next fall. With incredible drive and desire, Mike was the perfect kid to build a team around. I only wished I had a few more just like him.

Next to Mike was C.J. Hanson. Tall, scrawny, and inflexible, C.J. was the least athletic kid on the team. Sporting a long, unruly mullet, C.J., like many highly intelligent people, marched to a different beat. The fact that he grew up in the shadow of his brother Keith, a state cross country champion, Foot Locker national finalist, and Division I All-American, didn't faze him. C.J. was his own person, did things his own way, and never let his big brother's success become a burden. Clumsy, awkward, and slow-footed, he was definitely better suited for the longer distance and slower pace of cross country. C.J., now a junior, thought of track season as a time to improve his form, strength, and speed as he slowly and steadily evolved into a good high school distance runner. He was definitely a work in progress.

Curt Clausen sat one row over. Tall, blonde, and athletic, he was always easy to find. Blessed with a combination of intelligence and social skills rare among most high school juniors, Curt was a natural leader. A key member of our program, he was a talented runner who'd recently discovered race walking. Already among the best young walkers in the nation, Curt had big dreams, Olympic dreams, and he was determined to follow them. After a great season of cross country, he planned to use track to lay the foundation for a series of national race walking competitions he had lined up over the summer.

John Ceplina was next in the row. Among the distance runners he was the misfit. Athletic, muscular, and fast, he wasn't like the rest of our guys. He'd grown up playing football, basketball, and baseball before somehow taking a detour and ending up with us. An athlete with the rare combination of strength and speed, he could run any event and run it well. As the football coaches puzzled over the defection of their star sophomore quarterback, I made plans to move him from the sprints to the half-mile. John was unlike any athlete I'd ever worked with. I was happy to have him in our group and looking forward to the challenge of turning him into a distance runner.

Kim Lasecki, or Bones as he was known by his teammates, had the kind of physique normally found only in third world refugee camps. With a light frame, long skinny legs, and an efficient stride, Kim was a gifted runner. He knew from an early age he wanted to be good at this and having watched the older guys on our team train, he knew just how to do it. He ran twice a day, every day, in any weather as he racked up fifteen mile days and hundred mile weeks. Determined to be our next great runner, his dedication bordered on compulsive and even among distance runners his level of commitment was unusual. Anxious to make the most of his final high school track season, he'd done an incredible amount of winter running. He was ready, maybe too ready, I thought to myself as I watched him lead stretches from the front of the group. Outsiders thought he won races with talent, but I knew differently. Kim won because he worked hard. He simply ran more miles than most of his opponents ever thought of running. Among the top few runners in the state, he was the lead dog in our pack and we all knew it.

Positioned a few steps to Kim's right was Rob Sparhawk, our most unlikely distance runner. Growing up racing snowmobiles, dirt bikes, and anything else with a motor, Rob had developed a love of racing and a passion for winning. At his first 7th grade track meet he asked to run the two mile, but was turned away by a cranky old track coach who told him "track meets don't last that long." It was the kind of comment that in other cases might elicit a phone call from an angry parent, but Rob took it in stride. This was the story of his life. The ultimate underdog, Rob was the kind of kid people always seemed to sell short. But insults didn't bother Rob; he used them, like all good athletes do, as a source of motivation. Now in his final season, Rob had, against all odds, made himself into an elite runner and more importantly a leader who would do anything for his team and his teammates.

"Coach!" someone yelled loudly from the far corner of the room in an attempt to gain my attention. "Hey Coach!"

Jerry, our somewhat eccentric Phys. Ed. teacher, was headed my way through the sea of prospective track athletes dressed in the uniform of the day, gray cotton shorts and gray cotton t-shirts with a red winged foot and Stevens Point High School

Track printed across the front. With his right hand attached firmly to the arm of a young man who had the look of a child being dragged to the dentist's office, Jerry charged in my direction, grinning happily.

"Coach Behnke!" he called out, waving a hand in the air. "Look what I found!"

Sizing up the situation with a quick glance, I knew that the disheveled figure to Jerry's left was no ordinary student. In an instant, I could tell that this was a person with special needs. Tall with thick, heavy eyebrows, a haystack of wavy, unruly brown hair, and a chin covered with scruffy whiskers, he seemed like a kid in desperate need of a shave, a haircut, and a good long shower. Dressed in his wrinkled Phys. Ed. class uniform everything, including his well-worn Converse All-Stars, looked to be at least one size too small and just a little bit dirty. Wagging his head side to side as he approached, his awkward movements reminded me of an oversized puppy.

With nine years of coaching experience behind me, I knew immediately what was about to happen. I'd been through it before. A well-meaning faculty member, in this case Jerry, had found someone he felt would benefit from being part of a team. Thinking something along the lines of "here's a kid with some problems, maybe you can fix him," he showed up, out of the blue, at our first practice. It's a compliment of sorts given to coaches willing to work with anyone possessing enough athleticism to successfully find his way down the hallway and into the field house in time for practice. In a no-cut sport like track and field, where opportunities to participate are almost limitless and junior varsity meets give even the least athletic a chance to compete, virtually anyone can find a place to fit in. Track coaches, always in search of the next "diamond in the rough," seldom turn anyone away. But in my case, heavily outnumbered as I waited for my assistant coaches to arrive, I was not at all excited to see Jerry and his misfit friend headed in my direction.

Great! I thought to myself as I stood motionless, trying not to look too annoyed. Just what I need, another project, another kid to supervise, another potential problem, and to top it off he doesn't even look athletic.

"Coach," said Jerry cheerfully, "this is Scott. He likes to run. He'd like to be a distance runner."

"Oh really?" I said, extending my hand as I sized him up at close range. "Nice to meet you, Scott."

Who was I kidding, I thought to myself. Clearly this kid was being dumped on me, and I was determined to have no part of it. If Jerry wanted to do a little social work that was fine with me, but my list of responsibilities was already too long. It was nothing personal, I had nothing against Scott, but I wanted to coach, not baby-sit, and from the looks of this kid, managing him was going to be a full time job.

"So, you want to be a distance runner?" I asked somewhat harshly, in a voice designed to sound a little unfriendly.

"Yeah," he replied with a wide, toothy grin while nodding his head vigorously.

"Have you ever done any running?"

"Yes he has," Jerry said, jumping in quickly. "He leads the 5-minute warm-up run every day, third hour, and boy can he run."

Searching for a way out, I played my next card. "Well, that's all very nice, but he'll need to have a physical before I can let him practice. Scott, do you have a physical card on file?" I asked, assuming he didn't.

"Yep, he had a physical last week. It's all taken care of," Jerry assured me.

"How about the insurance form, the emergency card, the athletic code?" I asked, searching for another excuse to send him on his way.

"All done, turned them all in to the south office yesterday. He's all set."

"Equipment? Do you have sweats? It's pretty cold out there, you'll need sweats."

"Got it. He's got 'em in his gym locker," Jerry explained,

placing his hands on the back of Scott's shoulders while gently moving him in my direction.

"Well, Scott, looks like you're on the team," I said, lifting my clipboard with a sigh. "I'll put your name on the roster...oh yeah, I didn't get your last name."

"Longley, L-O-N-G-L-E-Y," he announced proudly, spelling it out as a broad smile spread across his face. "Scott Longley."

"Okay Scott, come with me," I ordered as I started off in the direction of Rob and Kim, two of my senior captains.

"Guys, this is Scott. He's going to run with us today."

"Scott! I didn't know you were a runner," said Rob, sounding somewhat shocked as he reached out to shake Scott's hand.

It made perfect sense I realized immediately. Even in a school of nearly 3,000 students, Rob knew everybody, the jocks, nerds, popular kids, rednecks, and even misfits like Scott. Always the first guys I looked to when I needed help, Rob and Kim were perfect for this assignment. Seeing no reason to waste any of my valuable coaching time with the new kid from third hour Phys. Ed. I placed him in the capable hands of my team leaders with instructions to "keep an eye on Scott" before quickly turning away. If Jerry thought he could pull me into his little social experiment, he was mistaken. I had no intention of getting involved with this new kid.

"Pay attention, Scott!" Rob shouted, doing his best to supervise our new addition as Scott joined the others stretching. With next to no flexibility, Scott struggled to follow along.

"NO! Scott, do it this way," Kim ordered while showing the proper way to do a hurdler stretch. Distracted by the activity around him, Scott was constantly off task.

"Hey! Stop screwin' around and pay attention," Rob demanded while reaching out to poke him on the shoulder. "I'm serious... stop screwin' around!"

It was instantly apparent that there was a natural connection between Rob and Scott. As our other runners looked on cautiously, not quite sure what to make of their new teammate,

Rob stepped up and took control. It all made sense. Rob and Scott both had learning disabilities and spent all or part of their school day in the classroom for students with special needs. A classic hands-on learner, Rob needed more activity than what was offered in a traditional classroom; he needed to move. With a natural talent for finding the path of least resistance, he became a master at working the system and concocting ways to get out of class. His learning disability had become his ticket to special treatment by the school staff, and his friendly, outgoing personality made people want to help him. Like Tom Sawyer, he had a knack for getting others to do his work and a way of making them feel good about doing it. Quick to volunteer for any errand that got him out of the classroom, Rob spent much of the school day wandering the hallways, linking one mission to the next, and beating the system. Scott had no way of knowing it, but today he'd met his match. His excuses for off-task behavior might fool some of his teachers, but they wouldn't work with Rob. Rob not only knew every trick in the book, he'd written the book, and knowing Rob, he'd probably convinced someone to write it for him.

"Alright guys," I shouted as our stretching session came to an end, "bring it in."

Surrounded by a sea of sweaty athletes seated on the floor, I read a series of announcements from the list on my clipboard before splitting the team into smaller, event-specific groups. As if drawn by some strange magnetic force, the distance guys headed immediately towards the northeast corner of the field house to pull on their sweats and ready themselves for a run in an early March snow storm. This was our little corner of the world, a few square yards of green rubberized tartan surface beneath the track record board just outside the locker room door. Each fall, winter, and spring for the last eight years, this is where we met, almost unnoticed, as we went about the task of producing successful track and cross country teams. On a shoestring budget with precious little support from school administration, our program had produced three state cross country team titles and two runner-up finishes in the last five years. We had no need for fancy, expensive facilities, just a tiny bit of floor space, a place for our eclectic group to meet before and after each workout. From here we would launch our attack on the narrow country roads north of town as we hammered out mileage and built the strength needed to compete with the best teams in Wisconsin. Anxious to get out the door, the guys milled about in nervous anticipation, knowing the hard work of a new season was about to begin.

"Bring it in guys," I said sternly, "let's go, hustle up, we need to get moving. LISTEN UP!" I shouted, using my deepest, most authoritative, "coach's voice." "The route for today is Double DuBay. I want you to do the seven or nine mile loop, but if you sat on your butt all winter you can do one of the shorter routes. Remember, sit-ups, push-ups, stretching, and check in with me when you get back. Let's keep the pace nice and easy for the first mile or so. There's a lot of snow out there so be careful, watch for cars, stay on the left side of the road, and try to run with a buddy, okay?" I ordered seriously while trying my best to make eye contact with each member of the group. "Oh yeah, and one last thing," I said, reaching out to tap our newest addition on the top of his head. "We have a new guy on the team. His name is Scott... Scott Longley."

Instantly a loud cheer and a burst of applause erupted from the group, making Scott suddenly the center of attention, something he clearly enjoyed. Smiling happily in the middle of the group, he had no way of knowing that this was how our guys reacted any time I announced the addition of a new member. Keeping their distance while donning hats and gloves on the way down the short hallway, Scott's new teammates studied him carefully, not quite sure what to make of him.

Happily, like kids turned loose at recess, we made our escape out the school's side door. Engulfed by huge swirling snowflakes, we headed across the snow covered parking lot. Several inches had accumulated already, but it was light, fluffy and easy to run on. One of life's great gifts, a snowstorm combines beauty with a little bit of danger, and today it gave our run a sense of adventure as we trotted off school property and headed west into the wind down Northpoint Drive.

Amid the loud banter and excitement, Scott somehow found himself at the center of our slow moving group. People in passing cars gave glares of disapproval as they grudgingly gave up a few feet of the roadway and wondered what possessed us to be out on a day like this and why in the world we seemed so happy about it. Like a mass prison break, our tightly packed group pushed forward against the wind to the sound of fresh snow crunching beneath our feet and the swoosh, swoosh, swoosh of C.J.'s nylon running suit.

The start of a run is always fun and full of energy. Everyone feels fresh, alive, and comfortable with the easy pace. We know this will change as the miles go by and the pace quickens, the pack thins, and conversation is replaced by discomfort, but for now we all enjoyed the feelings of unity and security that come with being part of a group.

With Scott positioned two steps ahead of me, I noticed his long powerful stride and pronounced forward lean. Small chunks of packed snow flew from the soles of his shoes and spun through the air before bouncing off of my gray sweats. His arms flailed about with elbows in tight to his body and his unusually large hands swinging wildly across his chest. With head high and his prominent chin leading the way, Scott smiled happily. Like a little boy allowed to tag along with his big brothers, he loped down the narrow, steeply crowned road head swiveling side to side in an effort to take in everything going on around him. Perhaps, I thought as I studied his movements, my assessment of Scott had been too harsh, too hasty. Less than a mile into the run I began to consider that perhaps Jerry was right about him; maybe this kid from third hour Phys. Ed. deserved a chance.

"Settle down guys, just relax," I shouted ahead as some at the front of our group, anxious to show off their level of fitness, began to push the pace. Our tightly knit pack began to string out as we turned onto Old Wausau Road, and conversation all but ended. The mood in the pack suddenly became more serious and as often happens on the first day of practice, our workout was beginning to take on the feel of a race. With Rob, our most famous "half-stepper," and Kim at the lead, we charged into the near white-out conditions heading north on the snow covered desolate stretch of road along the banks of the mighty Wisconsin River. Determined to establish their place on the team, our leaders edged the pace ever faster, testing themselves and those around them while stragglers, fearing the possibility of being lost in the blizzard, did their best to keep the group in sight.

With my attention focused on the sounds of those around me and the feeling of snowflakes as they hit and quickly melted on my cheeks, I settled comfortably, happily, onto the back end of the group. It felt good to get moving. I enjoyed teaching, but at the end of the day I needed to get away from my desk, out the door, into whatever Mother Nature had to offer and run. Flying down a narrow country road in a snow storm surrounded by serious runners was just what I needed.

The sky seemed to darken as a strong west wind drove large, sticky flakes into our faces. Finding the edge of the road became increasingly difficult as we paralleled a mile wide section of the partially iced-over river. Slowing briefly as we made the turn onto DuBay Avenue, I looked back down the road to survey the picket line of gray clad runners following along behind, hoping we hadn't lost anyone yet. In another mile I'd drop back and check on them, but right now, with the wind at my back, I put the problems of the day aside and enjoyed the moment.

"Good job guys!" I shouted as we neared the turn onto Second Street. "I've gotta check on the rest of the guys. Just keep it even…don't get carried away…don't be stupid!" I warned while stopping to reverse my direction.

"Keep it going guys!" I said, clapping my wet cotton gloves

together as the chase pack ran past. "Good job! Nice work!" I repeated over and over while straining to pick out the vague shadowy figures as they emerged from the curtain of driven snow.

"Alright, Scott!" I called out enthusiastically. "How you doin'?"

"I'm okay, Coach," he answered with a slight smile, "but… HOW MUCH FARTHER?"

"Well, if you turn right on Second Street you're about a mile from school."

"That's five miles?" he asked, sounding surprised.

"No, that's three and a half. The five mile loop goes over the overpass and down to the next crossroad."

"Coach," Scott said confidently as he picked up the pace slightly, "I'm gonna run five miles today."

"Really? Are you sure you're ready for that?" I asked seriously.

"Rob said I have to. Rob said only leakers run the three mile loop."

"Yeah, that sounds like Rob, but you don't have to go five. Rob's been a runner for six years. You've only been a runner for about an hour."

"No Coach," he said correcting me. "I run every day. I run a lot."

"I know Scott, but five minutes at the start of gym class isn't exactly a lot of running."

"No Coach," he said holding up his right hand to show me three fingers. "I've run the Special Olympics three years in a row."

"Really!" I said, trying to hide my shock at learning that I was now coaching a Special Olympian. "Well, good for you, Scott."

"Yeah Coach, and when I run the mile, I win. Coach, nobody can beat me."

"That's good Scott," I said as we ran the long gentle downhill of the overpass that took us to the second section of DuBay Avenue, committing to the five mile loop. "But you're running with the big boys now. Rob, Kim, and Mike are some of the best runners in the state. Let's just get you through five miles today, okay?"

"Okay Coach," he said, reaching his left hand up for a high-five. "It's a deal."

Over the course of the next few miles as we made our way back to school, I did my best to get to know Scott. Asking all the standard questions about school, favorite classes, and teachers, I listened carefully to his answers as I evaluated his cognitive and social skills. Normally as I try to get to know a kid I ask a few ridiculous questions like "So, can you hot wire a car?" or "Done any jail time?" but unsure that he would catch the humor, I moved on to questions about his family.

"So, Scott, where do you live? Got any brothers and sisters? Where do your parents work?"

"Coach," he said, casting his eyes to the snowy surface of Reserve Street as his voice acquired a serious tone, "I don't live with my parents. I live in a group home in Plover."

Embarrassed that my persistent questioning had hit a nerve, I quickly changed the subject to something safe and easy, sports.

"So, are you a Brewers fan?"

"Yeah Coach, I like the Brewers and the Packers and the Bucks, but wrestling's my favorite. I LOVE wrestling and Hulk Hogan…The Hulk. OH YEAH!"

There were no lulls in the conversation as we finished the last portion of our snowy run. If I ever needed to get him talking all I had to do was mention wrestling. Clearly Scott was an authority on anything and everything having to do with the absurd "sport" known as professional wrestling, and he seemed to have an advanced case of "Hulkamania."

Kicking the snow from our shoes outside the back door, we entered the locker room and made our way to the field house. Standing carefully on a large gray floor mat, I watched the swirl of activity in front of me as I peeled off my wet, heavy sweats.

"So, what did you think of your first practice?" I asked, still trying to get a handle on the nature of Scott's disabilities.

"Good Coach, but, boy am I tired! Coach, how far did those other guys run?"

"Those guys ran five," I said pointing to the small group stretching nearby, "but the others all went seven or nine."

"MILES! They ran nine miles? That's craaaaaaazzy, those guys must be nuts!"

"Yeah they are. Who else would think that running nine miles in a blizzard is actually fun? Now go stretch while I check on the rest of these guys."

Turning my attention away from Scott, I watched proudly as snow covered runners straggled into the field house and headed my way. The first run of the season had gone pretty well. The majority of the guys had taken the long route and, as far as I could tell, we hadn't lost or injured anyone. Taking a knee among the rabble of assorted runners stretching between the wet spots in our little corner of the world, I began the process of assessing how each of my guys had handled the workout.

"What's next Coach?" Scott asked, interrupting my conversation.

"Sit ups, pushups, stretches?" I asked.

"Yep, did 'em all, Coach."

"Great!" I said, rising to my feet and placing my hands on his broad, bony shoulders. "Scott, you had a really good first practice. You're gonna have a little muscle soreness tomorrow, but that's all a part of getting in shape," I explained while turning him toward the locker room and delivering a firm pat to the middle of his back. "You're done for today. Go get changed, eat a good meal, and get a good night's sleep. Tomorrow we'll do some interval training."

"What's that?" he asked, looking back at me with a puzzled expression.

"I'll explain tomorrow," I said with a nod as I watched him turn away. "Hey Scott!" I shouted to gain his attention one last time. "Welcome to the team. I'll see you tomorrow."

"Thanks Coach, see ya tomorrow."

Saddened by the thought of a seventeen year old without a family to go home to, I paused for a moment and watched as he walked off. An hour ago I tried to get rid of this misfit from third hour Phys. Ed., but strangely my attitude had changed. I'd invested an hour in this kid, I'd run a few miles with him, and suddenly he was one of "my guys." It would be no great loss if he didn't return, but I was hoping he would.

TWO

HEY ANIMAL

Armed with an updated team roster and a handful of completed forms, I left the coaches' locker room and jogged quickly down the main hallway toward the athletic office in search of Mr. Anderson. Andy, as most people knew him, was seated at a large gray steel desk in his cluttered office a few feet from the lunch room.

"Come on in, Donn," he invited as I leaned through the doorway. "How was your first practice? What do your numbers look like?"

"Good, really good," I answered. "We have over a hundred guys and we should add a few more when basketball ends. I think it's going to be a really good year for us."

"Good to hear," he said. "Now what can I do for you?"

As an assistant principal and athletic director, LeRoy "Andy" Anderson was respected and well-liked by all who knew him. Like his idol Vince Lombardi, he saw sports as a vehicle for developing character and had little patience with coaches who didn't share his point of view. Nearing the end of his long career as an educator, he was an excellent resource and role model for young staff members like me. Unfortunately, growing up at a time when high school sports meant football, basketball, and baseball, he was a little slow to adjust to some of the "minor sports" and the fairly recent development of girls' athletics. Andy and I had a good relationship, but with little background in cross country or track, he sometimes had difficulty grasping the concept of distance running. To a former football coach, the fact that a person could run ten miles, let alone wanted to, seemed an absolute mystery.

"Well," I said, pausing for a second as I pulled up a chair and set my clipboard on the corner of his desk. "I'm not sure what to do with this one. There's this new kid on the team, a special education kid, and I don't really know what his deal is. I just... I've never worked with anyone quite like him and...well, I don't know if he'll even show up again, but if he does I should probably know something about him. I just don't know where to begin."

"What's his name?" Andy asked.

"Scott Longley. I'm pretty sure he's a junior."

"Oh sure," said Andy with a nod and a smile. "I know Scott. He and Eric are friends." Eric, Andy's youngest child, had some of the same learning disabilities as Scott, and it turned out that they spent the majority of their days together in the same classroom. "Scott's pretty new here so I don't really know that much about him, but I think it's a fairly complicated case so I'm going to send you over to Ramone. He should be able to give you what you need."

Ramone Stade was a friend and former social studies teacher who'd moved up the ranks to become an assistant principal. Good with students and staff members alike, he was the type of guy you could always count on to know the answer or find one and get back to you promptly. As I poked my head through the doorway of his office, Ramone looked up from a stack of papers and stroked his short beard with one hand as he motioned me forward with the other.

"This won't take long," I said apologetically. "I'm just wondering if you know anything about a kid named Scott Longley. He joined the track team last night and I'd like to get some background on him."

"Well, I know a little about him, but give me a minute," he said, standing abruptly and stepping quickly into the outer office. "Here we go," he said, setting a thick file folder in the middle of his desk as he sat back down. Spilling it open, Ramone studied the contents for a few minutes as his face took on a look of deep concern. Looking up he asked somberly, "What is it you'd like to know?"

"Well, Scott seems like a nice enough kid, but at this point all I know is he has some learning difficulties and he told me he lives in something called a group home. So, I guess I'm just hoping you could explain some of that to me."

Scanning another page Ramone explained that Scott had been taken from his parents at an early age as a result of an abusive situation. Due to confidentiality issues he could tell me little else, other than describing some of the incidents listed in the file as "very serious and disturbing." A group home, he explained, was a facility run by the state where young men like Scott were cared for and supervised by social workers. Ramone said that in his experience these places offered a highly structured environment with very strict behavior modification plans, which was likely a good fit for those with behavioral issues like Scott. Paging further into the file he observed that Scott had been bounced around the state of Wisconsin quite a bit since being taken from his parents and that he was classified as learning disabled, emotionally and behaviorally disturbed, attention deficit, and hyperactive with a number of physical disabilities mixed in. The combination of L.D., E.B.D., and A.D.H.D. made Scott what some in education like to call an "alphabet soup" kid.

The file noted that teachers, counselors, and social workers described Scott as friendly and likeable with fairly good social skills. He fit in well with classmates and loved to get attention from adults. Many noted his strong memory skills, specifically his ability to remember names, numbers, facts, and just about anything pertaining to sports. Everyone, it seemed, knew that Scott was crazy about sports and obsessed with professional wrestling and in particular Hulk Hogan. Ramone summarized his grades as "pretty good" and best of all, the file made few mentions of disciplinary problems so apparently Scott knew how to follow rules and behave himself around school.

The biggest negative in the file centered on the fact that Scott seemed to have a rather loose grasp on reality. Teachers and supervisors noted numerous examples of his "tall tales" and times they had caught him "stretching the truth." Creating stories of places he'd been, things he'd done, and people he'd met, Scott seemed to have a talent for making things up in an effort to gain attention.

Realizing I'd already stayed too long, I thanked Ramone for his time and hustled down the hallway. I had only a few minutes to get to the field house before the first athletes would arrive, and leaving teenage boys unsupervised was something I knew could lead to trouble. Several years earlier one of our pole vaulters, a guy we called "Z-Man," had taught me this valuable lesson. Climbing a piece of electrical conduit up the wall, he grabbed hold of a ceiling I-beam and followed it hand over hand as teammates pushed a pole vault pit across the floor beneath him. As hundreds watched he reached the center of the field house, let go, and plummeted 30 feet to his target. It was the kind of story that had the whole school talking the next day. "Z-Man" got a lot of attention from classmates while I got to answer questions from both the principal and athletic director. Apparently there are few limits to the idiocy of teenage boys given a pole vault pit and unsupervised time.

Taking up my position outside the locker room door I awaited the first arrivals. These tend to be the excuse makers, guys who come through the door in street clothes, anxious to plead their case and get out of practice. Some have legitimate reasons like dentist appointments and make-up tests while others complain of vague or fictitious injuries they couldn't possibly practice with. Even on the second day of practice I could expect a few to engage in this verbal chess match between coach and athlete. For me it was a test of patience and diplomacy as I did my best to sort the trustworthy from the whiners.

"CHECKIN' IN, COACH!" Scott called out loudly as he burst from the locker room, arms stretched to the sky and flailing about as he worked to draw my attention. "Scott Longley is here and reporting for practice."

"Good to see you, Scott," I said with a hint of surprise in my voice. "How do you feel today? Any soreness?"

"Oh yeah, Coach. I could barely walk this morning it hurt so much right here," he said, pointing to his lower leg.

"Sore calves?" I asked.

"Yeah, Coach. REALLY sore calves," he said, reaching down to rub the back of his legs before running off to join a group of our younger guys throwing tennis balls at one another. Scott had his share of problems, but clearly shyness wasn't one of them.

Practice started the usual way with athletes lined up in rows and captains leading the stretching as I called names and checked my attendance list. Scott positioned himself in the front row facing Rob and Kim. Unaware that most of his teammates were keeping their distance, Scott was happy, smiling, and full of energy. As always, it would take time for the new guys to gain acceptance and in Scott's case that was especially true, even if he didn't know it.

Stretching was new to Scott and it wasn't easy. His long, well-muscled legs were naturally inflexible and his movements were clumsy and excessive. Doing his best to mimic those around him, Scott tried to stay on task, but the activity around him was distracting. Despite the repeated commands and encouragement of Rob and Kim, he always seemed to be out of sync. Rob moved ever closer to Scott, and each time he became distracted Rob redirected him by shouting his name. Like a drill sergeant, Rob stood nose to nose with Scott giving orders and accepting no excuses.

"Scott, pay attention. Scott, follow along. SCOTT! Do it like this!" Rob called out, repeating Scott's name louder and louder as he became increasingly frustrated. "HEY... ANIMAL!" Rob screamed out in desperation. "PAY ATTENTION!" Laughter erupted from those within earshot as they instantly recognized Scott's similarity to the drum playing Muppets character named Animal. From his dense pile of unkempt hair to his pronounced forehead, thick eyebrows, oversized mouth and huge teeth the resemblance was undeniable. Add to this Scott's deep raspy voice and hands that flailed about as if playing a drum set and it was, minus the pink hair, a near exact match. In that instant, Scott had earned a nickname.

Anyone who's ever been a part of a team knows the importance of nicknames. Even a bad one, something cruel and insulting, can help you become known and get you on the fast track to acceptance. From this moment on Scott was not just "Animal" but "The Animal." Like the professional wrestlers he so admired, he'd been given an alter ego, and to his delight, just like The Hulk, Jessie the Body and Andre the Giant, his nickname included the word THE. It made no difference that Rob had used it as an insult; in Scott's world there was very little difference between good attention and bad attention. He'd been noticed and that's all that really mattered. On a high school team the value of a nickname can hardly be overstated. Few things can get you into the group faster than a nickname and a good one, like "The Animal," can make you a legend.

Normally I avoid putting guys on our little 12-laps-to-a-mile indoor track during the first week of practice, but today I had few options. Yesterday's snowfall had become a hard packed frozen mess as temperatures dropped into the low teens and winds gusted to 30 miles per hour. Track is supposed to be a spring sport, but in Wisconsin, spring often looks an awful lot like winter. Today, weather conditions would force us to run our workout indoors in a very crowded field house.

With only four narrow lanes and little room on the perimeter, track space was at a premium, especially at the start of practice. Hoping to avoid some of the early congestion, our group, the distance guys, gathered our sweats and headed outside for a two mile warm-up run in subzero wind chills.

"Coach," Scott asked with a smile as we burst through the doorway into the harsh bite of a bitter cold west wind, "you're takin' us out in the cold to warm-up?"

"Yeah Scott, as crazy as it sounds that's what we're going to do," I said, noticing many around me chuckling and nodding as we adjusted our stocking caps and leaned into a powerful gust that attempted to impede our progress.

In theory there would be fewer people on the track when we returned, but more often than not we only managed to join in as activity hit its peak. In a flurry of activity, jumpers and vaulters covered the infield, sprinters and hurdlers used the straightaways, and distance runners were confined to lanes one and two as nearly 200 athletes did their best to stay out of each other's way.

As with sports like golf, tennis, and trap shooting, there is an etiquette to indoor running. Certain rules must be followed for the sake of courtesy and safety. Most are common sense things like look before stepping onto the track and stay out of the way of people faster than you. Others, like jogging your recovery on the infield and yelling "track" if someone steps into your lane, are taught by coaches and modeled by more experienced runners. Accidents are all too common on indoor tracks and when they happen it's usually because someone didn't know or bother to follow the rules. Today would be a learning experience for those new to indoor running and a busy day for me. Normally I would jump in and run the workout, but today it was more important that I teach, supervise, evaluate and keep a close eye on the new guys. Especially the one we now referred to as "The Animal."

"We'll do these in two groups," I shouted as we assembled on the infield near the starting line and prepared to join the flow of bodies circling the track. "Group one and group two, choose the one you want to run with, it's up to you." Scott stood silently at the back of the second group, listening carefully and looking just a little bit nervous as I finished my instructions. "We're going to run some halves today. A half mile, for those who don't know, is six laps," I explained loudly. "Group one, I don't want you any faster than 4:40 mile pace, so 23 second laps, 70 at the quarter, and 2:20 at the half. Guys in group two should be in the 2:35 to 2:40 range and for some of you it might be closer to 3 minutes. I'd like you to do 6 of them, but after the third one we'll see how you're doing. Just do the best you can. Okay, group one, ready? Remember no faster than 2:20. Up to the line. Set and GO!"

Kim jumped immediately to the front, hitting the lap in 21 seconds.

"Too fast," I yelled. "RELAX!"

Passing the quarter in 63, Kim looked smooth and comfortable on his way to a 2:07. Fast for the first interval of the season, especially fast considering our field house record was only 2:01. With the rest of the group finishing between 2:15 and 2:20, the workout was off to a good start. They'd run too aggressively, but it was good to see they'd done their off season training and were anxious to show off their fitness and test themselves.

As group one began their recovery jog clockwise on the crowded infield, group two stepped to the line. They were fourteen guys of varying ability and the majority had never run a mile faster than about 5:10. Some had done a little off season running but most had not and several, like Scott, had never run an interval workout before. I knew they weren't ready for this and they knew it too as they looked my way and listened for instructions. "Your goal is to be between 2:35 to 3:00," I reminded them as they stepped to the line. "Listen for your times. You should be 26 to 30 seconds a lap. Be careful, don't trip anyone, remember you're not racing, you're just trying to help each other stay on pace so work together."

Off and running at my command, they bolted from the line, starting fast, hoping to build a time cushion as they tried to hit their goal pace. Scott, following their lead, went out hard and placed himself toward the front of the group. Tucked nicely behind the leaders, he hugged the inside lane line, giving me a chance to study his form from my spot on the infield. With arms reaching forward and swinging wildly side to side he struggled to negotiate the tight turns and avoid getting tangled with the other runners. On the straightaways he looked better as he ran up the heels of the leaders. He wasn't graceful, but he was powerful and he ran with a sense of purpose. Something seemed to drive him forward. Controlled by the mysterious force that makes runners push back against fatigue and discomfort, Scott, to my surprise, had the look of a runner. In under a minute my evaluation was complete. In spite of all his problems, this kid could run. The kid from third hour Phys. Ed. could run.

As the leaders hit the quarter slightly ahead of pace, Scott slipped back slightly.

"Good job, Scott," I yelled excitedly. "Stay with the group!"

"Come on Animal, get back up there!" added Rob.

"Yeah Animal, you can do this." "Be tough." "Hang on Animal." Guys shouted from the infield. Reacting to each word of encouragement, Scott quickened his pace as he surged to maintain contact. His five minute gym class runs couldn't possibly have prepared him for this I thought as he crossed the line a few steps behind the leaders, finishing in 2:36.

"Nice work, Scott!" I said as I patted him on the shoulder. "How do you feel?"

Turning his head to the ceiling Scott gulped air, pointed to his oversized Adams apple and said, "Coach, my throat really hurts."

"Yeah, I know. The air in here is really dry, and your lungs aren't ready for this yet. Does it taste like metal?" I asked. Scott tilted his head, squinted and gave a quizzical look as he strained to understand my odd question. "I'm not sure what causes it but a lot of guys get a weird taste in their mouth after a hard effort, kind of like the taste of copper or rusty metal," I explained before turning my attention back to the track.

There's a rhythm to a workout like this. Step to the line, set and go, work your way into lane one, relax, listen for your splits, and stay on pace. Don't think about what's been done or what lies ahead, just run in the moment and stay with the group. Cross the line, listen for your time, quickly slip onto the infield, break into a jog, and keep an eye on the other group. As coach it was my job to choreograph the chaos, keeping track of not just my groups but sprinters, hurdlers, the girls' team, and the many random students who, for whatever reason, end up walking aimlessly across the track.

Standing at the starting line, group one found a gap, jumped onto the track, and awaited my count down, set, and go. Kim made the workout look easy. Running like a finely tuned machine, he dialed in the pace and hit his splits precisely. He crossed the line with barely a trace of discomfort on his face.

"This is way too easy, you gotta let me go harder," he pleaded. "C'mon Donn," he added, addressing me by my first name as most of my athletes did. Having started my coaching career while still in college, formal titles had never quite fit me. During the school day they called me Mr. Behnke, but at practice I was pretty much just one of the guys.

"Sure," I yelled in his direction, "if the state meet was next week. But since its three months away don't you think we should be patient?"

"Yeah, I know, but I just feel so good. I've never felt like this," he responded excitedly as he turned to jog away.

At the halfway point of the workout our group formed into a tight circle on the infield.

"Decision time," I announced. "I'd like you to do a couple more, but some of you have probably done enough. You decide. Remember, if you're done, go jog a mile cool down in the halls and finish with some stretching. If you're going to hang in with the big guys, take a jog on the infield."

Scott stood silently as half a dozen guys took me up on my offer and headed for the door. Turning to watch as half of his group walked away, he contemplated the situation. Choosing between less work and more work was something new for Scott. Caught between the desire to be done and the fear of disappointing his coach and teammates, he paused, not sure what to do next.

"Come on Animal," said sophomore Michael Morgan, tapping him in the middle of his back. "Do the last three with me. You can do it, you know you can."

In an instant Scott's decision was made. All it took was a little encouragement and a simple invitation. The fact that he was being invited to do more work was beside the point. This was about being included and he couldn't possibly refuse. Scott didn't have to finish the workout; he chose to finish simply because a teammate had invited him.

Averaging just slightly under 3 minutes on his last three intervals, Scott struggled to hang on to the back of the second group. His form broke down and it wasn't pretty, but he did the full workout when a lot of his teammates had not. Crossing the finish line for the final time, Scott hunched over, placing his hands on his knees as his legs wobbled beneath him.

"Coach, that was SO HARD!" he gasped.

"I know it was," I said, walking in his direction. "But Scott, I have to tell you…that was a great workout. For a guy with practically no running experience at all, that was amazing."

"Coach, I got experience! Every day in gym, and last summer, the Special Olympics."

"Oh yeah, I forgot all about that," I said, nodding my head while reaching out to shake his hand. "I'm proud of you, young man."

Kim, Rob, Mike, John, Curt, C.J. and several others formed a line to congratulate Scott with a procession of high-fives. "Nice workout," "Good job," "Way to go Animal" they offered sincerely as they filed past.

"Animal, you really are an Animal," Rob concluded as we walked slowly towards the last pile of sweats heaped on the field house floor.

Members of the baseball team stood leaning against the north wall near the locker room doors, waiting to start practice and looking somewhat puzzled by what they'd just seen. The concept of running without being forced to was strange enough; the fact that we seemed to enjoy it only added to the mystery. Watching as we headed outside for our cool down, they cast looks of disapproval our way. Baseball guys had no way of knowing that cool downs are fun, comfortable, and easy, a time to celebrate the completion of a good, hard effort. It's a kind of victory lap, minus the cheering crowd.

Exiting the school into the cold air and fading pink light of sunset we broke into a slow jog across the parking lot. Predictably, it didn't take long before the pace began to quicken.

"Hey, do any of you guys know what the term COOL DOWN means?" I shouted sarcastically as Rob and Kim pressed the pace. Like so many good distance runners, the concept of running easy was often hard for them to grasp.

"Coach, how far are we going?" Scott asked loudly.

"Just two miles."

"Two miles? COACH…I'M TIRED! I can't do two more miles."

"Yeah, you're right, Scott. C'mon, we'll do a shorter loop," I said as we turned off from the main group and followed the edge of the parking lot toward the back of the building. Running alone with Scott, I quizzed him on the workout he'd just run. What did you think of the workout? Do you know how many miles you ran today? What was your fastest half? What was your time on the last one? Scott answered them all without difficulty, leaving me impressed with his cognitive skills. Finished with the running portion of my interrogation, I moved on to questions about Scott's living situation as I worked to understand him better.

The group home in Plover, he told me, was the best of all the places he'd lived. He described it as a big four bedroom place with a huge kitchen and a well with the "cleanest, coldest water in the world." He got along well with most of the other residents and called the staff "good guys," adding that they were "really strict but pretty fair." His only complaint was that violating house rules landed him on K.P. duty for days on end.

"Coach, I spend lots of time on kitchen patrol, so if you ever need someone to peel potatoes, I'm your man. I'm an expert with a potato peeler," he said while quickly flicking his right hand forward in front of him.

"I'll keep that in mind," I said as we entered the back door of the locker room. "Get to bed early tonight, drink lots of that good Plover spring water, and remember, tomorrow's workout won't be nearly as tough as this one."

"Good, 'cause I don't think I could do that again," he said before flashing a big toothy smile and heading off down the hallway.

"Hey," I called out to gain his attention. "That was an excellent workout you ran today young man. We are definitely going to make a runner out of you. And one last thing…be careful with that potato peeler tonight."

"No problem, Coach. Look, still got all ten," he said proudly with his hands extended in my direction.

On my short drive home I had the chance to reflect on the events of a very busy day. Kim had run the best workout I'd ever seen on our indoor track, with Rob, Mike, and C.J. not far behind. With quality front runners and good depth, I knew we were on our way to a very good track season and in the back of my mind I was already looking ahead to the cross country team we would build in the fall. It had been a great practice; no collisions, conflicts, or injuries and best of all no one had done anything too stupid. For me, any practice where I didn't have to yell at someone was a good one.

Rounding the corner onto Meadow Street I pulled into the driveway of our story-and-a-half, shingle-clad cottage. Referred to as the "Red Cross House" by those old enough to know it had been the organization's headquarters during World War I and II, it had been moved to our quiet neighborhood sometime in the 1960's. Cheaply priced and in need of major renovation, it was a classic "fixer upper." Perfect for a young married couple, it had two small bedrooms downstairs and an upstairs apartment we used as a rental unit to supplement our income. Located a few blocks from my alma mater, the University of Wisconsin-Stevens Point, we always had a list of college runners interested in becoming our tenants. In our lives, it seemed, almost everything had a connection to running.

Late as usual, I entered the kitchen from the back hallway, dropped my duffel bag on the oak parquet floor and greeted my wife, Cheryl. Slightly more than a year into our marriage, she knew better than to expect me to be on time during cross country or track season, and she did her best to adjust for that as she prepared our meals. Testing my powers of observation, I studied her carefully as she walked in my direction. Having recently learned that we were expecting our first child I watched excitedly for any changes to Cheryl's tiny frame.

"So, how was practice?" she asked happily while working to transfer our now slightly overcooked meal from the stove to the dinner table. "Did Scott show up?"

"Yeah, he was there and he ran a pretty nice workout."

"Really? So the kid can run?"

"Yeah, he's awkward as can be, but he can definitely run."

"That's good, but how do the guys feel about him?"

"Well, it's a little hard to tell. Rob, Kim, and Mike are good with him, but most of the others are still keeping their distance. A bunch of guys lined up and high-fived him after the workout and you should have seen his face light up. Oh, and Rob gave him a nickname; he's now known as The Animal, you know, like the Muppets character."

"So, is that a good thing? They're not picking on him, are they?" she asked, sounding rather concerned.

"No, I don't think so. Well, maybe just a little, but the name fits him and he seems to like it. And after the workout he ran today, I'm pretty sure he earned some respect. I know I was impressed."

"So the problem kid that Jerry brought you yesterday is now on his way to being the next great SPASH runner," Cheryl said, with a smile as she placed a large glob of Hamburger Helper on my plate.

"No, I'm not saying that, but he's a big strong kid, he likes to run, and well, this might just work out okay. If nothing else, he should dominate the Special Olympics next summer."

THREE

THE PANTHER
INVITATIONAL

Always a case study in physiology and personality type, a track team is a very unusual organism. Guys who barely acknowledge one another during the fall sports season suddenly become teammates in the spring as coaches attempt to blend skinny, mild-mannered distance runners with loud, aggressive shot putters, free-spirited pole vaulters, laid back high jumpers, and temperamental sprinters into some sort of cohesive unit. Anyone who's ever tried to coach track understands the difficulty of assembling a team from such a strange collection of dissimilar parts.

The first weeks of practice had passed quickly as we worked to condition and evaluate our athletes. After losing our first two meets of the season, we were not off to a great start, though wins and losses had not been our concern to this point. We had no interest in scoring team points in early season dual meets. I knew we had a good team; we had nothing to prove...until today.

Our home meet, The Panther Invitational, was a bit of a throwback to earlier days. Held on a Friday night, it was the kind of meet you might have seen in the 1950's or 60's at schools lucky enough to have an indoor track. A standing room only crowd would pack our field house as the first big meet of our season attracted not just the friends and families of our athletes, but people from the community who enjoyed watching high school sports. In truth, it was a rather modest eight-team meet on a slippery little twelve-lap track, but we did our best to make it seem like a big deal. We charged admission, sold concessions, handed out printed programs, and most importantly we let the guys elect "track queens" to present awards. The Panther was a meet we wanted to win, and for young trackmen few things could provide greater motivation than the chance to ascend the awards stand and kiss a pretty girl in a prom dress in front of a crowd of cheering fans.

Anxious to start setting up for the meet, I raced from my classroom at the sound of the bell and wove my way down the crowded halls toward the field house. Janitors awaited my instructions on the placement of roll-out bleachers as varsity runners strolled in to help with set-up before heading out in search of a pre-meet meal. Port-a-pits were moved quickly into position and runways were roped off as equipment was gathered and correctly placed. In a matter of minutes, we were ready.

"Alright guys," I shouted, turning toward the group of distance runners assembled near the locker room door. "Time to stretch."

These were the guys who hadn't made the lineup, the left overs, junior varsity, or "scrubs," as they sometimes called themselves. Many were good enough to be in the meet, but with only nine positions in distance races I just couldn't find a place for them. Earning a varsity spot on our team was never easy; getting your name listed in the program as an alternate was, for many of our guys, the best they could hope for.

"Here Scott," I said, pointing to his name in print on page three of the official program. "I have you listed as an alternate in the two-mile relay."

"REALLY? I'm in the program?" he shouted, sounding surprised and excited as he jumped to his feet to take a look.

"Yeah, well after that 2:16 you ran in here last week I thought you earned it," I explained as he studied the list of names, seemingly unconcerned that he was the number three alternate.

With his own unique combination of strength and mental toughness, Scott had made huge progress over the first few weeks of the season. His awkward form was improving, he worked hard, was a great competitor, and after a poor initial reaction by many of us, he was quickly beginning to fit in.

As someone who had never before been a part of an organized team, Scott found everything new and exciting. He enjoyed every aspect of track practices. From our poorly organized stretching sessions to the long hard road runs, indoor intervals and easy recovery days, he loved all of it. However, his true passion for sports became most evident on meet days as teammates urged him on in his races and he returned the favor during theirs. Like a little boy proudly encouraging his big brothers, he ran back and forth across the infield cheering wildly as those in attendance looked on and smiled. In just a few short weeks Scott had learned to mimic the encouragement doled out by his coaches as he turned himself into an athlete, cheerleader, and mascot all rolled into one. His silly antics drew a fair amount of attention, but never in a bad way. Cautioned by coaches as to the limits of his sideline behavior, he seemed aware that the trash talking he'd seen so much of as a fan of professional wrestling was out of place at a high school track meet. Directing his comments only at teammates, he shouted encouragement with uninhibited passion as they passed. His enthusiasm was not only good for us, it was infectious.

With Scott positioned happily in the middle of the group as they began what might be described as stretching, I walked over and took a knee.

"You are staying for the meet tonight, aren't you, Scott?"

"Yeah, Coach. I got it all worked out."

"What about supper?"

"No problem, Coach. I brought one of my extra special peanut butter and banana sandwiches."

"Do you have a ride home later?"

"COACH! I got it all worked out. No problem."

"Good! I'm glad you can stay. It's gonna be a great meet!"

"You got that right Coach. And just wait till ya see what I got planned," he said, nodding his head vigorously as he looked up and smiled.

What could it be, I wondered for an instant. Something silly and fun no doubt, certainly nothing to worry about, I thought, as I stood to address the group:

"Okay guys, listen up. This is a short, fast workout —seven miles. Remember, this should be a good hard effort. Go easy the first and last mile, hang onto the group as long as you can, alright? Check in with me when you get back, then catch a shower, get something to eat, and meet on the back side of the track, ready to make some noise. Running events start at 5:30. Okay, let's get moving," I ordered while pointing to the doors the guys would exit to begin the loop we called "in-town."

"Who's in charge of The Animal?" I asked, knowing that this would be Scott's first run without me.

"I got him!" Dan Morgan called out, waving his hand in the air. "I'll be the Animal keeper."

Dan and his brother Michael were ideally suited for the assignment. Blessed with good looks, great personalities, and self-confidence, they were natural leaders. Today they would replace Rob and Kim at the front of the pack, taking on my role as Scott's chaperone while I awaited the arrival of the first teams.

Through the tall hallway windows I studied Scott's highly animated movements as the group climbed a small embankment at the edge of the parking lot and headed in the direction of Second Street. Flanked by Dan and Michael, he'd taken up his usual position, mid-pack, right where he wanted to be in the middle of all the activity.

It all looked so perfectly normal, I thought, standing in the silence of the hallway as I watched them turn the corner and disappear. Yet, like a parent sending a child off for the first day of school, I felt a small sense of concern. The Morgans were great kids, mature and trustworthy, but this was new to them and as I turned toward the locker room, I couldn't help wondering if they were ready to work with someone like Scott.

Surrounded by the wonderful aroma of burgers and fries, assistant coaches sat on folding chairs with feet propped on the large oak desk in the center of the coaches' office as they ate their supper. The unmistakable smell of greasy, delicious fast food traveled through the locker room attracting teenage boys like crows to road kill. In a Pavlovian response my mouth immediately watered and hunger pangs gripped my stomach.

"Have a burger," offered sprint coach John Zellmer, pointing to a white paper bag on the desk.

"No thanks, got my supper right here," I said, pulling an orange from the top shelf of my rusty locker.

"Looks like Oshkosh West is here," John said, bringing our few minutes of relaxation to an abrupt end as athletes dressed in blue and white sweat suits flowed curiously among the lockers before pouring out into the field house. Some stood beneath our track record board, studying it carefully, quietly pointing up at some of the outstanding times and distances. Soon other teams arrived and the track became a colorful swirl of activity as athletes jogged warm-up laps, sprinted down runways, and checked out field event areas. Every inch of floor space seemed to be occupied by athletes and their equipment. The unmistakable smell of analgesic balm was in the air and bleachers began to fill with the first spectators. At the scorer's table coaches made lineup changes, workers were assigned to event areas, and the starter, dressed in black and white stripes, cleaned his pistol.

"First call, all field events," the head scorer announced over the P.A. system. "All field event contestants must check in."

We were off to a good start. Things were running smoothly, and all we needed now was the box of stop watches I kept carefully stored in my locker.

"I'll get the watches," I yelled in the direction of the head timer before hustling off at a fast jog.

"How was the run?" I shouted curiously in the direction of my loud, excited J.V. runners as they filed into the locker room through the back door. Surrounded by the smell of the cool, fresh air they'd brought in with them, they strained to hold back laughter while forming a tight circle around me.

"Oh, it was GREAT!" Dan replied as those around him broke down in laughter. "It was just GREAT!"

"Okay, let's hear it...what happened?'

"She was out there again. Crazy Shovel Lady was out in her driveway again."

"Yeah and she started swearin' at us," added Michael with a laugh. "She called us a bunch of...well...fatherless children."

"You didn't say anything to her, did you?" I asked hopefully, giving the group my most serious glare.

"No! No really, I promise, we didn't say a word. But Donn, it was so funny, we couldn't help it. We all just cracked up. MAN! We had to walk a block after that one."

"Yeah Coach, I never heard an old lady talk like that. What's wrong with her?" Scott asked excitedly. "Coach, I thought she was gonna throw her shovel at me!"

"Well Scott, she's got some problems, and evidently scraping ice from her driveway makes her pretty angry. We're not the only one's she does it to. I hear she swears at a lot of people."

"Next time I'm runnin' on the other side of the street," Scott announced.

"Yeah, well, next time I'll deal with the shovel lady," I answered as I watched him turn and race off to catch the group.

"Hey guys, running events start in 20 minutes!" I shouted while unlocking the door to the coaches' office. "HUSTLE UP!"

"Last call, all field events!" the announcement blared from the overhead speakers as I returned to the field house with the box of watches tucked safely under my arm. The meet was about to start, finally. After the introduction of track queens and the national anthem, the long awaited Panther Invitational could begin.

Queen selection had been the talk of the school in the days leading up to the meet.

Twelve girls were nominated, ballots were printed, and votes were cast, with the chosen few given the chance to wear their prom dress, complete with corsage, one more time as they were escorted to the awards stand with all the pomp and ceremony a group of track coaches could pull together. Six beautiful young girls in flowing gowns, escorted by handsome young men in track suits, marched toward the awards stand as the winter formal theme song "I Wanna Know What Love Is" rained down from the P.A. system. For a few hours on a Friday night they were track royalty. They, along with a few select runners, jumpers, and throwers, would be the center of attention. Ascending the podium, they turned toward the crowd as athletes stopped in their tracks to study them like judges evaluating livestock at a county fair. Free from the normal concern of being caught staring, guys moved in close to take a good long look, making every effort to give the queens the proper amount of respect.

To those unfamiliar with our sport it must have seemed an odd spectacle, but for track people it was an expected part of many big meets. The activity on the awards stand was just part of the drama as the crowd watched with interest to see who would lean in for a kiss and who would settle for a handshake. Predictably, distance runners took the handshake or accepted a quick peck, as if kissing their mom, while sprinters and pole vaulters locked on until the very limit of what might be viewed as appropriate. In this strange, time-honored track tradition, pretty girls and sweaty boys were placed on a pedestal to exchange a kiss in front of hundreds of watchful eyes. A kiss, so simple and so innocent, that if not for a small amount of cleavage it might well have been a scene from a Norman Rockwell painting.

With introductions complete, silence fell over the crowded field house as athletes and spectators came to their feet and turned to face the large American flag on the north wall. With a microphone held close to an old phonograph on the scorer's table, the meet announcer carefully dropped the tone arm onto the scratchy 45 recording of the National Anthem.

Standing tall and proud along the east wall, a collection of J.V. distance runners, freshly showered and neatly dressed, stood with hands over their hearts, singing proudly. A few mouthed the words softly, but most in the group sang with enough volume to be heard across the field house. Dressed in the uniform of the day, khaki pants and button up shirts, I couldn't help smiling as I proudly studied this fine group of young men. These were my guys, the ones I hadn't been able to squeeze into the meet. They didn't need to be here. They wanted to be here to cheer on their teammates, to be a part of something special.

Having run their workout and devoured a sandwich, they'd now taken their place where distance runners gather, on the back-side of the track. While others pack themselves tightly near the finish line, distance runners seek out places closer to the action, places where their shouts of encouragement might be heard. From here we strain our lungs shouting ourselves hoarse, hoping to push our guys to run just a few fractions of a second faster. Scott stood happily between his new friends Dan and Michael, a look of joy and excitement on his face. Now part of this wonderfully eclectic group, he waited eagerly for running events to get under way, ready to create some noise along the far turn.

Weight men puffed out their chests as they entered the circle and launched 12 pound shots across the track at the far end of the field house. High jumpers, long jumpers, and pole vaulters finished their run throughs and were given final instructions while sprinters and hurdlers headed toward the starting line to check on their heat and lane assignments.

After circling our small track to check on each of the field event areas, I jogged to the back-side to join the line of my guys wedged between the outside of lane four and a wall of unopened bleachers, waiting anxiously for the start of the mile run. Pushing my way into the middle of the group, I could feel the excitement of the impending race as I scanned down the line of smiling runners. Scott, having taken on the job of cheerleader, jogged from one end of the group to the other, slapping hands and issuing numbers as he went.

"Sixty-three, sixty-four, sixty-five," he shouted loudly while I watched and wondered.

"He's collecting high-fives," Curt said with a nod of his head. "Said he wants to get to one hundred before the mile starts."

Reaching out as he passed, I offered my hand.

"NO!" he yelled, suddenly retracting his arm. "I'm savin' number one hundred for you, Coach."

Laughter erupted from our group as he hurried along, counting "seventy-two, seventy-three, seventy-four" as he added to his collection. Smiling happily, he wove his way among athletes, spectators, and anyone else willing to lend a helping hand before looping back my way.

"Ninety-eight, ninety-nine, here it comes Coach," he warned, pulling his hand back in a wildly exaggerated wind-up motion. "ONE HUNDRED!" he announced to the amusement of those on the back-side while slapping my hand with enough force to produce what sounded like the report of the starter's pistol. The resulting cheer and laughter from our group caused all in attendance to cast a puzzled look our way.

"All right, that's enough," I said with a smile as I grabbed him by the elbow and pulled him out of lane four and into our line. "It's just about time for the mile."

"Okay Coach, one question," Scott asked quite seriously. "Is Kim gonna win?"

"Yeah, he's gonna win. The question is can he break our field house record?" I responded. "We've had some very good runners on this track and no one has ever gone sub 4:25," I said loudly enough that all in our group would hear. "Kim might just be the first to do it. Hey guys, do the math, what does he need to average per lap?" I called out as a challenge.

"22 seconds," someone answered almost instantly.

"22.1" added another.

"22.08," said C.J. with the authority of a math league member.

It's good to be around runners, I thought to myself. Not just guys who run, but guys who love the sport as much as I do. Our distance program, our tight knit little group, our team within the track team, made me proud. We had a group of highly motivated young men determined to be good runners and good teammates. It was a great environment for all of us lucky enough to be a part of it, and the Panther Invitational gave us a chance to show off what our program was all about.

With the sound of the starter's pistol echoing among the ceiling beams, the crowd erupted as Kim shot from the line and into the lead. Cheering loudly each time he passed, we evaluated his form and carefully checked his splits. Twenty- two seconds at the lap, forty-three, then sixty-five at the quarter, he was locked onto his pace. Well out front, looking smooth and efficient, he clipped the half in 2:11 on his way to what would surely be a great time... until it happened. On the crowded turn, near the hallway doors, not far from the awards stand, as happens all too often on indoor tracks, someone stepped carelessly into lane one, right in front of him. The collision was slight, a quick side step and a little stumble, but just enough to disrupt Kim's rhythm, costing precious seconds he could not recover. With the record out of reach he could have jogged in for the win, but instead chose to charge full speed to the finish, crossing in a respectable time of 4:28. Ignoring the fact that he was scheduled to anchor our distance medley relay in less than an hour, he'd attacked the race fearlessly, determined to chase the meet record at all costs. This was our style and exactly how I wanted all of our guys to run, pressing the pace from gun to tape, more interested in running fast times than merely picking off points or collecting medals.

Despite the disappointment of the collision, Kim's all-out effort had made us proud. Excited and energized, we cheered loudly as he jogged slowly in our direction, shaking his head side to side. He shrugged his shoulders as he said "I had it...I felt so good. I could have done it, I just know it!"

Teammates circled in close, offering handshakes and high-fives to the race winner now standing among us.

"ONE HUNDRED AND ONE!" Scott cried out as Kim reached high above the sea of hands to slap his palm. "Eye of the Tiger, Kim. Eye of the Tiger!"

With a puzzled look and a wide smile, Kim laughed and turned away to begin his cool down. No doubt someone would explain this odd episode to him later.

The meet moved along quickly, as relay meets tend to do, with Appleton West dominating the sprint events and our distance guys matching them point for point. It was a close meet, very close, until high jump and pole vault points tipped the balance in our favor. With the outcome determined, I worked my way around the perimeter of the track, shaking hands and congratulating athletes as mile relay teams assembled at the starting line. Specifically seeking our J.V. runners, I thanked them for their enthusiasm and asked for their help putting equipment away after the meet.

"Hey, has anyone seen Scott?" I called out while scanning the group positioned along the outside lane line.

"Yeah, he went to the locker room a few minutes ago," Michael answered. "Said something about getting changed."

Giving little thought to the statement, I cleared my stopwatch and quickly headed off in search of a place to watch the final race. Few events generate more excitement and interest than a well contested mile relay. In a classic test of speed, endurance, and mental toughness, teams combine sprinters, hurdlers, jumpers, and distance runners to finish off the meet in what many track fans think of as a grand finale. Athletes and spectators pushed their way to the edge of the track to cheer their athletes on. Runners bolted from the line, sprinting madly before tying up on the third lap and straining to reach the exchange zone. Amid the deafening noise anchor runners flailed their arms as they rounded the last turn and lunged toward the finish line, bringing the meet to an end as sudden quiet fell over the field house.

Reaching the scorer's table, I found the head scorer working quickly to pencil in the results of the last event while the starter leaned over his shoulder, watching carefully and waiting eagerly to check the scores, apply his initials, and bolt for the door.

"I'll be right back with copies for the coaches," I announced as I scooped the officially verified result sheet from the table. "You can hand out the M.V.P. awards and the team trophy whenever you're ready."

As the only person in the building with permission to use the copy machine, I headed at full stride down the hallway toward the main office. Unlocking the door to the darkened room, I flipped the toggle switch on the side of the Xerox and shuffled my feet impatiently as I waited for the green light to come on.

With spectators and athletes filtering slowly through the field house doors, mile relay medals were distributed and coaches cast their votes for the most valuable performer award. As good hosts we gave a Co-MVP award to the top two athletes, hoping to avoid looking bad if one of our guys won. Today Kim, with victories in the mile and the distance medley, shared the award with a sprinter from Appleton who anchored three winning relays. The small crowd still in attendance applauded politely while track queens presented the MVP awards and listened as the final team scores were read.

Standing in the dimly lit office, I gently rocked the stubborn copier like a pinball machine in hopes of inducing a green light. Anxious to get back to the field house to distribute results, congratulate athletes, and help put equipment away, I waited in agony, helpless as the annoying machine did whatever it is a Xerox machine must do before making copies.

Standing in a semi-circle in front of the scorer's table, the team awaited the trophy presentation and the start of a time honored tradition known as the victory lap. There were relatively few people left to witness the procession, but our guys, standing shoulder to shoulder, didn't seem to mind. Parents stood in small groups scatted around the field house while coaches waited patiently for my return from the office and visiting athletes exited into the dark parking lot to board their busses. Only a few dozen remained to watch the presentation of the team trophy and the special performance that Scott, with help from some teammates, had planned.

With a cassette tape cued to the song "Eye of the Tiger" by a band called Survivor, Dan set a large boom box on the edge of the scorer's table as the announcer began reading the final team scores. The rock anthem of the 1982 movie *Rocky III* seemed appropriate for a victory celebration, a popular song that the entire team would enjoy as they circled the track. But for Scott, it held an even greater significance. "Eye of the Tiger" was not just his favorite song, it was the theme song of his favorite athlete and idol, professional wrestler Hulk Hogan.

"And in first place, with one hundred and twenty- nine points," the announcer read before winding up for one final emphatic statement, "THE PANTHERS OF STEVENS POINT AREA SENIOR HIGH!"

Modest applause burst from the sparse crowd as one of the queens, carrying out her last responsibility, struggled to hoist the oversized team trophy in the direction of the onrushing mob of teenage boys. Repositioning the microphone next to the boom box, the announcer pressed 'Play,' and to the sound of four hard cords, BOMP...BOMP, BOMP, BOMP, Scott burst from the locker room right on cue. Dressed in a pair of red running shorts, a tight fitting white t-shirt, and a yellow headband, he raced across the field house with his distinctive long, loping stride. His t-shirt had its sleeves torn off, four horizontal rips across the chest, and "Hulkamania" scrawled across the front with black marker. On the back in large, nearly illegible letters, was Scott's new nickname: The Animal.

Positioned at the front of the group, Rob accepted the trophy from the queen and turned quickly to pass it to Scott in his "Hulkesque" costume as the team erupted in joyous celebration.

It seemed like a perfect plan, simple and harmless. The thought of asking permission hadn't occurred to those who'd organized the celebration. Knowing that Scott's brand of enthusiasm would make for a fun lap, they simply sought to include him. For a few minutes Scott would be the center of attention and in their minds that was a good thing.

With a huge grin Scott took the trophy from Rob and hoisted it over his head as crackly, distorted music blared from the P.A. system.

It's the Eye of the Tiger; it's the thrill of the fight, rising up to the challenge of our rival...

Scott, with trophy held high above him, bounced on his toes and shuffled his feet like Rocky Balboa on the steps of the Philadelphia Art Museum. Responding to the cheers of his teammates, he lowered the trophy, gave it a big hug, and used a portion of his t-shirt to shine the golden figurine. Stopping abruptly after moving only a few yards, Scott bent forward and carefully set the trophy on the floor while his teammates watched and wondered. Straightening up quickly he placed his fingers in the pre-made rips in his t-shirt, drove his elbows outward, and tore it from his body. Dancing happily in a tight circle, surrounded by cheering teammates clapping in unison, he twirled the tattered shirt high above his head, celebrating as he'd seen Hulk Hogan do so many times in the ring.

In the world of pro wrestling this kind of demonstration was expected; it was part of the show. After punching, biting, and beating your opponent senseless with a folding chair, you were expected to taunt the loser with an over the top celebration designed to incite the crowd. For Scott, the celebration seemed perfectly normal. In his view of the world there was no reason to do otherwise. Years of watching pro wrestling in group homes around the state had taught him this.

Rob and Kim stood motionless, watching the spectacle unfold in front of them, unsure of what to do next. This wasn't part of the plan. They knew about the boom box, the song, the t-shirt, and the victory lap, but the rest was Scott's idea. Draping his torn t-shirt over the trophy, Scott held it aloft with both hands, rotating it for all to see as his teammates cheered and urged him on.

From the perspective of a bunch of teenage boys, the whole thing was just good fun, but to the adults in the room it looked like something else. A victory lap was one thing, but this had gone too far. This reeked of poor sportsmanship as the rowdy mob carried out an excessively loud celebration. At best it was a show of disrespect by a team so confident of winning they'd pre-planned their victory lap; at its worst, it was a team making fun of the shirtless kid dancing with a trophy above his head, a kid from the special education classroom.

Risin up, straight to the top. Had the guts, got the glory. Went the distance now I'm not gonna stop. Just a man with the will to survive…

The music continued as Coach Zellmer hurried across the infield.

"Alright guys, that's enough!" he shouted, inserting himself into the group to pry the trophy from Scott's firm grasp. With a look of stern disapproval, he quickly transferred the award to the nearest athlete and sent the group off to complete the victory lap with some degree of humility.

Placing a gentle hand on Scott's shoulder, John guided him across the infield in the direction of the locker room while giving a quick lecture on good sportsmanship and the importance of showing respect to other teams after a victory. Unfortunately, for Scott the idea of a moderate celebration was an entirely new concept. To this point in his life, winning was something he'd only experienced through the eyes of people like Hulk Hogan who had no reason to modify their behavior or show respect to their opponents.

Returning from the office with copies in hand, it became instantly apparent that something had gone wrong during my absence. Athletes scattered quickly in all directions at the conclusion of the victory lap, grinning and laughing as they ran off. Kim and Rob stood quietly, with Mike, John, Curt, and C.J. close behind, waiting while I passed out result sheets and shook hands with departing coaches. Dan and Michael waited a short distance away, still red faced from minutes of sustained laugher. Turning in their direction, I listened carefully as they attempted to unravel the combination of events that had happened a few moments earlier.

"Really," said Kim apologetically, "We didn't know he was gonna do that. We were just trying to include him, make him feel part of the team, like we always do, like you always tell us."

"Yeah, well you know what it looked like, don't you?" I asked sternly. "You had the new kid, the kid with disabilities, dancing and stripping off his shirt while you guys cheered and laughed. I know YOU GUYS didn't mean to make fun of him, but I'm afraid some of your teammates didn't get the message. Just think of how that looked to the coaches and parents who watched that little celebration," I asked the quiet, somber group standing in front of me, with just a hint of anger in my voice. "Is that how we act when we win?"

"Donn, we're really sorry, but we weren't making fun of him. You know that, right?" Kim asked.

"Yeah Donn," Rob added. "We wouldn't do that. We like the kid."

"I know, Rob, but I leave you guys alone for a couple of minutes and look what happens. Okay, we need to fix this. He's probably still here, so let's see if we can find him," I said, leading the group quickly toward the locker room.

Thick, soap scented steam rolled from the shower room and mixed with the sounds of excited young men still in the mood to celebrate on a Friday night. Amid all the commotion, Scott stood almost motionless in front of his Phys. Ed. locker, quietly buttoning his blue and gray plaid shirt.

"Animal," Rob began. "Hey, we're really sorry! You know we weren't making fun of you, right?"

"Yeah Rob," Scott answered quietly, still facing his locker, refusing to look in our direction.

"Really," added Kim, extending a hand in Scott's direction. "We were just trying to have fun. We never thought you'd get in trouble."

"Sorry, Animal," Mike said, leading a procession of teammates who'd lined up to offer a handshake and an apology.

"Yeah, sorry Animal."

"Sorry, Scott."

"We're really sorry, you know… the whole thing just got outta hand."

"Yeah, I know, thanks guys," Scott said, turning to give a partial smile.

"You understand why people are upset, don't you?" I asked, stepping over the narrow maple bench as I placed my hands on Scott's shoulders and looked in his eyes.

"Yeah, Coach. Coach Zellmer said it's 'cause I took my shirt off."

"Well, that's part of it. The victory lap was fun, the music was a nice touch, but ripping your clothes off and dancing around like that….well, you just can't do that. The Hulk gets to do it 'cause it's part of the show, but when you do it in school, someone's gonna get in trouble."

"Am I in trouble?" Scott asked, wide eyed.

"Look, I don't want to make a big deal out of this. Nobody got hurt and there was no real damage done, but there's always a chance that someone could get the wrong idea. People might think that some of the guys put you up to this so they could laugh at you."

"Coach, nobody told me to take my shirt off. That was my idea!"

"Yeah I know. And what did you learn today?"

"Coach Zellmer said we have to show respect to the teams we beat."

"And?"

"Keep my shirt on," Scott said with a vigorous nod of his head.

"Good answer. See, you learned something today," I said, patting him on the back as we exited the rear door of the locker room and walked toward the dark colored van waiting under the orange glow of a lone, sodium vapor street light.

"Other than that, it was a great meet, wasn't it Coach?"

"Yeah Scott, other than that, it was," I responded as I watched him walk away.

Stopping abruptly a few feet from the van, he turned around and with a look of deep concern asked, "One question Coach. I'm still on the team, right?"

"Yes, you're still on the team. You belong here. You made a little mistake, you learned a lesson, and we move on. Just peel a couple potatoes when you get home and we'll call it even."

"Sure Coach, got it covered," he said with a smile.

"Okay, Scott, I'll see you on Monday."

"Yeah Coach. See ya Monday."

FOUR

FINAL DECISION

Quietly slipping into the unattended main office, I checked my mailbox by the red glow of an exit sign and headed off to start my day. Moving down the dark, lonely hallway with a bag of running gear slung over my shoulder and a stack of folders pinned under my arm, I hurried along, like a man on a mission. Track season was, by far, the busiest part of my year as I struggled to balance teaching and coaching with being a new husband and soon to be father. Unlocking my classroom door, I flipped on the lights and, as the first teacher in the building, set out to make use of some uninterrupted work time. Time was precious. In an hour and a half, 30 sleepy students would drag themselves through the doorway of my first hour social studies class and I needed to be ready. Somehow, by 7:55 A.M., I had to organize the jumble of papers strewn across my desk and pull together a well-organized, engaging lesson about the world wide depression of the 1930's and the rise of the Nazi Party in Germany.

However, lesson plans were far from the only thing on my mind this early Monday morning. As I shuffled papers, positioned equipment and stacked books I couldn't help wondering if the story of Scott's little performance last Friday would find its way to the attention of the administration. Strangely we'd reached the mid-point of the track season without serious incident and I was starting to worry. Usually by this point something would have gone wrong, an athletic code violation, a pulled hamstring, or a stress fracture, but so far nothing bad, not even a slightly sprained ankle, had happened to our team. It all seemed a little too good to be true, I thought, while fighting the nagging feeling that I was about to be called to the athletic director's office. After all, this was Monday and I knew very well that if I was going to get bad news, it would happen on a Monday. If one of our guys was going to do something stupid and get in trouble, it usually happened on a weekend. The same was true for kids who quit the team; they usually do it at the start of the week. They don't often come and tell you they quit, they just don't show up. Sometimes they have a friend relay the message and they might even send back their equipment, but most often they just assume that by not showing up you'll figure out they've found something better to do. Usually it has something to do with a job, trouble at home, or a girlfriend, but in a state like Wisconsin it could be that some would rather go fishing, ride motorcycles, or just walk the streets aimlessly.

The school day came and went without, as far as I knew, any trouble arising from the victory lap incident. There was some discussion about it around school, but making it to the end of eighth-hour without being summoned to the office was a very good sign. After all, it had been a pretty harmless act, Coach Zellmer had ended it quickly, and it was in no way a violation of any team or school rules. Heading down the hall in the direction of the field house, I felt confident that the whole thing had blown over. If something bad was going to happen, I would have certainly learned about it by now, at least that's what I kept telling myself.

As practice time approached I assumed my usual position near the locker room door and watched as athletes filed past. Most paid little attention to me as they chattered excitedly about events of the day, track queens, and Scott's now famous trophy dance. Distance runners formed a circle around me with questions about the day's workout, weather conditions, and my thoughts on the Milwaukee Brewers' upcoming season opener.

"Where's Scott?" I called out to no one in particular as the flow of athletes began to slow and I realized he hadn't checked in yet. Usually one of the first and loudest through the door, it was unlikely he'd slipped past me. We were five weeks into the season and he'd never missed a practice. He'd never even been late.

"Rob," I shouted, thinking the worst, "where's the Animal? Was he in school today?"

"Yeah, he was here. I saw him this morning."

"Did he say anything to you about missing practice?" I asked hopefully.

"No, he didn't say anything to me, but I think Dan talked to him this afternoon."

"So, what's goin' on?" I asked as Dan emerged slowly from the group and stepped toward me.

"Well, Scott said he was going to come and tell you this… but…he has to quit."

"What? Well, that's just great!" I said sarcastically. "This is about Friday, isn't it?"

"Yeah, I guess. He said the guys at the group home heard about his little Hulk Hogan thing and they weren't too happy."

"I knew this would happen, I just knew it. The poor kid's probably been peeling potatoes all weekend," I speculated while shaking my head. "Rob, Kim, get the warm-up started. I have to make a phone call," I said, turning toward the locker room with my clipboard tucked under my arm.

Nervously drumming my fingers on the cinder block next to the wall mounted telephone in the coaches' office, I waited for someone to answer.

"Hello."

"Yeah, are you one of the counselors?"

"Yes I am."

"Well, this is Coach Behnke. I'm Scott Longley's track coach and I'm just wondering why he's not at practice today."

"Sure, well, we had a meeting with Scott last night and, well…
we decided that track just wasn't working out for him."

"Really. Why is that? I mean, well, from my perspective I think
things have gone pretty well. Scott really seems to like it, he
works hard, he's improving, and I think he's really beginning to fit
in. So what is it that's not working?"

"Well, it's mostly about the time he's spending away from here.
Bottom line is, he's not getting his chores done around the
house."

"Okay, I get that," I said, trying to conceal my anger. "Couldn't
you just adjust the schedule a little? After all, it's not like he's
goofing off. He's doing something positive here, getting some
serious exercise, and the social aspect is just so good for him, you
know that, right?"

"Sure. That's all probably true, but some of our other residents
feel he's not pulling his weight around here."

"Really? 'Cause from what I've seen, Scott's a pretty good
worker. Couldn't you just shift some of his responsibilities to the
weekends when we don't have practice? There must be a way to
work this out. I'd hate to think you're going to make him quit
because of a few complaints from the other kids."

"Well, there's a little more to it than that. Let me be perfectly
honest. We've caught Scott telling some pretty tall tales lately so
we're trying to address that issue. We've already taken away most
of his T.V. time and he's on pretty much permanent K.P., so
taking him out of track is the logical next step. You need to
understand, we're just following Scott's behavior modification
plan. When he lies we have to take action."

"Yeah, I get that, but don't you think this goes a little far? He's
in a very positive situation here with us. To me this seems like a
step in the wrong direction."

"Look, we've given Scott quite a few chances and I hear what
you're saying, but we've talked to him time after time and he just
continues to come home with all kinds of ridiculous stories."

"Sure, so what kind of things has he been telling you?"

"Ahh, let me see, there's so many. Oh yeah, he told us he made varsity, he's going to earn a varsity letter, he's going to get a letter jacket, he's going to run in the state meet, and he says he's got a girlfriend. It just goes on and on."

"Okay. Now, I don't know about the girlfriend thing and Scott's never going to run in a state meet, but if he keeps working, he might actually reach our letter standard in the half mile. And he's really not that far off of our varsity. In fact, last Friday I had him listed as an alternate for our big invitational," I explained, stretching the truth only slightly.

"Last Friday, yeah, well, that's another issue," he said with his voice taking on a lower and more serious tone. "Scott told some of our residents that he'd gotten into trouble after the track meet. Something about tearing his shirt off and running around the track with the trophy on his head. He said he got yelled at. It all sounded pretty strange."

"Okay, sure, I know it sounds kind of bad but trust me, it just wasn't a big deal, the whole thing lasted about thirty seconds. At the end of the meet, on the victory lap, Scott did this little Hulk Hogan thing with an old tattered T-shirt, but one of my assistant coaches stepped in and stopped it right away. Yeah, it was inappropriate, but we talked to him about his behavior and the importance of being a good sport, so really, in the end I think it turned out to be a good lesson for him."

"Well, from what we've been able to find out, it sounds like some of your track guys were having a few laughs at Scott's expense, and that's a really big concern for us, so I'm sorry but we've made our decision. We just can't have Scott in a position where he's being made fun of. After five weeks we feel like we've given this a fair shot, but we just don't think it's in his best interest to have him continue."

"I understand what you're saying, but he's building some friendships here, and I don't think any of the guys intended to make fun of him. Really, they like Scott. I'm not trying to tell you what to do, but I think it's worth another shot."

"I appreciate your input, but you need to realize that when we enforce a rule we can't backtrack. It would send a bad message to Scott and the rest of our residents. So, our decision is final."

"Look, I'm a teacher. I know the importance of rules, but in this case I don't think the punishment fits the crime. I think if you came to a practice you'd see how good this is for him. I really think if you saw the bigger picture you'd reconsider," I said, pleading Scott's case one last time as the conversation seemed near its conclusion.

"Well, I'll bring it up to the other staff members, but like I said, our decision is final."

Angrily I hung up the phone, slammed the door to the coaches' office behind me, and stalked off in the direction of the field house.

"What'd they say?" Rob asked eagerly as I rejoined the guys waiting anxiously to start our usual mileage Monday run.

"Unbelievable!" I shouted, throwing my hands in the air as the group closed in to hear my explanation. "One little incident. The kid takes his shirt off for a few seconds and they make a big deal out of it. Suddenly we're a bad influence on the kid, just a bunch of mean guys on the track team pickin' on the poor kid. They don't bother to call me. None of them ever came to a meet or a practice. They never saw the good side. One thing goes wrong and they make him quit. It is unbelievable. I gave it my best shot, but it sounds like they've made up their minds. They might reconsider, but I really doubt it. Anyway, let's get moving," I ordered, pulling on my hooded sweatshirt while leading our now silent group toward the field house doors.

"Look," Dan called out, pointing to the large trophy case in the hallway. "Look at the Panther trophy."

"What is that?" someone asked as we moved in together for a closer look.

"It's Scott's shirt, the Hulkamania t-shirt," Dan explained. "Someone tied it around the trophy."

"Someone?" I asked, casting a questioning look his way.

"Really?" Dan said, putting his hands up as if being held at gun point. "You think I had something to do with that? Come on, Donn. Really?"

Laughing as we walked away, I looked back at the torn and tattered shirt and imagined Scott, in the kitchen of the group home, peeling potatoes. He should be here with us, I thought to myself as we pushed through the doorway into a cold, gray, damp Wisconsin spring afternoon and started our run.

Scott's problem was set aside as we quickly shifted our attention to the task at hand. Suddenly the air was filled with the joyful noise of young men excitedly headed out for a ten mile run on a loop we called Junk Yard. Laughing loudly, they jostled for position, threw insults, and kicked discarded soda cans while crossing the student parking lot. Scott was not mentioned again. The guys knew very well that on a track team things like this happen all the time. Guys join and guys quit. New guys are welcomed while others quickly disappear and are soon forgotten.

For me it wasn't quite that simple. Despite my initial reaction to Scott, I'd become attached to him and absolutely hated the thought of losing him. Like all the young men I herded along ahead of me, Scott was one of "my guys" and pulling him from the team was, in my mind, the worst possible decision. He'd earned a spot on the team, he belonged with us, and he'd been accepted. Once we'd learned to overlook his disheveled appearance and sometimes strange behavior, we began to realize he wasn't all that different from the rest of us. He only wanted what we all want—a place to belong.

Scott needed us and in many ways we needed him too. From his silly habit of collecting high-fives to the now infamous Hulkamania dance, he was fun to have around. He brought energy and enthusiasm to our group but most of all he served as a daily reminder that we should appreciate the things around us that many of us took for granted, like a home, a family, lovingly prepared meals, clean, fresh clothes and even the crappy, dingy gray, school-issued sweats everyone else seemed to complain about. Those of us who'd gotten to know him had begun to see the world a little differently through the eyes of someone who never complained about what he didn't have and seemed to appreciate anything good that came his way. Losing Scott would never cost us team points, I thought, while striding comfortably behind our tightly packed formation of runners; it would, however, cost us in other ways, ways that never show up in a box score.

"Settle down, Rob," I warned from the back of the group, noticing his two stride lead as he pushed the pace into the strong, cool, west wind that hindered our progress. Instinctively trying to shorten the time until we turned out of the annoying headwind, we were all guilty of running too hard in the first mile.

Except for an occasional car, there were few signs of life as we headed north of town on this unusually bleak spring day. A thin layer of frozen slush along the edge of the roadway cracked beneath our feet, producing a steady rhythm as we passed under the arched branches of towering oaks, maples, and white pines. Slowly the troubles of the day, like many of our J.V. runners, began to melt away.

The pace quickened with each passing mile and conversation all but ceased as we began our long, hard pickup. This, we all knew, was the cornerstone of our program. Pushing the pace for three, four, or five miles in the middle of a long run is what set us apart from many other high school teams. Here on the narrow rural roads outside of town we set out to build the strength and toughness that allowed us to compete with the top teams in the state. For runners like us, mileage, especially long fast mileage, is the great equalizer. While those blessed with natural talent honed their skills on the tight turns of indoor tracks, we preferred to hammer out miles on roads with names like Old Wausau, Casmir, Jordan, and Woodview. Our success wasn't the result of "something in the water" as people were prone to suggest; we were successful because of runs like this one: a long run at a brutally hard pace, on a deserted country road, surrounded by teammates pushing their limits, trying desperately to make themselves better runners. Trained to mask our feelings, hide our fatigue, and show no fear, we secretly wondered who among us will be the first to break as we passed a large open field and climbed the highway overpass that overlooked piles of rusty, discarded automobiles. As if chased by a pack of baying hounds, we flew down the road at a pace faster than any of us ought to be running. For true distance runners like us, this is what we thrive on, the challenge of doing too much and doing it too fast. Silently we crossed Haymeadow Creek before entering the vast openness of empty farm fields on both sides of the road as we neared the end of our long pickup. Past a large, stately white barn we turned right onto the long stretch of road called Reserve Street.

"Alright guys, shut it down," I yelled to Kim and Rob, ten yards ahead of me, before turning to check on the line of runners trailing along behind. "Cool down," I ordered, gasping for breath. "Let's group it up."

"Wow, that was great. Man, did I feel good!" Kim said, stating what the rest of us had already figured out.

"Holy crap," Mike added, "that was nuts!"

"Great workout!" I shouted excitedly as the pace slowed to a jog. "You guys are really fit. I can't wait to see what you can do on a good indoor track and an outdoor track… if we ever get some decent weather."

"So, Donn, what are you going to do about Scott?" Kim asked, jogging slowly as we waited for our stragglers to catch up.

"I don't know. I'm not sure there's anything I can do. It sounded like they'd made up their mind."

"The whole thing just sucks," Rob added bluntly. "A kid finds a place where he fits in a little and they make him quit, and why? Just because he took his t-shirt off? Big deal! He didn't do anything wrong. The whole thing is just stupid!"

"Rob," I said, knowing that by now we had the attention of the entire group, "I agree with you. What he did was pretty minor, but once they heard about it they had to do something. Scott has a written behavior plan so when he screws up they drop the hammer on him. The guys at the group home don't have a choice; they're just doing their job."

"Well then they suck at their job," Rob said to the amusement of his teammates.

"Problem is, they're not Scott's parents. Rob, you screw up all the time, your mom gets mad, you apologize, and you get another chance. That's what parents do, but the group home guys are like policemen. They just enforce the rules to the letter of the law. They don't get to make the rules."

"Yeah, well, maybe they should, maybe if they came to a practice or a meet they'd change their minds. I'll tell you what I think, I don't think they care. I think they got tired of drivin' all the way up here every day to pick him up after practice. I think the t-shirt thing was just an excuse," Rob said angrily.

"Yeah, I don't know, Rob. Maybe that had something to do with it. I'll make another phone call, but I'm pretty sure we've seen the last of The Animal."

Our run ended with the sound of running shoes scuffing the sand covered asphalt parking lot outside the locker room door.

"Great run, nice workout, good work," I rattled off while offering high fives and handshakes as my guys filed through the door.

"Scott!" I heard C.J shout. "Where you been, man? What's goin' on?"

Turning the corner I could see Scott standing at his locker, surrounded by teammates, head down, eyes cast to the floor, with a pile of neatly folded gray sweats cradled in his arms. With little doubt as to what was about to happen, I issued a loud, happy greeting.

"Hey, Scott! Great to see you. We missed you today."

"Thanks Coach, but I got bad news. Coach, I gotta quit," he said softly, shaking his head, unable to look me in the eyes.

"Coach, I tried real hard to talk 'em out of it, but they said no."

"Yeah, I called 'em, but it seems like they had their minds made up. I think it's a really bad decision. I think it does more harm than good, but...."

"Here's my sweats, Coach. I washed 'em last night. All nice and neat."

"Thanks, Scott. You didn't need to wash them, but it was nice that you did."

"No problem Coach, I do lots of laundry. I'm very good at laundry," he said with his usual confidence. "But Coach, just one question," he said, pointing to the t-shirt on the top of the stack of items he'd just handed me. "That's my lucky shirt, and I was wonderin'...."

"This is a lucky t-shirt?" I asked, noticing the number 70 printed on the winged foot beneath the words SPASH TRACK.

"Yeah Coach! Don't you remember? This is the exact shirt I wore in the race that I almost won!"

"Oh yeah, the one you led till the last half lap. You ran 2:16. I didn't forget; that was a great race."

"Thanks Coach. So, do you think?"

"Well, I'm not allowed to give away school equipment, but now that I look at it, this shirt is in really bad shape. I think maybe it needs to be retired."

"Yeah," he said as a smile quickly replaced the somber look on his face. "Good idea, Coach. Maybe I should retire it for you."

"Sure, why don't you take care of that," I said, holding it out in his direction.

"THANKS COACH!" he cheered, bouncing happily on the balls of his feet, "and don't worry, I won't lose it. I'll take good care of it."

With one hand placed firmly on Scott's shoulder, I reached out to shake his large bony hand.

"Scott, I just want you to know how much I enjoyed being your coach. You worked hard at every practice and I respect that. You earned a spot on this team and you belong here, so if anything changes at the group home, you can always come back.

You're always welcome here. Remember that, okay?"

"Yeah Coach, thanks."

"Now, you better get moving. Those potatoes aren't going to peel themselves, you know."

"Sure Coach, I got it covered. You don't have to worry about me. I'll be okay," he said, flashing his trademark toothy grin before turning toward the back door of the locker room and slowly walking away.

Our track season ended as one of the most successful in the history of our program. With individual state champions in the high jump and the pole vault along with outstanding efforts in the 3,200 meters by Kim (9:19) and Rob (9:33), we earned a sixth place finish at our state meet to end what we all considered a fun and rewarding season.

Sadly, Scott was never allowed to return to the team, and after the initial angry reaction by his teammates, he was seldom mentioned. Seeing him in the hallways just wasn't the same. At practice he was one of us; around school he was just another loud, awkward kid. You can't be part of the group unless you show up, and Scott "The Animal" Longley wasn't allowed to show up.

FIVE

GOOD NEWS COACH

The tiny air conditioner in our bedroom window whined continuously as an early August heat wave entered day six. July had been hotter than normal, and the record setting trend continued, driving all but the heartiest souls in search of relief. Each morning I scanned the sky, hoping for any sign of a change in the weather as skinny young men clad in shorts and t-shirts assembled on my front lawn for our morning run group. We could shorten the run, slow the pace, and find shadier routes, but little else could be done. Television weathermen warned of the dangers the heat wave posed for those who worked outdoors, dogs left in parked cars, babies, and pregnant women like my wife Cheryl. Now eight months pregnant, the current string of hot days was beginning to wear on her. Having spent most of the last week trapped in the two semi air-conditioned rooms of our small home, an uncomfortable feeling of confinement was beginning to set in. The shade of the small silver maple in our back yard offered little relief beyond early morning, and the hard wooden chairs in the cool quiet of our public library seemed an uncomfortable choice for a pregnant woman.

"How about going to a movie this afternoon?" I shouted to her as I searched through a stack of old newspapers.

"Really, a movie? Who goes to a movie in the middle of the afternoon?"

"Oh just kids, old folks, and people like us who need to get out of the heat." Scanning page two of the *Stevens Point Daily Journal* sports section, I added, "Here, how about this one? It's called *Back to the Future* with Michael J. Fox."

"That sounds awful!" Cheryl said, entering the kitchen with a puzzled look. "Yeah, and you know how much I hate science fiction, but the guys on the morning run have been talking about it non-stop for the last couple days. They say it's really funny."

"So you're going to trust the opinions of a bunch of teenage boys?" she asked.

"It's not just the young guys; the college guys liked it, too." I reminded her.

"Well then, who am I to argue with a thumbs up from the college guys," she responded with just a hint of sarcasm in her voice.

Normally having no interest in horror movies, car chases, or, in this case, time travel, I did my best to avoid movies marketed to teenage boys. Somehow this one sounded different. The idea of a comedy about a mad scientist and his time machine made from a 1981 DeLorean captured my interest. Each morning for the last week I had listened to the guys throw movie lines back and forth as only teenage boys can do. Things like Flux Capacitor, 1.21 Gigawatts, and "I'm your density" had been flung around all week, along with shouts of "It's the Libyan Nationalists!" each time they sighted a white van. Since I hadn't seen the movie, these quotes meant nothing to me, but I enjoyed the dialogue and wanted to be in on the joke. I didn't want to be like the guy on a golf outing who couldn't quote *Caddie Shack* verbatim, or at least recognize the reference.

Conversation and constant banter are important parts of a running group and to fit in you need to be able to contribute something to keep the conversation ball in the air. Quoting the first sentence of the U.S. Constitution or the Gettysburg Address is all well and good, but not knowing what the Dalai Lama said to Carl Spackler after hitting his drive into a 10,000 foot crevasse could make you a social outcast in the 1980's.

The line at the Campus Theater box office wove into the parking lot, indicating the popularity of the movie and the desire of people to escape the oppressive heat. For the next two hours we enjoyed a clever comedy, cool air, and the pregnancy-friendly combination of lemonade and lightly salted popcorn. Putting my doubts about time travel aside, I was taken in by the absurd concept of a young man given the chance to witness his parents' first meeting 30 years earlier. Quirky, believable characters and oldies music made a great combination as the two hours passed without the slightest temptation to check my watch. Best of all, Cheryl greatly enjoyed both the movie and our short parole from the confines of our house.

As we pulled into our driveway I took special notice of the rolled up newspaper leaning against the bottom step of our front porch. Reading the newspaper, always a highlight for me, was especially important today. The date, August 6, 1985, was the 40th anniversary of the bombing of Hiroshima. As a history teacher, I was anxious to read about the annual memorial ceremony and perhaps acquire some new material for my classroom bulletin board. A two page article complete with before and after pictures held my attention as I spread the paper across the kitchen table. Our new cordless phone rang loudly on the counter just a few feet away. Cheryl answered it on the first ring as I looked on, trying to interpret the puzzled look on her face.

"Sure, I'll get him," she said as she held the phone in my direction. A shrug of her shoulders told me she had no idea who might be on the other end of the line.

"Hello," I answered.

"Coach Behnke!" a loud, raspy voice shouted. "Good news, Coach!"

"Who is this?" I asked, somewhat annoyed by the ringing in my ears.

"It's me Coach, The Animal," came the loud response from

Scott who was clearly disappointed that I hadn't been able to guess. to hire

"Well hey, Scott, good to hear from you. Sorry I didn't recognize your voice. How've you been?"

"Coach, I've got really good news for you. I'm gonna run cross country this fall!"

"Oh really? Well, that is good news," I said as I tried to process what I'd just been told. "Are you sure you're ready for this, Scott?"

"Yeah Coach, I've been running every day. I made my own cross country course in the backyard, and I run for an hour every day."

"In your backyard. You run around your backyard for an hour?"

"Yeah, Coach."

"Every day?"

"Yeah, Coach. Except for sometimes I run with one of the new counselors. And if I have a really good week they let me run to the Moto Mart, and I get to buy a soda before I run back."

"That's great, Scott," I said cautiously. "Sounds like you're pretty serious about this. Do you know when the season starts?"

"Coach, it's in the paper, front page of the sports section. Next Monday at eight o'clock sharp."

"That's right, Scott," I said flashing a partial smile at Cheryl who stood several feet away trying to break the code of my conversation. "Remember, you're going to need to turn in some paperwork before the first practice."

"No problem, Coach. I was at school last week. I talked to Mr. Anderson, and I got everything taken care of."

"Good, nice work taking care of that. But remember last track season? That didn't work out so well, did it?"

"I know, Coach. But that won't happen again. I'll never tear my shirt off again. I promise."

"I know, Scott. I'm not worried about your t-shirt. But if you start the season with us, you need to be ready to finish it. It's bad for our team when guys come out for a couple weeks and then quit. So I need you to think about this. I'm glad that you want to run, but this is a serious decision. I need you to promise me that you'll be at every practice and work hard every day."

"C'mon Coach, this is me, The Animal. I've got the Eye of the Tiger. No one works harder than me."

"I know, Scott, and that's great, but I'm actually more worried about keeping you out of trouble at the group home."

"No problem, Coach. We have a new counselor here. He's a runner and he's helping me. He's getting me in shape, and he said he'll pick me up after every practice."

"That's good because I think that was a problem during track," I said, working towards the conclusion of our conversation. "Scott, it's really good to hear from you. I'm looking forward to seeing you Monday. I think it will be a good season."

"You got that right, Coach. Just one question. Are we going to win state? And if we win, do we get white tuxedoes and a big limousine?"

"Where did you hear about tuxedoes and limousines?"

"From Mike. He said the team that beat you last year wore white tuxedoes and got their picture taken sitting on a big shiny limousine. He said that if we win this year you promised you'd get us white tuxedoes, too."

"Well, if I said that I was just goofing around. We're going to have a good team this year, but we're not going to be state champs. We have Mike and C.J. to build around, but after that, well, we have a lot of work to do."

"Coach Behnke! Come on! Ya got The Animal now. Ya gotta have a positive attitude."

"Okay, well in that case I better start pricing tuxedoes this afternoon," I joked.

"There ya go, Coach. That's it, ya gotta believe."

"Alright, Scott. Hey it's good to hear from you. I'll see you Monday at eight."

"Gotcha Coach, Monday eight o'clock sharp."

"Well, that was interesting," I said to Cheryl as I hung up the phone. "Remember Scott, the kid we called Animal? Evidently he's been running around his back yard for an hour every day. He says he's gonna run cross country with us, and he thinks we'll be state champs. Said I should start pricing tuxedoes and limousines."

"Really, and the guys at the group home are okay with that?"

"Yeah, it sounds like it. He said he has his paper work turned in, and he seems to have some support from one of the new counselors who's into running, so that's good. I don't know, maybe he's making this stuff up, but he sounded really serious."

"So what was all that about tuxedos and limousines?" asked Cheryl with a puzzled look.

"I guess Mike told him about the guys who beat us last year having their picture taken wearing white tuxes and, well, that kid's got some sort of memory."

"Really?" said Cheryl. "How weird is that?"

"Yeah that's a pretty big bombshell he just dropped on me," I said, smiling as I scooped the newspaper from the kitchen table and pointed to the picture of the mushroom cloud above the city of Hiroshima. "But after all, it is August 6th."

Six

Six Foot Pizza

Kim and Rob stood against the east wall of the field house along with a few other alumni, studying the chaos of the first cross country practice as they waited for the run to begin. No longer the team leaders, they were here to evaluate and support us for a few days before heading off to join their college teams. Watching quietly from the sidelines, they knew that the torch of leadership was about to be passed. Today, the next group of seniors would inherit the program.

Mike was clearly the guy we would build this year's team around. Tough, driven, and highly competitive, he was determined that the success of our program would not end on his watch. Ready and eager for the season to begin, Mike was our most vocal leader.

Curt, who by this point was among the nation's best high school race walkers, would have to miss the first two weeks of practice to participate in a series of national level events on the east coast. As one of our top returning runners, his absence was reason for concern, and while none of us wanted to interfere with his Olympic dreams, we all knew we needed him back soon.

C.J. had few of the leadership skills that Mike and Curt possessed. Giving a rah-rah speech to the team was never going to be his thing. He preferred to let his actions speak for him. We all knew that when the gun went off C.J. was always ready to race.

We were a team of only three seniors until Scott entered the field house. Certainly we couldn't expect him to be a leader. He'd never, to my knowledge, even seen a cross country meet, and his entire running career amounted to a couple of indoor half-miles and apparently several hundred loops on some sort of course in the group home's backyard. Scott was, for the most part, just here for the social aspect. This was a chance for him to spend time with guys far different than the ones at the group home and in his "special" classes. I knew there would be challenges along the way, but there was never a doubt that our team environment would be good for him. He might require a little more supervision and effort on my part, but after what I'd seen during the track season I knew it was worth a try. •

Approaching quickly from across the field house, Scott looked just as shaggy and unkempt as the last time I'd seen him. Charging my way, excited and full of energy, he called out in his loud, raspy voice, "COACH BEHNKE! I can't believe it. I'm here, at a SPASH Cross Country practice. FINALLY!"

"Scott! Hey, it's great to see you. Welcome to the team," I said as I offered a handshake.

"Coach," he said, shaking my hand with a forceful, exaggerated motion, "this is going to be a great season. I just know it is."

"Well Scott, you know, every cross country season is a great season."

"No Coach, I mean this one's gonna be somethin' special. I can just feel it."

"That's what we're here for, to build something special, but it's not going to be easy, I can tell you that."

"I know, Coach, and I'm ready. I mean I'm really ready. This team is going to surprise you, Coach. You wait and see."

Glancing at my watch I realized it was 8:05. "Time to stretch!" I yelled as the season officially began.

With our small group spread randomly across our corner of the field house, Mike and C.J. took on the task of leading our stretching routine with Scott positioned front and center. I stood off to the side, chatting with a few of our recent graduates.

"Have you ever had a team this small?" Kim asked me as we stood overlooking a group of only 19 runners.

"No, not in the eight years I've been here. This is definitely our smallest group ever."

"So, we've won three of the last five state meets and the team gets smaller?" Rob asked angrily. "I don't get it."

"I don't know what to tell you, Rob. I talked to a lot of kids at junior high track meets, and I sent out a bunch of letters this summer. I really thought we'd get at least eight or ten new guys."

"Yeah, how many did you get?"

"Well, right now just three and only one freshman."

"Wow, that's incredible. I mean that's just awful. I can't believe that," said Kim quietly.

"Yeah, but you know how freshmen are. If they weigh 100 pounds they think they can play football and the new soccer program is gaining momentum, so that hurt our numbers too."

"Soccer? Soccer sucks!" added Rob.

"Hey, this is nothing new. You've been around long enough to know that we're the sport of last resort. We're bottom feeders, a place for guys who've been rejected by every other sport, the place for guys like you two," I said, directing a smile their way. "The way I see it, I can sit here and whine about it or I can do my best with whoever walks, limps, or crawls through the door on the first day of practice."

As what passed for stretching came to an end, I took my position in front of our small, eclectic, collection of runners. We didn't look like much, but then again good cross country teams often don't. Admittedly we had a sort of *Lord of the Flies* look to us, but I didn't care. I wanted guys to show up every day, work hard, and contribute something to the team. Appearances mattered little to our raggedy little group, and Scott was a perfect fit. From his trademark pile of untamed hair to his bushy eyebrows and unshaven chin, he had an almost permanent "just rolled out of bed" look. Dressed in his black cotton gym shorts, dirty, nearly worn out Brooks shoes, and his "lucky" SPASH Track t-shirt, he was definitely one of us.

"Just a few announcements," I said as I ran down the list on my clipboard, rattling off information about our schedule, paperwork, and the athletic code as the group sat quietly listening. Having described in detail the course we were about to run, I gave instructions on pacing and finished with a few reminders. "The goal for the first week is to run as many miles as you can handle. It could be 20 or 120, that's up to you. If you don't already know, we have an afternoon run and I'd like to see most of you show up, but I'll leave that up to you, too. This week is all about breaking down barriers, getting over your fears and building strength. Just remember, the only difference between teams that succeed and teams that fail is hard work. The surest path to success is to simply run more than the people you compete against. All those trophies in the case," I said, pointing to the hallway, "that's no happy accident. We didn't get those by having guys run three or four miles a day. Don't ever forget that. Those trophies are the result of a lot of hard work by the guys who came through this program ahead of you. If you're one of the new guys, you might want to take a look in the trophy case as we head out and study our collection. It's a history lesson, and I'll quiz you on it tomorrow."

A slightly warm, humid morning greeted us as we filed out of the school and began a slow jog across the empty student parking lot.

"Scott!" I yelled, realizing I'd already lost track of him. "Where IS he? How can he be lost already? We haven't even gone fifty yards…ROB!"

"Hey, it's not my job. I'm not a captain anymore," Rob reminded the group.

"Coach," said Dan, "this is just a guess, but I think he's just doin' what you told him to do. He's probably in the hallway looking at the trophy case."

Turning my face to the sky, I closed my eyes, smiled, and

nodded. "Yep, just like I told him." Backtracking quickly as the team waited, I entered the hallway and found him, face pushed up against the glass, studying the trophies in the case.

Noticing my approach, Scott proudly announced, "Coach, I got it. There's five trophies in the last five years. Three gold, two silver, and I know the dates, too."

"That's great, Scott, but we need to get the run started. We'll talk about trophies later."

"Okay, Coach. I just want you to know I'm ready for your quiz."

A loud round of applause greeted us as we exited the building and rejoined the group. Scott beamed, seemingly unaware that clapping can sometimes be used sarcastically.

With everyone now accounted for we headed down the road at a comfortable pace in a tightly formed pack. For many in the group the pace was far too slow, but they knew the rule: the entire group had to stay intact for at least a mile. We started each run at the pace of our slowest runner. The goal was not to burn the new guys, at least not right away.

An odd silence fell over the group as we shuffled down Northpoint Drive. The new guys, not sure what to expect, had the good sense to keep their mouths shut, but even the older guys were much too quiet, uncomfortably quiet.

"Hey," I shouted loudly, "didn't anyone do anything exciting this summer? Any Sasquatch sightings? Alien abductions? Liquor store robberies? Your first kiss? Oh yeah, I forgot, you guys are cross country runners, you don't get girlfriends. Come on, someone must have had an interesting summer job," I pleaded. "Kim, you painted fire hydrants, didn't you?"

"Yeah, I painted 14 the first day and got yelled at by the boss. He told me that at that rate I'd be out of a job in a week. So I painted one in the morning, took a three hour lunch, and painted another in the afternoon. Yep, your tax dollars at work!"

"You know, I used to work at the fire hydrant factory, but I had to quit. Could never find a place to park," I joked lamely, trying my best to get any sort of reaction.

Several guys admitted to the kind of dull low paying jobs that only a high school kid would do. Several worked at fast-food joints while others mowed lawns and one told of the misery of trimming Christmas trees. Rob had spent the summer selling sun glasses from a kiosk in our local mall while John stocked shelves in a grocery store with a guy who claimed to be in the professional baseball Hall of Fame with the record for the most bratwurst eaten during a nine inning game.

"I delivered pizzas!" Scott announced proudly.

"Pizzas? How can YOU deliver pizzas?" Rob demanded. "You don't even have a driver's license."

"I don't need one…I run!" Scott explained.

"You run? You run and deliver pizzas?" Rob asked as he moved closer to Scott. "No one runs to deliver a pizza."

Suddenly the entire group focused its attention on this curious conversation as they strained to hold back their laughter.

"Yeah, that's right," said Scott, defending his claim, "and these are big pizzas."

"Oh, I'm sure they are. So how big are they?" Rob demanded to know.

"A large pizza is six feet across."

"Six feet? Animal, do you even know how big that is? Six feet is like THIS!" Rob shouted as he stretched his arms out to their full width.

"That's right, that's how big they are," said Scott without backing down.

"How do you carry a pizza that big?"

"Right here!" he answered, hands spread wide above his head.

"So you're telling me you run down the road with a six foot pizza on your head?"

"Yeah, and sometimes I have to run five or ten miles!"

"Animal, do you know long that would take?"

"Yeah, it takes about an hour," Scott said proudly.

"You can run six-minute pace with a pizza on your head?"

"Yeah, and then I have to run back."

"Animal! This is why you get in trouble all the time. You can't just go around makin' stuff up. You're lying and everyone here knows you're lying. Just keep it up, and they're going to make you quit again. Is that what you want?"

"No, of course not," Scott answered, then quietly added, "but I did deliver pizzas."

"Animal! Just shut up and run," Rob shouted as we staggered down the road, laughing.

It was a comedy routine worthy of Abbot and Costello, and it became an instant classic to all who'd been there to hear it. Unfortunately, it was also an example of Scott's somewhat loose connection with the truth. For many of our younger guys, this was their first introduction to Scott and they weren't sure what to make of him. Should they laugh with him or at him, they wondered, or just stay away? Scott was not the only misfit on our team, but he was definitely the most complex. While I was as amused as anyone by his exchange with Rob, I knew I couldn't let things get out of hand. At some point I'd have to address his penchant for exaggeration, but right now it was time for the workout to get a little more serious.

Reaching the first turn off point, our group became slightly smaller and the pace gradually quickened. Dan was clearly the most anxious to show his level of fitness, with Mike and C.J. close behind. Rob, an infamous "half stepper," took up his usual position at the front while Kim and I stayed at the back of the group with Scott between us. This was my first chance to assess his level of fitness and whether he'd really run an hour a day in his back yard or simply created another one of his stories. Settling into a slightly quicker pace, I could feel a sense of unity in our tightly bunched group. A few guys struggled to hang on, but most looked pretty comfortable with our fairly ambitious pace. Scott lopped along at my side with his characteristic forward lean and pronounced arm swing. He certainly wasn't efficient and his foot strike was by far the loudest in the group, but he looked strong as we made the turn that committed us to the long loop.

"How you doing, Scott?" I asked, feeling as if I already knew the answer.

"Great Coach, I told you I was in good shape."

"Yeah, I can see that. What do you think? Are you ready to go with the long group?"

"Coach, come on! Of course I can go with the long group, no problem."

"Okay, but the pace is going to get a little quicker, so just let me know if you need to back off a bit."

"Sure Coach, got it."

Nearing the midway point of our nine mile loop, I liked what I was seeing. As concerned as I was about our lack of numbers, I had a good feeling about having nearly half the team still in the front group. As the leaders, itching to go harder, increased the pace ever so slightly, several of our younger guys began to fall back. I kept a watchful eye on Scott and our talented freshman, Johnny Hyland. If the pace was too fast for them, it was hard to tell. They looked good and seemed determined to hang on at all cost.

"Hey," I shouted from behind as I decided it was time to split the group. "I'm going to take Scott and Johnny and back off a bit. The rest of you guys, remember this is ONLY Monday, the first day of a really big week, so let's not be stupid. Keep it sensible."

"I got it," said Kim, once again assuming the role of team leader.

Comfortable with Kim and Rob in the lead group, I slowed the pace slightly with my two inexperienced runners in tow. Sensible, I thought to myself, is clearly a term open to interpretation, especially on the first day of practice, when guys want to test themselves, measure their teammates and stake out their place on the team. I could warn them, but I couldn't really control them, at least not today. I knew that good runners have to be willing to push their limits and run a little too fast sometimes. This was something they needed to get out of their systems, and Double DuBay loop on the first day of practice seemed like a good place to do it.

Some of the new guys struggled a little, but the majority of the team looked pretty good. Our leaders had run an excellent workout and several others really impressed me. Johnny was new to cross country, but his talent was unmistakable. He had been dominant on the track in junior high, and I knew he was fluid and fast, but now, after one long run, I was sure we had found one of our next great runners.

Despite the initial shock and disappointment of such a small turnout, our first practice had been a great success. We wouldn't be a big team, but we definitely had some guys who could run. Mike and C.J. were strong, fit, and ready to lead the rebuilding process. Dan Morgan and Bill Kleckner looked lean and strong after a summer of serious training, and John was determined to apply his considerable track talents to cross country. Dan's younger brother Michael and a new kid named Chip Carlson had drawn the attention of all in the lead group by hanging on to the back of the pack for most of the run.

Beyond our top three returners we had few guys with race experience, but clearly we were a team with potential. We would never be among the top teams in our state, but with Curt's return from his race walking tour I felt we could build a respectable team.

Without a doubt Scott had been the biggest surprise of all. Having finished our nine mile run within shouting distance of the leaders, he entered the field house at my side with a smile on his face. Somehow, the big awkward kid Jerry had forced on me a few months earlier had turned himself into a runner. Evidently, I thought to myself, those hour-long runs in the back yard and Moto-Mart sodas had done the trick.

SEVEN

DEAL

As always, the start of our season was an odd combination of fun mixed with a nearly insane amount of hard work. Spending hours together each morning and afternoon had made us closer and helped us feel and act like a team. Guys worked together, encouraged one another, pushed those ahead of them and pulled along those who fell behind.

Concentrating almost entirely on mileage during the first week, Mike and C.J. recorded more than one hundred miles and several others in the group totaled well over eighty. Scott, unable to join us for the soft surface afternoon runs, racked up miles in his backyard, on his way to what, by his count, was a seventy-five mile week. It's hard to tell much from just a few practices, but with Scott wedged in the middle of what was becoming a closely knit, dedicated group of guys, we seemed to be heading in the right direction.

From tennis ball games before practice to cool downs and gab sessions at the end, he was always included. Sure, the nickname Animal could be seen as derogatory and the phrase "shut up and run" came his way with some frequency, but that was about it. A few guys were still cautiously trying to figure him out, but for the most part he was treated like any other kid on the team. Maybe it's the more the merrier philosophy of our sport or something to do with the way distance runners tend to view the world, but

Scott had found a home simply because he worked hard. Showing up for practice and jogging a few miles will get your name on the roster, but that's about it. Respect, as Scott had learned, is earned by giving an honest effort at every practice.

"Long run today, Coach?" Scott asked as he bounced happily into the field house for the first practice of the second week of our season.

"No Scott, today we're going to do a ladder."

"A ladder? Coach, are ya kiddin' me? We're gonna climb ladders?"

"No Scott, it's just a term for an interval workout we do at the park. This week we still do a lot of long runs, but we're going to add in a little pace work, like we did last track season, remember?"

"Yeah Coach, we did half-miles."

"Right, except today we'll run a quarter-mile, half-mile, three-quarter, and a mile, like climbing up a ladder," I said, making a step-like motion with my hand.

"Sounds hard, Coach."

"No, really this one's not bad. This is just a half ladder. Wait till we do the full one—that's when things get tough."

Jogging along toward Bukolt Park, I made a point of reminding Mike and C.J. about their pace-setting duties. "Eighty second quarters, that's the pace. Eighty, two-forty, four minutes, five-twenty...got it?" I asked sternly.

"Yeah," Mike answered. "Piece a cake."

At this early hour on a hot and humid Monday morning, the park, except for a couple of anglers on the river bank, was nearly empty. T-shirts were quickly removed and cast aside as the group assembled at the stone pillars that marked the park entrance, ready to begin the first step of the ladder.

"I could run this pace all day," Scott announced proudly in the middle of our first interval.

"Yeah, that's how you're supposed to feel," I explained as we crossed the line with the main group, right at eighty seconds.

"Anyone can run a bunch of quarters and half-miles at this pace," I explained as we began our jogging recovery. "The trick is to run 5,000 meters just like that. Do that and you'll be a very good high school cross country runner."

"And you're going to make me into a very good runner, aren't you, Coach?"

"No, Scott, I'm not going to," I said to his surprise. "You're going to make yourself into a good runner. All you have to do is stick right with me, run everything I run, every day. Think you can do that?"

"I don't know, Coach. You're pretty good for an old guy," he said cautiously.

"Oh!" I said, amid the laughter of our group. "So, are you saying a strong, healthy, young guy like you can't stick with an old man like me? Come on," I said, extending a hand in his direction. "It's not a bet, just a gentleman's agreement."

"Okay Coach, it's a deal! I'll do every workout just like you," Scott said, shaking my hand to seal the deal.

Surrounded by a group of attentive witnesses, Scott had just committed himself to a season's worth of hard work, and, without giving it much thought, so had I.

EIGHT

PORTAGE

Travel bag slung over my shoulder, I quietly pulled the back door shut and faced the pre-dawn darkness of the early September morning. It was already uncomfortably warm and humid, and I wondered what conditions would be by race time as I pedaled my Raleigh ten-speed slowly through the warm, light fog.

This is ridiculous, I thought to myself, 82 degrees at 5:45 on a September morning. Having spent all 32 years of my life in Wisconsin, I knew this could happen, but I had no recollection of anything quite like it. Already worried about putting a young, inexperienced team on the course for our first meet, I now had to consider the safety of my athletes. My stomach churned nervously as I biked past the tennis courts and through the faculty parking lot to the locker room door.

The Portage Invitational was going to be an ugly introduction to cross country for those new to our sport, and a potentially dangerous situation for any who didn't show proper respect for the conditions. With a temperature forecast in the upper 90's, I had to be ready to pull guys off the course mid-race if I felt they were in trouble. As much as I hated the thought, today would be more about survival than posting fast times.

Always the first to arrive at school, I parked my bike, propped the back door open with my travel bag, and set out to find one of the football team's many five gallon Igloo coolers. Filling it with ice, I carried it back to the parking lot, placed it against the brick wall near the bike rack, and sat in the quiet early morning haze, waiting for others to arrive.

The morning calm was soon broken by the roar of a four-cylinder engine attached to the rusted-out exhaust system of a Toyota pickup. Entering the lot at a decidedly unsafe speed, Mike, an intelligent and responsible young man in most instances, cranked a hard right turn, locked his brakes, and sent loose gravel flying as he skidded to an abrupt halt. Jumping quickly from the cab of the small truck, he turned his face to the sky and shouted, "What a great day for a race! I am soooo ready for this!"

Pulling a huge travel bag from the bed of the truck, he slammed the driver's side door forcefully and headed my way at a trot.

"Morning, Donn," he said happily. "How are you on this beautiful morning?"

"Great, Mike," I said, holding off a strong desire to lecture him about his driving habits. "I'm a little worried about the weather, but it's great to finally get the season started."

"You got that right. I'm so excited I barely slept. Hey, anything you need help with?" he asked as he tossed his bag to the ground next to mine.

"Yeah, could you grab some of the boards from the training room?"

"Sure, how many do you think we'll need today?"

"Oh, I think half a dozen should do."

"Boards" referred to the pieces of three-quarter inch plywood we placed between the bus seats to accommodate a few more passengers. With only one bus for both the boys' and girls' teams, Mike Olson, the girls' coach and wood shop instructor, had improvised a way to add a fifth seat to each row. For a couple teams on very tight budgets, it seemed to be a logical solution to our shortage of seats. Rather than press the issue and ask for a second bus, each year as our programs grew Ole simply cut up another sheet of plywood.

Fortunately, the Wisconsin Department of Transportation never learned of our little innovation, our bus drivers didn't seem to mind, and outside of an occasional Rosa Parks reference, our runners didn't complain. There was a good attitude on our crowded bus, and the girls, led by three-time state champion Suzy Favor, added to it. The boards provided a way to keep both teams on one bus and brought us closer together both literally and figuratively. Just remember, as we told the new guys, keep the smooth side facing up.

Standing at the bus door in the dim morning light, I checked my attendance sheet as the runners boarded. A small crowd gathered a few feet away as Rob arrived in the brand new Ford Escort he'd won at a church raffle a few weeks earlier. Although officially a college student, Rob's heart was still with his high school team and he wasn't about to miss the first meet of our season. He also knew I'd appreciate his help with The Animal.

Watching carefully as Scott emerged from the group home van stopped nearby, I paid close attention to how he was dressed and the items he carried as he walked my way. With the "lucky" gray t-shirt I'd given him last track season tucked deeply into his black cotton Phys. Ed. shorts and red, white, and blue striped tube socks pulled up to just below his knees, he smiled like a lottery winner as he approached. He had a light blue duffel bag slung over his shoulder, a red one gallon thermos jug in his right hand, and a brown paper grocery bag in the other.

"Coach Behnke," he said excitedly, "I got all my gear, just like you told me. I got a dry shirt, extra socks, and the spikes given to me by the great Keith Hanson."

"Good job, Scott," I said as I patted him on the shoulder.

"And Coach, look," he said proudly holding up his thermos. "Cool, refreshing Plover Spring water. It's like you always tell us, Coach, ya gotta stay hydrated."

"Yeah and that's going to be especially important today. So, what's in the bag?"

"Coach," he said as he placed the thermos on the ground and opened the paper bag to reveal a green Tupperware bowl, "it's a salad and I gotta tell ya, I toss a mean salad."

"Looks like you're all set now. Get on the bus, it's time for us to get moving."

"Should I give him a board?" Mike asked as Scott neared the bus steps.

"No, he'll sit up front with me."

Climbing on board, Scott sat directly behind the driver and watched intently as C.J. lugged a huge boom box down the center aisle. With both teams packed aboard, the bus lurched into gear as I wedged my Igloo cooler between the first row of seats and planted myself next to Scott and Rob. With windows in the full down position and the bus radio tuned to our driver's favorite station, we began to move forward. The first road trip of our season had begun.

Heading south on Highway 51, we settled in for the hour and a half trip to Portage as the sounds of country music and excited voices filled the bus. Few paid any attention to the barely audible country western songs and morning farm report. The weather forecast was the only thing of interest to us today as we headed down the road with wind whipping our faces. How hot would it get we wondered as we listened intently to some guy named "Mornin' Bob" read the news and weather report. Curious to hear the current temperature and the projected high for the day, the front half of the bus fell silent as "Bob" told of a plane crash in Milwaukee and an upcoming Farm Aid concert at the University of Illinois organized by Willie Nelson.

"Shut up! Everybody SHUT UP!" Mike demanded as "Bob" finally began the weather report.

"Currently 84 degrees with 96 percent humidity and record highs in the forecast," "Bob" reported, warning those who had to be outdoors to use "extreme caution." The National Weather Service predicted highs in the upper nineties with the possibility of 100 degree readings in parts of northern Illinois and southern

Wisconsin. Rob could see the look of concern on my face as I processed the numbers in my mind and tried to think of something to say.

"Well," Mike said with a smile, "I guess I won't be needin' these!" as he held up a blaze orange stocking cap and a pair of light cotton gloves. Suddenly, almost as if pre-planned, C.J., Curt, and Dan held up similar winter gear. These were the veterans. Prepared for anything, they had heard me say on many occasions that Wisconsin has only two temperatures, too hot and too cold. Evidently they'd been paying attention.

The weather was definitely going to be a factor today, and as worried as I was it didn't seem to bother the guys. They knew better than to shy away from adversity. Successful runners learn to face bad conditions head on, with some even believing it gives them an advantage. That's the attitude I wanted to foster on our team. In intense heat, bitter cold, rain, sleet, or snow, our approach didn't change. I wanted our guys to be ready for any conditions, but this, I worried, might be a little too extreme.

Turning to Mike first, I questioned him on his race plan for the day. After finishing fifth at our time trial last weekend, I was concerned that totaling nearly three hundred miles in three weeks had been too much for him.

"Yeah," he said, "I was pretty beat down last week, but I feel great today. I'm goin' right to the front. Screw the weather, I'm ready."

The response was classic Mike, and I wasn't the least bit surprised. He was always one to meet a problem head on and was eager to test himself against whatever the day had to offer. Searching the stack of papers on my clipboard, I studied the result sheet from our time trial the previous Saturday.

"Here," I said as I handed them to Rob, "take a look."

"Wow, slow times," he said at a near whisper.

"Yeah, but it was pretty hot and it's a new course. I think it's accurate, but after seeing those times I'm hoping it was long."

"Me too. So are you worried?"

"Maybe a little, but the guys were pretty worn down. Mike and C.J. ran it pretty much as a workout. I never worry about them, but the rest of the guys — it's really hard to know."

"Well, I was shocked when I heard that Dan won it and Bill got third."

"Yeah, I'll admit I was surprised too, but they put in a lot of miles this summer. I knew they were fit, but still...I didn't expect that."

"Ever had a freshman run a better time trial than Johnny?"

"No, but that kid is just so talented," I said in a soft voice as I leaned in Rob's direction. "He's gonna be our next great runner, just wait."

"And what's this all about?" Rob asked as he pointed at John's name on the list.

"Oh, yeah. Well, John just cut the lead group loose and ran with Scott. It was Scott's first race and he was just lost out there, so John paced him in."

"Alright, so are we good enough to win today? What's your prediction?"

"Based on last year's results, I'm pretty sure LaCrosse Central is the team to beat. I think we're better than Fond du Lac, but most of our guys have so little varsity experience it's hard to know. Mike and C.J. should be in the lead group, but after that who knows. I don't think it's a real tough field and with this heat I just hope no one gets hurt."

"Still, don't you think we should put a couple more guys in the top ten?"

"John should, he's run enough varsity races. Johnny could, but he's never even seen a cross country meet before. Dan and Bill looked really good last week, but it's so hard to know how they'll react in their first varsity race. We'll just send them out conservatively, try and run an even pace and see how they hold up."

"What about Curt? Is he ready?"

"I don't know," I said, shaking my head. "He just won a

national title race-walking a 10k, so he's gotta be fit. He told me he's ready, so I've got to give him a chance. It was either Curt or Scott. What would you have done?"

"No offense," Rob said, turning in Scott's direction, "but I woulda picked Curt too. He was on varsity all last year and he ran great at the state meet; in fact, he almost won it for us."

"That's okay, Rob," Scott responded. "Coach said I might have a chance to win the J.V. race and look," he said, pointing to the tattered gray t-shirt that served as our junior varsity uniform. "I get to wear my lucky shirt."

"And remember," I added, "today we're only allowed seven in the varsity race. Next week we get to run eight, so our first J.V. runner today earns a varsity jersey."

"I can see it now, Coach," he said as he straightened up in his seat, puffed out his chest, and pointed to himself. "The Animal in a varsity uniform…oh yeah!"

Like a kid on a Disney vacation, with a bowl full of salad and a big jug of "cool, refreshing Plover Spring water," he sat back in his seat and smiled. Paroled from the group home for the day and surrounded by people he thought of as friends, life was good for Scott "The Animal" Longley.

Leaning in my direction, Rob asked, "You don't think they'll cancel the meet, do you?"

"I suppose they could. It's up to the meet officials. If they think it's unsafe, maybe we just took a long bus ride to a fast food place," I said, shaking my head in disbelief. "But assuming we do run, you and I are going to keep a close eye on them. We need to stress that if they run into problems out there, they have our permission to step off and they need to know that we're serious about that. I have no problem pulling a kid off the course if I think he's in trouble, even kids from other teams. That's our job today, Rob. We need to make sure everyone survives."

Pulling into the parking lot at Portage High School, we climbed from the bus, gear in hand, and set out to find a shady spot near the start and finish area. The heat of the morning was amplified by the black pavement, and the still air reminded me of the horse latitudes encountered by seafaring explorers. Finding a strip of shade along the north wall of the school, we staked our claim and dropped our equipment.

"Stay out of the sun as much as possible," I advised. "Rob and I are going to talk to the meet officials; we'll be back to hand out numbers so don't wander off. Somebody keep an eye on The Animal," I said to no one in particular as I turned to walk away.

"So, how many teams are here today?" Rob asked.

"Probably ten or twelve, but I'm not sure. This was a big meet when we started coming here seven years ago, but for some reason it gets a little smaller every year."

"Maybe because we win it every year," Rob suggested.

"Could be, but that might end this year. We could be second or third, maybe worse," I said quietly as we entered a side door that opened into an industrial arts classroom.

Meet officials informed us that the meet would go on as scheduled. Water would be available at several places out on the course, teams would be allowed to seek refuge in the hallways of the school and they would shorten the time between races if possible in an effort to avoid some of the mid-day heat.

Returning to our team area, we found them motionless, littering the ground like the carnage of a civil war battlefield as they did their best to conserve energy.

"Alright!" I shouted. "Come and get your numbers. Warm-up starts in fifteen minutes. I don't think you're going to need sweats. In case you haven't figured that out."

Normally we would jog the entire course, but given the conditions and the fact that it was a fairly simple course to follow, I decided we could shorten our warm up. The course began at the far end of the school's athletic fields before heading slightly uphill through a beautiful stand of oaks. It then followed the perimeter of a large corn field before working its way back to a gravel road winding through a farm field and re-entering the school grounds on the way to the finish.

"Remember, YOU are responsible for knowing the course, so pay attention," I said sternly as we started our tour of the course at a very slow jog.

Heat radiated upward from the sandy soil as we worked our way up the first of two very small hills on the course. Dry grass seemed to shatter under our feet as we slowed to a walk near the stand of oaks, seeking a few steps in the welcoming shade. Just past the mile mark, we heard the faint report of the starter's pistol and the cheers of the crowd as the girls' race began. Breaking into a jog, we completed the back loop of the course and found a position to cheer on the girls' team as they ran past. Our own Suzy Favor, as always, was the first to appear on the sandy trail near the mile mark. A full two-hundred meters ahead of the next runner, our defending state champion didn't seem bothered by the heat, giving me hope that just maybe conditions were not as bad as I had feared. Reality would soon set in as I watched the rest of the field file by in what was already, for some, taking on the unpleasant look of a death march. The harsh conditions punished those of lesser ability and those who had not prepared themselves. Predictably, the effect on the truly gifted, like Suzy, was far less dramatic.

With twenty minutes until the start of the J.V. race, we jogged the last section of the course down a farm lane in the blazing sun before stopping in the shade of a large red oak. Pointing out the flags marking the final left hand turns before the finish, I gave a few last instructions before asking if anyone had questions.

"Coach!" Scott said waving his hand wildly over his head. "One question, Coach. I'm wonderin' why a red flag is a left turn. Shouldn't red be right?"

"Good question, Scott," I said, impressed by his observation. "That's a great mystery to all of us. I can't explain it. I guess a hundred years ago someone did it that way and we've been stuck with it ever since. But hey, don't think about it, just follow whoever's leading. You can do that, can't you?"

"Sure, Coach, but this sure is a confusing course."

"Rob and I will be out there to help you. You'll be okay."

After sending the guys off to prepare for the start of the race, I jogged to the finish area to watch the end of the girls' race and attempt to evaluate the condition of the incoming finishers. The heat had taken a heavy toll on many of the runners, it was plain to see, but all were able to exit the finish chute under, mostly, their own power. Meet workers assisted some as they wobbled their way to the tables where tiny paper cups of water were being distributed. Nearby an ambulance and paramedics stood ready to handle any serious problems, but as far as I could tell no one needed their service. Maybe, I thought as I jogged in the direction of our team, I should do a little less worrying and a little more coaching.

Jammed together in the quickly narrowing strip of shade near the building, our J.V. runners sat quietly, tying their shoes. Taking a knee in the middle of the small group, I gave a few last words of advice.

"Don't get too excited early, be patient in the first mile, DON'T get in over your heads," I emphasized. "Central should have the deepest team here, so let's see if we can break up their pack. And remember, if you have trouble with the heat, you can step off, and if I think you're in trouble I'll pull you off the course. And I'm serious about that!"

As we headed to the line, I grabbed Scott by the shoulder to give a final instruction. "I want you to follow Lee, Chip, and Michael. They'll take you out at a sensible pace. Don't go sprinting like a wildman, okay? Ready?"

"Risen' up, Coach, straight to the top. I got the eye of the tiger today," he said with a broad smile as he raised his hand confidently to the sky, delivering a powerful high-five before sprinting away.

Minutes later the sound of the starter's .32 caliber pistol launched a flurry of action as 130 J.V. runners, ignoring any advice about running a smart race, sprinted from the line. Some were caught up in the excitement and rush of adrenaline while others simply wanted to show their face at the front before slowly sliding to the back of the pack. Junior varsity races offer a wide variety of athletes, and in some cases non-athletes, participating for a multitude of reasons. A few are just here because they enjoy a Saturday morning bus ride and some social interaction. Others use running to lose weight, improve their health, or in a few cases to burn off an athletic code violation. Only a small percentage of these J.V. runners will ever move up to the next level, earn a varsity letter, or have their name in the paper. Most are content to give their best effort and knock a few seconds from their best time, something few were likely to accomplish on a day like this.

For Scott, today would be an experiment, a chance to add to his limited resume as a runner and gain valuable experience. His summer backyard regimen had prepared him and he'd run well at the time trial, but we all wondered how he would react today.

At six-foot-one with a brush pile hairdo, Scott was easy to pick out. Positioned a few yards back of the lead group, he was surrounded by teammates doing their best to help him run evenly as they approached the first turn 300 yards into the race. Pace was always difficult for Scott. On long runs, intervals, or even warm-up jogs, he surged ahead and drifted behind in a fairly predictable pattern. Now with guys ahead of him, he looked anxious to move up, like a hound on a scent he wanted to chase. Today there would be medals awarded to the top finishers and he was determined to get one.

The lead group had thinned considerably as they neared the mile mark. Three LaCrosse runners pushed the pace up front as a thin picket line, including Lee and Scott, trailed along behind. Lee's face was so red it almost glowed, indicating a level of body heat that would exact a price in the final two miles. Just to his right Scott showed no sign of stress as he maintained contact with the leaders. He had the appearance of an experienced runner and he looked good. Positioned squarely in the middle of the group, his awkward form contrasted with the more efficient runners around him as they headed off to circle the corn field.

"Looks good, Scott. Stay on that group!" I yelled as he passed.

"That's it, Animal," added Rob. "Run with those guys."

Waiting until the last of our J.V. runners had passed, we angled through a portion of the corn field and waited on grassy farm land for the leaders to return from the far portion of the course. Several hundred yards way we could see that three runners had broken the rest of the field, two in maroon jerseys, and Scott, wearing the only thing our limited budget could provide, a faded gray t-shirt.

"Can you believe it?" Rob shouted, giving a puzzled glance my way.

"He's a tough kid, but, I don't know…that last mile could get ugly," I warned.

Scott looked in our direction and gave a slight smile as we shouted words of encouragement. On the dusty gravel road in the farm field a few hundred yards later, Scott moved into the lead. He had made his own decision and it was a good one. With less than a half mile to go the race had come down to two runners, and Scott was not interested in finishing second. His varsity teammates positioned themselves on the edge of the field near where the course reentered the school grounds, loudly shouting encouragement. "Come on, Animal!" "You can do it, Animal!" "Eye of the tiger Animal, EYE—Of—THE—TIGER!" Each cheer brought an immediate and noticeable reaction as he stretched a two meter lead to three, then four. He might actually win this thing I began to think as he approached the second to last flag still looking fast and strong.

Two final turns stood between Scott and the finish line, two red flags, and with no one to follow it was up to him to figure it out. Seeing him slow slightly, I yelled "Left turn! Left turn! ANIMAL…TURN LEFT!" Unsure of what to do and confused by people shouting from all directions, he slowed to a near stop. He knew he had to turn, but which way? Lifting both hands to face level he stared at his left hand and then the flag before making his decision. Choosing correctly he turned left, but as he hesitated the LaCrosse runner flew past and built an insurmountable lead on his way to the finish. Scott's mistake had been costly, but his effort was impressive as he sprinted across the line just two strides behind the winner.

With his hand on the shoulder of a meet worker, Scott reached the end of the chute and came to an abrupt stop as a silver medal was pressed into his palm.

"Coach, I got a medal!" he exclaimed as I approached. "Look, a silver medal." Examining his new possession as a collector might study a rare coin, he flipped it from hand to hand to study both sides.

"Scott," I said, extending my hand, "great race. That was just awesome!"

"Yeah and look…on the back…it says, Second Place Portage Invite. 1985."

"Nice. Is that your first medal?"

"Yeah, and if I had a letter jacket I could sew it on the letter… if I had a letter."

"Maybe someday that'll happen," I said, knowing it might. "Should I hold on to that for you?"

"No Coach, I'll take good care of it. I won't lose it, I promise."

Holding the medal high above his head with his left hand, he high-fived teammates with his right. "Nice race, Animal," "Good job, Scott," "Awesome," they said as they filed past.

As we knew from the Panther Invitational trophy disaster during track, Scott loved awards and the small silver medal was more important to him than any of us knew. For guys with comfortable homes and loving families, an award like this might have little significance, but to Scott it was a treasured possession he could hold in the palm of his sweaty hand for the rest of the day.

In the final race of the day, with temperatures in the upper 90's, our varsity team squeezed out a close win over La Crosse Central. Mike and C.J. ran with the leaders for two miles before fading slightly to place third and fifth. Bill, the surprise of the day, moved up well late in the race to finish an amazing sixth place in his first varsity race while Johnny, showing the poise of an upperclassman, followed close behind in eighth. John suffered badly in the heat, struggling home in sixteenth, with Dan and Curt finishing well back in the pack.

Under the conditions, it was hard to evaluate our performance. Times were extremely slow and our fifth, sixth, and seventh runners were too far back, but there were also many positives. Somehow we'd won the meet and beat a couple of decent teams, and we did it with a very inexperienced group under some of the worst conditions I'd ever seen.

With the team trophy tucked under Mike's arm, we walked past two air conditioned motor coaches on the way to our big yellow toaster oven at the far end of the parking lot.

"Forty-five," Mike said, pointing to the trophy that looked like a fruit bowl bolted to a block of walnut.

"Forty-five what?" someone asked.

"Invitationals. We haven't lost an invitational in five years. The streak is at 45 and counting," he announced proudly.

"Mike," I said quietly as I placed a hand on his shoulder, "that streak was built by some really good teams. Seems like a lot of pressure to put on a bunch of first year guys, don't you think?"

"I suppose, but I really think we can keep it going," he said confidently as he handed our latest trophy to me.

"Here Scott, take care of this," I said, quickly passing it his way. "Monday morning I want you to take it to the office and give it to Mr. Anderson. You know who that is, right?"

"Yeah Coach, I know Mr. Anderson, but what am I supposed to say?"

"Tell him we won the Portage Invitational, and then tell him that you are now a varsity runner."

"I am?" he shouted as he threw his arms in the air. "Coach, are you kiddin' me?"

"No, I'm not kidding. You ran a great race today. You would have been our sixth runner and look on the result sheet. Your time would have put you in twenty-first place in the varsity race, that's how well you ran."

"I can't believe it! I get to wear a varsity uniform? I get to run in the varsity race with Mike and C.J. and Johnny? I won't let you down, Coach, I promise."

"I know you won't, Scott. Now let's go get some food," I said as we climbed the bus steps and slid onto the hot vinyl seats.

As the bus began to roll, Scott lifted his thermos jug above his head and gulped the last of his Plover Spring water.

"How's the water, Scott?" I asked.

"Good and good for you. It's the best," he answered as if doing a Saturday morning television commercial.

Retrieving his grocery bag from the floor of the bus, he carefully removed its contents. Ignoring the commotion on the rest of the bus, Rob and I watched closely as he set the Tupperware container on his knees, peeled back the cover, and peeked inside. A sudden look of profound sadness came over him as he tilted the bowl my way to show that after six hours in our yellow inferno, his "mean salad" had morphed into a tan, gloppy stew. Scott paused for a moment and then, like a child discovering his dead hamster, slowly resealed the container and tenderly placed it back in the bag on the bus floor. Fighting the temptation to laugh and cry at the same time, I studied Scott as he performed this solemn ceremony for his dead salad and contemplated the thought of going hungry.

"Scott," I said, reaching over to tap him on the knee with the back of my hand, "don't look so sad. I'll get you some lunch."

"Really, Coach? No, I can't let ya do it. Thanks but I'll be okay."

"You've got 40 minutes!" I shouted as the bus came to a halt in the parking lot of a Hardees, knowing very well that with two other buses in the lot we were unlikely to meet that time limit. Like a Chinese fire drill, runners poured out of both ends of the bus and dashed across the parking lot, anxious to secure a better spot in line. Everyone seemed to be in a hurry except Mike, C.J.

and Curt, who stood patiently waiting for me at the bus door.

"What's with The Animal?" Curt asked.

"Yeah, he looked really upset," added C.J.

"Is someone pickin' on him?" Mike asked angrily.

"No, it's nothing like that. You know the lunch he brought? It was a big bowl of salad and well, it pretty much decomposed on the hot bus."

"So, does he have lunch money?" Rob asked.

"No, I'm pretty sure the group home doesn't allow him to carry cash."

"Well, we can't let him eat that salad," said Curt with a laugh. "I've got a couple of extra..."

"Here," Rob said, taking off his baseball cap and inverting it at waist level. "We'll take care of it!"

Positioned at the counter near the cash register, Rob announced the newly established "Feed the Animal Fund" and encouraged all to contribute their spare change. The hat fund earned enough to provide a lavish feast for Scott, with the leftover money placed in my care for a future meal.

Surprised by his teammates' generosity, Scott stood smiling happily at the counter as Rob helped him place his order.

"Get two Animal, get two," Rob coaxed.

"Two? Two chocolate shakes? Are you crazy?" he asked with a loud laugh.

"Yeah, get three if you want, we got plenty of money, see?" he said, lifting the hat to Scott's face.

With burgers and fries jammed into our new "fruit bowl" trophy and Rob following behind with two large shakes, Scott walked proudly past his smiling teammates. Dan stood motioning him over to a spot in a corner booth as I flashed a smile their way. This is what a team should be, I thought to myself as I watched Scott arrange his silver medal and our trophy on the table in front of him. Holding one of his chocolate shakes in the air, he shouted, "Thanks everybody! This is the best day EVER!"

As we pushed aboard the crowded bus and moved the boards

into place, C.J. lifted his massive boom box and placed it across the seat backs. In what had become a tradition dating back all of four years, music would rock the bus until the eight D-cell batteries gave out. After suffering through the pounding bass of several nearly identical rap "songs," C.J. gave in to Suzy's pleading and played her favorites by the B52's. As the front half of the bus grew restless, he queued up more of our traditional bus ride tunes by Van Halen and an old standby from the Stones called "She's So Cold," directed at every girl on the bus who had ever jilted a guy.

As the hot wind swirled our hair and the bus clanked and bumped along at the required 55 miles an hour, Mike stood up. Putting his entire body into it, he shouted, "Hey everyone, this is for The Animal! Scott, this is your song, man."

Silence fell over the bus as we waited for the sound. BOMP… BOMP, BOMP, BOMP…. *Rising up…back on the street. Did my time, took my chances. Went the distance, now I'm back on my feet, just a man with a will to survive…*

With our team trophy above his head and his t-shirt firmly in place, Scott stood and swayed to the music as those aboard, feeling his joy, sang along loudly.

It's the Eye of the Tiger; it's the thrill of the fight rising up to the challenge of our rival….

As our trip neared an end and the D-cell batteries gave up the last of their voltage, a new tradition had been born. From now on we would finish every road trip with this song. "Eye of the Tiger" was now our anthem and the theme of our season as we prepared each week for the challenge of our rivals. Scott's trademark toothy grin infected all of us with gladness as we rocked slowly down the highway at the end of a long day.

NINE

LOST

As we slowly assembled for practice, I could sense a change in our team. Guys stood a little closer together, talked a little louder, and laughed a little more. Everyone was in on the joke as Mike described Scott's "mean salad."

"Man, Scott," he said with a laugh, "it looked like a bucket of puke! It's probably still sittin' there... a big steamin' pile in that parking lot."

"Yeah, it's probably still there!" Scott added somewhat awkwardly. "A steamin' pile."

Somehow, strangely, a Tupperware bowl full of wilted lettuce had brought our team closer together.

Team building is a curious thing. It can happen in the hot parking lot of a fast food joint or on a bus to places with exotic names like Manitowoc, Fond du Lac, and Menomonee. A team can be built to the sound of Springsteen, Van Halen, or the annoying, redundant beat of a rap song blaring from a boom box. Almost any activity can fall into this category, including silly things like swamp runs, stick races, and pushing unprepared young runners down steep hills or into scrubby little jack pine trees. Traditions like Friday morning donut runs and Saturday night ice cream parties help us build a team, but in the end it's hard work that makes the team good. Hard intervals at the park on Monday and long hard runs on Tuesday are at the core of our program. This is where we lay the foundation for success.

Today, Mike and C.J. were anxious to test their teammates on a big square route known as Wilshire. This is where those two could shine, hammering away at a sustained hard pace for three, four, or five miles in the middle of a long run, pushing themselves and their teammates to become stronger, tougher, and more determined.

Trotting comfortably down a long straight stretch of Northpoint Drive, we began our nine mile run. Amid the sounds of excited young voices, two miles down the road we made the first of three left hand turns that would take us back to school. Working our way up the only hill on the route, we headed for the sparsely populated roads north of town. As the pace steadily quickened, our weakest members began to peel away from the group. Hardly a word was spoken as we pushed on through a cattail swamp and into the cooling shade of a stand of mature white pines. Past a small, poorly maintained dairy farm, Mike led our ever shrinking group, pushing all of us to the breaking point as we wondered how much faster he might go and how much longer we could hang on. It was a test of mental and physical toughness that, once started, had to be finished.

C.J. matched Mike stride for stride with John, Bill, Dan, Curt, and Johnny tucked close behind as we churned along at what for some was approaching race pace. Positioned a few steps back with Lee at my side, I studied those ahead of me, wondering who would be the first to break as we ran to the rhythm of running shoes hitting blacktop.

Young, strong, fit, and confident, we hammered along at a punishing pace past woodlots and farm fields, eyes fixed on the horizon, shoulders relaxed, breathing deeply and hanging on. This was our trademark — long, hard pick-ups on the rural roads north of our town, pushing hard, sometimes too hard. No one said a word. No one dared ask "When does this end?" Focused only on their arm swing, their foot plant, and the stretch of road ahead, they ran on without complaint.

"Okay, guys. Shut it down when we get to Jesus!" I announced, referencing the shrine built by a local farmer half a mile ahead.

"Thank you, Jesus!" Dan groaned as we neared the twelve foot white crucifix guarding the next intersection.

"That was great, guys!" I said as the pace began to slow. "Nice work. Now group up and go easy on the way back. I'm gonna go check on Scott."

Reversing direction, I studied the long, strung out line of runners headed my way. As the first small pack approached I shouted, "Where's Scott?"

"He's back there someplace," Michael answered. "We caught him near the farm and he was goin' pretty slow. You guys must a run him into the ground."

"No, he was doing okay. He wasn't ready to run that hard for four miles, so I told him to back off. I thought he'd hook up with you guys."

"Well, he did for a while, but he fell back. He must be back there someplace. He couldn't have just disappeared," Michael concluded, as others in his group nodded in agreement.

"How could we lose him?" I moaned, placing my hands on the top of my head. "He could have turned around and headed back or he could have turned right, but why? He must have seen you guys turn left so why would he go right? Who would turn right? It doesn't make any sense."

"Maybe the aliens got him," joked Michael, "or a car full of college girls."

Ignoring the attempt at humor, I continued my rant. "This could be bad. I'm supposed to be in charge of him. He's not supposed to be unsupervised. I know we're going to find him, but this could be really bad. If this gets back to the group home, they could pull him off the team...again," I said, beginning what would be a very fast three mile run back to school.

"Get your car keys!" I ordered angrily as I threw open the field house door. "We lost The Animal. Somewhere out there, we lost him. If you have a car, go get it."

With search areas divided and routes assigned, I headed quickly to my rusty Buick Skylark. Team members were stationed at the front, back, and side doors of the school as I headed out to drive the course in the same direction we'd run an hour earlier. With eyes fixed on the horizon, I sped down the road, doing my best to estimate how far he might have wandered since the last sighting. Like the Coast Guard searching for a lifeboat, I calculated the parameters of my search area as I drove on nervously.

Squinting to block the harsh, low angle glare of the golden sunset, I strained to make out a small figure at the very limit of my vision. It must be a person, I thought, growing suddenly hopeful. And if it is, it has to be Scott. After all, who else would be out here standing in the middle of the road as this figure seemed to be? With the distance between us closing rapidly, I could tell it was him. Holding something in both hands, he stood squarely in the center of the three way intersection so transfixed he was oblivious to my approach.

Slowing to a stop, I watched as he studied what appeared to be a map, turning it one way and then the other. Which direction would he choose, I wondered, rolling my window down to get a better look as he worked on the problem. Shuffling his feet as he pivoted his body, Scott's eyes grew suddenly wide as he realized I was parked a short distance away. He'd only been missing for an hour, but you wouldn't have known it by his reaction.

"Coach Behnke!" he yelled excitedly as he sprinted towards me with hands extended. "BOY am I glad to see you! I got lost!"

"Yeah, I'm glad to see you too, Scott. Now get in. Let's get you back to school so we can call off the search."

"Coach, I went the wrong way. I went way down there and then I turned. And then I went way down that next road till I came to a fire station. And I went in and this real nice lady took the phone book and she put it on the Xerox and she exploded it."

"Exploded it? Exploded what?"

"This map," he said holding it in my direction. "She exploded it on the Xerox and drew this red line on it and gave it to me. Oh, and the sign said ten cents, so we owe her ten cents."

"Alright, as soon as I find out who the nice lady is, I'll take care of it," I reassured him. "Now let's get you back to school. Your ride is probably waiting and wondering where you are."

"Yeah, just wait till they find out I got lost."

"Scott...I'm not sure....well, maybe you should just say that you decided to run a few extra miles. I think that might be a better way to explain it. After all you were never really lost, you just made up a new course."

"Yeah, a new course. Can we call it the Animal loop?"

"Sure, from now on it'll be known as the Animal loop," I said with a nod.

"Coach?"

"Yes, Scott."

"Remember, we owe the nice lady ten cents."

The lost Animal story circulated around school the following day, but as far as I know it never came to the attention of the group home counselors. The "nice lady" at the Town of Hull Municipal Garage laughed politely at my offer to pay off our debt before inquiring, "That young man...is he okay?"

"Yes," I answered, recognizing that she was asking about more than just his safe return to school. "He has a few learning disabilities, but he does pretty well in his classes and," I said, sounding slightly like a proud parent, "Saturday in Madison he'll run in his first varsity cross country meet."

The Madison West Invitational was one of my least favorite. Run on the greasy clay of the city's landfill site, it was one of the least interesting courses I'd ever seen and with only eight teams in the field I wondered if it was worth the two hour bus ride. Scott bounced and rocked in the seat next to me as our bus pushed through the thick, humid, early morning air. Dressed in a black and white sweat suit with STEVENS POINT stitched across the front, he could hardly contain himself.

"Sit down, Scott," I reminded him.

"Relax Animal. Save it for the race," added Curt, slightly annoyed at his inability to sit quietly.

"Here, look at this," I said, removing a copy of the course map from my clipboard and leaning in his direction. "It's pretty easy, just follow the dashed line," I explained, tracing the route with my index finger.

"One question, Coach," Scott interrupted. "Is this another course where they use yellow flags for right turns?"

"Yes, Scott, yellow is always a right turn and red is always a left. At every race and every meet it's always the same."

"Okay, Coach, but I really think they need to change that."

"Animal!" C.J. added harshly, leaning over the seatback. "It's not that hard. Here, I've got a pen. I'll write it on the back of your hand. It's the same every meet so just get used to it. Now sit still, shut up, and let me sleep."

Harsh words I thought as I watched C.J. pull his cap over his face and slump in his seat. Like a big brother chastising a younger sibling, he'd laid down the law. Knowing better than to argue, Scott twisted in his seat, placed his hands on his knees and stared forward at the long straight stretch of highway as he'd been ordered. Amazingly a few words from an angry team captain had done in an instant what years of medications seemed unable to accomplish. Scott was still and absolutely quiet as we rolled past the countless acres of potato fields on our way south.

Today was going to be a big test for our young team. Ranked eighth by the first Coaches Association poll, we were up against fifth ranked Madison Memorial and several other strong programs. I had very little information on the teams we were about to race, but I really didn't care. This was simply the next step on our journey to become a competitive team and a chance to gain valuable race experience.

As we rolled down the Interstate, not far from the meet site, I slid into the seat next to Scott and offered a few clear, concise instructions. "Don't even think about running with Mike and C.J.," I said firmly looking straight into his eyes with my hands on his shoulders. "All you have to do is find a bunch of our guys, tuck in the group, and hang on. Think you can do that?"

"No problem, Coach. Eye of the Tiger Coach. Eye…of…the…Tiger."

It was a confident, simple response to my incredibly simple advice, and Scott followed it with the tenacity of a Spartan soldier carrying out an order. Latched onto a tightly packed group of teammates, he matched them stride for stride as they pulled him steadily through the field of eighty-six runners. Elbows extended far to each side, jaw bouncing loosely, he loped along, determined to stay in close contact with the group. Mike and C.J. spent much of the race in the lead pack, looking strong before fading to 4th and 8th place, respectively, in the last half mile. John, having led our pack the entire race, crossed the line in 20th overall with Bill at his side in 21st and Scott one second back as our fifth runner in 22nd place. With Johnny and Curt close behind, we bunched five guys across the line in five seconds to complete a solid team performance claiming second place behind Madison Memorial in the team scores. We'd run well, but the streak was over. Exactly five years after it began, our string of 45 consecutive invitational victories had come to an abrupt end.

"Hey, it happens," I said to the sad faces around me, knowing very well that none of them had ever seen us finish second at anything short of a state meet. "We ran a good race so keep your chin up. Nobody died. It's not the end of the world. We're heading in the right direction, Memorial's a pretty good team and they only beat us by ten points. We did okay and we'll get better. We just have a lot of work to do," I concluded while leading our quiet group in the direction of the awards presentation area.

With a crowd of onlookers watching curiously, Scott marched proudly forward to accept our award, a silver trophy. Puzzled by his disheveled appearance and exaggerated movements, they couldn't help but be amused by his childlike excitement. How had this scruffy looking kid, this obviously "special" young man, won the honor of accepting a trophy, they seemed to wonder. We knew Scott had been chosen simply because it meant so much to him.

Having learned the etiquette associated with accepting a trophy, Scott understood that too much or too little celebration can be disrespectful. Too often I'd watched as one of our guys accepted a trophy with all the excitement of taking a cafeteria tray from the lunch lady. Scott knew better. No matter how big or small the meet, he treated them the same, with the respect and excitement they deserved. After politely accepting the trophy from the presenter, he pretended to shine it with the sleeve of his sweatshirt before proudly hoisting it high in the air and rotating it for all to see as he walked slowly in the direction of his teammates. Scott enjoyed every part of the process and we enjoyed watching him. The broad smile on his face helped ease the sting of a second place finish and put things in perspective. We'd lost a meet, a streak had ended, and now, no longer attached to the coat tails of our previous teams, we were on our own. If we wanted to be part of a legacy, we'd have to create a new one, and it wouldn't be easy.

TEN

THE BIG LADDER

Wind driven rain pounded against the wall of windows lining the hallway as we stood quietly gazing out at the student parking lot.

"You might want to wear a second layer today," I warned loudly, "and a hat if you have one."

As luck would have it, the first foul weather day of the season had coincided with our toughest practice, a workout we called the big ladder. Scanning the group as we stood waiting for the last of our members to exit the locker room, I noticed that most were ill prepared for the conditions we were about to face. Some looked apprehensive as they stood clad in only shorts and t-shirts. Watching as the wind whipped the flag atop the school's flagpole, they knew they were about to pay a price for their lack of planning.

As sympathetic as I was to their plight, I dared not show it. This is how teenage boys learn. For them life is lived by trial and error. Having ignored my many warnings, they would now have to deal with some horrendous conditions and I could not help them. Scott was the lone exception. With no one at home to warn him of the impending weather, and lacking the resources to acquire the proper gear, he needed someone to take care of him.

"I'll be right back," I said to the group as I headed in the direction of the south office.

Jogging slowly down the hall, I considered my options and thought about altering the workout. We could do a short, quick run. Five miles and a hot shower seemed reasonable. A nice, simple, safe workout, good enough for most high school teams under these circumstances but not, I reminded myself, good enough for us. Not after the race we'd run two days earlier at the Wausau East Invitational. In our best race to date, we earned the team title with an impressive point total of 27. C.J., Mike, and John finished in the top five, and our next five runners were tightly packed between eighth and fifteenth. We were improving steadily, and I was beginning to believe we could run with most of the better teams in the state. Ranked sixth in the latest poll, we would have a chance to measure ourselves against top ranked Manitowoc at their home invite on Saturday. Taking the easy way out was not an option; today we would do the big ladder in whatever conditions Mother Nature could whip up.

Reaching beneath the south office counter, I sifted through the collection of lost and found items. Amid the backpacks, textbooks, and folders I hoped to find something for Scott to wear. Every school has a place like this, a box filled with items carelessly left behind, waiting sadly to be reclaimed by their young owners. With a dark green sweatshirt and a black stocking cap in hand, I stood up and after a short examination and a quick smell test I headed for the door. The strong odor of smoke told me both items had likely been left behind by the "window people." Window people was the term given to the unfortunate members of the student body who spent much of the day sitting dazed and disinterested along a large bank of windows in the cafeteria. Whether the result of impairment, irresponsibility, or apathy I didn't know, but at the end of each day they always left things behind. Things I could loan to Scott and return in the morning, in the unlikely event that anyone came looking for them.

"Here," I said, launching the hat and sweatshirt at Scott. "Put these on, complements of the window people."

"Thanks Coach," he said as a smile of relief crossed his face.

"Hey, if any of you guys don't want to do this, you don't have to," I said, offering them a way out. "If you're not dressed for this, you can stay in, run in the halls, or just go home."

Silence surrounded us as I waited for a response, scanning the worried faces around me.

"Really, it's ugly out there. You don't have to do this," I said, feeling the sudden rush of cold air as Mike kicked a door open behind me.

"Let's run!" he shouted angrily, making the decision for all of us as he led the way into the gray, miserable, conditions we would endure for the next hour and a half.

Powerful wind hindered our progress and cold rain stung exposed skin as we began our ordeal.

"This wind sucks," Michael shouted angrily.

"Hey, don't say sucks!" Dan responded angrily. "The wind blows!"

"Sure is a good day to have a sweatshirt," I taunted while pulling the hood of my sweatshirt over my head. Instinctively we pressed the pace, trying desperately to generate protective body heat as we made our way to Bukolt Park past vacant soccer fields and an empty school yard. The entire population seemed to be hiding indoors. Conditions were bad and we all knew things would be worse along the wide open stretch on the banks of the Wisconsin River. Nervous laughter and shouts could not conceal the obvious fact that this workout was going to be extremely difficult.

Huddled beneath the slight protection of towering pines at the park's main entrance, we studied the monsoon conditions as sheets of rain rolled in over white caps smashing against the river bank. This was the kind of weather that sent people running for the couch and reruns of *Gilligan's Island*. Even fearless football players sought the dry comfort of indoor facilities on a day like this. We had no such option. We would steel ourselves to the conditions and meet the force of nature with all the willpower we could muster. Rain pounded against my back as I motioned for the group to huddle up.

"This is it guys, the big, ugly, nasty ladder...the full ladder," I shouted as the wind did its best to push the words back down my throat. "I know it's miserable out here, but this will make us a better team," I reminded them. "No excuses, be tough, give your best effort, and help each other through it. Five minute pace, here we go...up to the line. Set...and...go!"

Tucked close behind Mike as he powered from the line, we sought protection from the wind. In wedge formation we leaned unnaturally forward, heads down, shoulders slightly twisted as we tried to cut through the wind. Normally this was the easy part of the workout, but not today. Four hundred meters straight into the teeth of the storm was a brutal way to start.

"Seventy three, seventy four, seventy five," I called out as we lunged at the crack in the pavement that served as a finish line and came to an immediate halt. With great effort, the lead group managed to finish on pace.

"That was the easy part!" I yelled loudly as we reversed direction to begin our recovery jog with the wind and rain pushing at our backs.

"Easy? Coach, that wasn't easy," Scott said, clearly missing the sarcasm in my voice as he lifted his head to peer out from under his droopy, wet stocking cap.

"Nothing's going to be easy today. Monday's never an easy day!" I reminded them on the jogging recovery. "Okay, up to the line," I shouted through cupped hands as rain pelted my face. "This is a half, two thirty, stay on it. Set... and...go!"

The swirling wind grew fiercer, the rain intensified, and temperatures seemed to drop as we began the second of seven intervals. Exposed skin turned pink and, in Lee's case, bright red as conditions took a toll on all of us. Mature red oaks gave slight relief from the wind as we turned to run parallel with the river on our way to the guard rail post that marked 800 meters.

"Two twenty-six, two twenty-seven, twenty-eight," I announced while turning back up the course to cheer on the rest of our group. "Two thirty-five, thirty-six, thirty-seven…come on, finish, stay on it, let's go!"

"Come on, guys!" Mike demanded as others around him joined in. "Be tough guys, you can do this, finish it!" they yelled to the wet, determined, teammates heading our way.

"The next two are always the toughest," I warned as we began our jog back to the start, dodging deep puddles along the way. "Talk it up! Help each other. No one can do this alone. Stay in the group, work together."

"Coach, how far is this one?" Scott asked.

"It's a twelve hundred, three quarters of a mile. Just stay right here," I said, pointing to the ground next to my left foot. "Remember our deal."

"Got it, Coach. If an old man can do it," he said with a laugh as we stepped to the line once again.

"Three-forty-five, stay on the pace, set…and…go!"

Charging into rain that seemed to be falling horizontally, I found myself surrounded by a phalanx of runners spitting out words of encouragement with each exhale. "Come on, Animal." "That's it." "Hang in, Scott." "Eye of the Tiger." "Animal." "Animal." "Come on, Animal," they said, expending precious energy to assist their teammate. Past the half mile point, pushed by a welcome tailwind, Mike and C.J. led our tight pack toward the speed limit sign that signaled the end of our journey. Surging ahead at the urging of those around him, Scott pushed to the finish, dragging me along with him. Positioned just off his right shoulder, I did my best to honor the agreement we'd made at the start of the season. Having failed to account for Scott's improvement or my fatigue after a full day of teaching, I struggled to hang on.

"Three forty, three forty-one," I gasped at the group ahead of me as I veered to the side and stopped a few steps short of the line to continue reading times.

"That tailwind was nice," John observed as we broke into a jog on the partially flooded road at the edge of the park.

"Yeah, remember that," I added. "If we get off pace in the first half we can make it up when we get the wind at our backs."

Rain came at us in sheets as nature seemed determined to drive us from the park. Walking the last few yards as we neared the starting line, I studied the wet miserable figures around me, casting a smile and a nod of approval in Mike's direction. Something good was happening on this gray, crappy day. Surrounded by young men staring blankly ahead like soldiers on a battlefield, I couldn't help but enjoy this display of mental and physical toughness. Stoically, without complaint, they marched to the line to await my orders.

"This is it, guys...the toughest one of all. One mile, into the wind, into the rain, into the volcano. To the line, set...and...go."

Weighed down by drenched sweats and waterlogged shoes, we began our attack on a five minute mile. Challenging for many in our group under the best of conditions, staying on pace today would be difficult.

"Seventy-eight!" I called out at the crack in the pavement. "Two thirty-five!" at the guard rail, and "Three forty-seven!" at the speed limit sign. "Keep it even," I ordered at the final turn as we set our sights on the small maple by the corner of the city bus garage.

"Five minutes!" I shouted from a few yards back with Scott and Johnny at my side as Mike, C.J. and John finished their last few strides.

"Great job, guys," I managed to spit out while leaning forward to put my hands on my knees. "Great effort!"

"Huddle up," I ordered as the last of our J.V. runners struggled across the line. "Hey! You guys have been great, but maybe it's time to call it quits. This is just awful."

Gazing my way with a thousand yard stare, Mike looked as if he had no idea what I'd just said. Dan, quoting Carl Spackler from *Caddy Shack*, responded with "But Donn, I don't think the heavy stuff's gonna come down for quite a while."

"Really," I repeated, "you can go back. It's okay, I mean it. Hey,

I'm all for being tough, but this is getting ridiculous. I don't want your parents to think I'm nuts."

"Too late for that," Mike added with a partial smile. "They already know you're crazy, so let's just get on with it."

"I think some of you need to go back. I'm serious. Go get a hot shower and some dry clothes. You've done enough. Really!"

Scanning the group as the cold wind hammered rain against my back, I waited for an answer. Water streamed from their chins and noses as they gazed in my direction, but no one moved, no one said a word, no one wanted to be the weak link in the chain that was our team.

"Well, there's your answer," Dan said, clapping his hands together loudly while flashing a huge grin. "Now let's finish this thing."

Fatigue joined with the wind, rain and dropping temperatures to push us to our limits as we descended the last steps of the big ladder. Rainwater forced its way into open mouths, shoes expelled water with each foot plant, finger tips wrinkled, and body parts chafed, but no one complained. In a country where whining may well be the national pastime, nobody uttered a discouraging word. They didn't have to do it, I'd given them a way out, but they stayed and they finished. This tough workout, this brutally tough workout in absurd conditions, was over, and now, somehow, as we began our jog home it didn't seem so bad. With the wind at our backs we celebrated our little adventure and laughed at the weather, knowing that we'd taken the worst it had to offer. On a Monday afternoon in an empty city park with no one watching, we'd passed the test. We'd done the big ladder.

Eleven

The Battle

Their body language told me they were up to something. Walking shoulder to shoulder, they smirked as they exited the locker room and walked in my direction.

"Okay, what's going on?" I asked, stopping them in their tracks.

"Nothing, nothing at all," Dan answered, turning his face to give me a sideways look. "Why would you think somethin's goin' on?"

"Well, it could be that you're all standing so close together, or maybe it's the bag you're trying to hide behind you."

"Bag, what bag?"

"The grocery bag Bill has behind his back."

"Oh, that bag, well….that's just a little something we found for the Animal."

"What, a Tupperware bowl full of salad?" I said, taking my best guess.

"No, but that's not a bad idea," Dan answered, nodding as he put his thumb to the bottom of his chin.

"Really, what's in the bag?" I asked, pressing the issue.

"It's something good, I promise."

"Yeah Donn, it's good. You're going to like it," John said, reassuringly.

"Okay, but if it's road kill, you guys are gonna be in serious trouble."

"It's not road kill, I'll tell you that much," said Mike, his voice taking on a more serious tone.

"Wait and see, just wait and see," Dan added as the group walked slowly away.

Practice began with the usual series of warm-up activities as I worked my way up and down the rows of runners sprawled across the green rubberized floor.

"So Scott, what did you think of yesterday's workout?" I asked, taking a knee directly in front of him.

"Coach, that was Craaaazzzzyyyy! Sometimes I didn't know if I was runnin' or swimmin'."

"Yeah, sometimes it was hard to tell, wasn't it?"

"You got that right, Coach."

Placing my hand on his left shoulder, I looked into Scott's eyes and said, "That was an amazing workout yesterday. For a guy who's only been a runner for six weeks...I can't believe you did that. That was unbelievable."

"Thanks, Coach."

"Really, you made me run so hard I could barely get out of bed this morning."

"Sorry 'bout that Coach, I was just doing what you told me."

"Yeah, runnin' the old guy into the ground."

Leaning in closer I said at a near whisper, "Scott, you are definitely our secret weapon, and Saturday we're going to turn you loose."

"Ohhh yeaahh, an Animal on the loose," he said loudly as a broad smile lit his face.

"Okay Dan," I called out as our stretching session reached its conclusion, "you have something for show and tell?"

"Sure," he said as he scrambled to his feet, grocery bag in hand, with Bill, John, and Curt at his side. "Well, a bunch of us found something and well, we thought it was something Scott should have. So, here Scott...come on up here."

In an instant Scott was on his feet and moving quickly to the front of our silent little group.

"Here, this is something you really need," Dan said, holding the wrinkled paper bag at arm's length.

Was this really a gift, I wondered, turning to watch Scott's reaction, or some sort of practical joke. Reaching out with both hands, Scott silently took the bag from Dan and with a confused look, turned in my direction, seemingly asking my permission to proceed.

"Really," I said, shrugging my shoulders, "I have no idea what it is, go ahead."

As if handling a sack of poisonous snakes, Scott cautiously unrolled the top of the bag. Eyes growing wider by the second, he peered inside as his curious teammates looked on.

"Coach, it's A LETTER JACKET! I can't believe it, I GOT A LETTER JACKET!"

Quickly pulling it from the bag, he held it high above his head as we applauded loudly and chanted, "An-na-mal, An-na-mal, An-na-mal."

A quick smile in Dan's direction signaled my approval as Scott eagerly jammed an arm into the beige leather sleeve of the red wool jacket. Tattered and a little bit faded, it didn't look like much, but Scott didn't seem to notice or care as he happily extended his arms to check the fit. Rescued from the sale rack at Goodwill, it was not an expensive item, but like many gifts its real value was best measured by its thoughtfulness.

"Thanks everybody!" Scott announced loudly before turning in my direction. "Can I wear it now, Coach?"

"Now? You mean at practice? You wanna run in it?"

"Yeah, of course, can I?"

"No," I said firmly. "You can wear it after practice, wear it to school, wear it on the bus Saturday morning, heck, sleep in it if you want. But no one runs a workout in a letter jacket. Now go put it in your locker…and lock it up. Okay?"

"Sure Coach," he responded as he turned in the direction of

the locker room, picking up the crumpled "gift bag" as he went. "It's a perfect fit," he said as he passed Mike and C.J. "This is great. I still can't believe it."

Without the help of his teammates, it was unlikely that Scott could have obtained such a treasure. With no money of his own and no parents to turn to, a letter jacket was something he'd never even dreamed of owning. The guys hadn't taken any of those things into consideration; it was simply the time of year when they started wearing their letter jackets and they decided Scott should have one, too. Somehow they'd stumbled on the perfect gift, something that immediately became Scott's most prized possession. With cuffs pushed all the way to his elbows he wore it in the halls, the classroom, and as he peeled potatoes at the group home. With no varsity "S" attached to the left chest, he drew some puzzled looks from the football guys in the locker room, but to Scott it didn't matter. For him it was more than just a generous gift. This raggedy jacket was his ticket into the popular group. In high school, he knew very well, if you want to join a group you have to dress the part.

Beneath the glow of a single street light we filed aboard the tightly packed bus for our longest road trip of the season. The Manitowoc Invitational was a relatively new meet that each year managed to attract many of the state's best teams. With the top three teams from last year's state meet in the field, this year was no exception. Senior heavy and number one ranked Manitowoc Lincoln would present the biggest challenge, with the defending state champs from Green Bay Preble adding to the excitement. After our solid performance in Wausau a week earlier, we'd been mysteriously assigned the number two spot in the state coaches' poll.

By mid-season the polls usually identify the top ranked teams with a fair degree of accuracy, but something about this seemed out of place to me. Undefeated Manitowoc was the clear choice at number one, but I wondered how in the world we'd been ranked second. Maybe it was based on the success we enjoyed in previous years, or the fact that we'd won three of four invitationals so far this season. Our low point total at Wausau the week before and the fact that we were a young and improving team were probably factored in, but in my mind we hadn't done enough to warrant our ranking. We were over-rated and in my opinion that was even worse than being under-rated.

I expected us to be the second best team at today's meet, but beyond that I made no predictions. There were far too many questions yet to be answered about our team to even think about such things. Today we had the opportunity to measure ourselves against a better team and a chance to see how we would respond to the challenge.

Rolling out of the parking lot at 5:30 a.m., we were packed shoulder to shoulder for a nearly three hour bus ride. With many of our younger runners bouncing along on the plywood boards, it was an uncomfortable and difficult trip. The rough ride combined with our hardest week of practice and the best field of teams we'd see short of the state meet represented a challenge I wasn't sure we were ready for.

The bus was dark and except for the occasional "Awwwh, who did that?" each time the foul evidence of someone's nervous bowel wafted through the air, it was quiet. Some wrapped themselves in blankets and despite the cramped conditions managed to catch some sleep, while others stared nervously out the windows, scanning the eastern horizon for the first sign of morning light. Each would handle the excitement and nervousness in his own way as we headed for battle on a beautiful 5,000 meter course along the shore of Lake Michigan.

"Scott," I said quietly as I shifted my position on the blue cooler that served as my bus seat, "you ever been to Manitowoc?"

"Coach, I never even heard of it before. Where is this place?"

With my left hand held up as a visual aid, I answered, "Here, this is Wisconsin, and this right here is Manitowoc." Touching the base of my thumb with my right index finger I mapped out its location. "And you know what this is, don't you?" I asked as I circled my finger in the space to the right of my hand.

"Lake Michigan, Coach, and here," he said as his finger stabbed the air "is Lake Superior, Huron, Erie, and Ontario."

"Wow!" I gasped, trying not to sound too surprised. "That was amazing. You named all five Great Lakes and put 'em in the right spots. What, are you some sorta genius?"

"Hey, I pay attention in class. And I like maps. I got 'em on the walls all over my room."

"Good. Here, study this one," I said as I peeled a copy of the course map from the cluttered stack on my clipboard. We don't want another "lost Animal" incident. You could end up in Lake Michigan if you're not careful."

"Yeah, or maybe Lake Superior," he joked as he motioned toward the bus ceiling.

Surprised by this display of knowledge I watched carefully in the dim light as he hunched over the crumpled map. What are the chances, I wondered, that this unusual person would end up with us. What infinite combination of events had landed him here? Of all the group homes scattered around the state, somehow he'd been assigned to one in our district. Maybe this was all just meant to be. Was this fate, I wondered as we slowly rolled past an enormous snow blower factory in the center of a small Wisconsin town, or just some sort of happy accident?

The silver light of low angle morning sunshine reflected brightly across the peaceful waters of Lake Michigan as we climbed stiffly from our crowded bus. Greeted by the fresh scent of a mild lake breeze, I stopped for a moment to enjoy the beauty of this perfect fall morning.

"Hey, look, it's the ocean," someone yelled from behind me, "Animal, it's the Atlantic Ocean!"

"Ha, nice try but…that's Lake Michigan," Scott shot back.

"Yeah, the fourth biggest freshwater lake in the world and one of the five Great Lakes…name 'em, Scott," I added loudly.

"Superior, Michigan, Huron, Erie, and Ontario," he answered quickly as shocked teammates stopped dead in their tracks.

"Listen and learn guys. Nice to know that someone stays awake in class. Oh and by the way," I said, pointing in the direction of the city's center, "we're about a mile away from where part of a Sputnik crashed in 1962, if any of you know what a Sputnik is."

Trudging through the dew soaked grass we headed for the starting area in search of a place to drop our gear before joining the long lines at a row of blue port-a-potties. Time stood still for a moment as I soaked it in, creating a picture in my mind. The shimmering lake, trees in near peak fall color, and a line of yellow school busses served as background for excited young runners who scurried about like ants on a sticky picnic table. Like all great moments in life, I knew this would be over too soon. Frozen atop a small mound near the finish chute I reminded myself to appreciate the day, no matter what the outcome.

"Varsity guys! Warm up in five minutes, meet on the hill behind the start," I ordered while collecting finish numbers from our J.V. runners.

Our young guys had gotten us off to a good start with a narrow win over Green Bay Preble, one of our biggest rivals. Lee Hacker surprised us all by emerging from the pack to win convincingly in the last mile with a career best time. A win by the J.V.'s was always a good sign, and with perfect conditions and great competition it looked like a good day to run fast.

A nervous silence fell over our group as we began our tour of the course at a slow jog. Like a religious order of skinny people under a vow of silence, we listened to the sound of our feet scuffling the ground and the occasional "thwack" as a gob of spit was launched from someone in the group. Except for my occasional, "settle down" reminder each time the pace quickened, hardly a word was spoken. We glared straight ahead as we jogged, sending a message of intensity. There was no time for joking around today. We were here to race.

"Hold up," I ordered as we reached a soccer field just beyond the mile-mark. "Hey, this is what we've been waiting for — great weather, a fast course, and a chance to race the top ranked team. You saw what our J.V. guys just did. Now it's your turn. Just remember, there's a lot of downhill in the first mile so the pace will be fast early, but we don't play that game. Be patient, and don't get too excited. We'll do our work in the second half of the race. The real race starts back here, on the far loop, away from the crowd. Three teams to watch today: Manitowoc in red and white, Preble in green and gold, and Sheboygan North in blue and gold. We're not going to win this meet, but I think we can give Manitowoc a good race. We've won a few meets, but we haven't seen a really good team until today. I think we can get within fifteen or twenty points and with some help from the other teams maybe even closer. Okay, let's jog."

Mike ran close at my side. With eyes cast to the ground, he shook his head in disagreement. He knew very well that I was trying to take the pressure off of our younger guys, but he hated to hear me talk this way. Mike's intensity dial was always turned to the full on position, ready to tear someone's head off. I did my best to keep him calm until race time.

C.J. was just the opposite. Calm and even tempered, his mood changed little. He didn't need a lot of screaming and fist pumping to get ready. A quiet handshake and a reminder that, "Your team needs you today," was all it took. For C.J., preparation was more cerebral than emotional; he would get ready in his own way.

Scott jogged happily along at the front of our group, occasionally moving a few strides ahead.

"Animal, settle down," someone shouted, sounding slightly annoyed.

"Yeah Animal, RELAX!"

"I am relaxed, you guys are too slow," he answered happily, grinning back at us.

"Are you paying attention, Scott?" I asked. "Cause if you get lost back here, no one's going to Xerox a map for you."

"Coach, I got it. You think I'm gonna take a wrong turn?"

"Well, it wouldn't be the first time," I reminded him as I reached out to pat him on the back of his bony shoulder. "Just remember, if you find yourself chest deep in Lake Michigan, it's time to turn around."

"COACH!" He growled with a laugh. "Do you really think I'd run into the lake?"

"I don't know, Donn," added John, "maybe we should get him a life jacket just in case."

Our mood was lighter as we entered the final stretch of the warm-up. My playful discussion with Scott had broken the silence and loosened us up a bit. It was hard to know how our younger guys would react to what, for most of them, was their first high pressure situation. Mike, C.J., and Curt were not my concern. As seniors with state meet experience, they knew what to expect. The rest of our guys were relatively untested and were about to be thrown into the fire.

"Relax out there, run smart, be patient," I reminded them sternly as they filed past me for a final handshake on their way to the line. "And remember," I added as I turned to jog away, "when you get to the lake, turn right."

As runners assembled at the starting line, I found a spot near the first turn and nervously shuffled my feet as I cleared my watch. It was up to them now. There was nothing left for me to do but watch…and cheer. Starting my watch at the puff of white smoke, I studied the crowd of runners funneling down to the first turn. Caught in mid pack, our guys chopped stride and did their best to keep from being knocked to the ground as the mob swallowed them up. This is the price we would pay for a conservative start. This was our style.

"Relax! Relax!" I shouted as they passed amid the chaos. "Just relax! Be patient!"

The pace was fast as the lead group headed downhill toward the lake. Mike and C.J. forced their way into the top twenty as our pack, stuck in the bottom third of the field, did their best to improve their position. Paying little attention to a group of Manitowoc runners as they passed, I scanned the field in search of our pack.

"Look Donn," one of our J.V. guys shouted in my direction. "Manitowoc guys, five of 'em, right there behind Mike and C.J."

"Doesn't matter," I shot back. "It's early."

At this point I was only interested in finding our guys, and our guys were buried. Nearing the mile mark, they were well off of where I wanted them to be, but they were together and moving up. Positioned to the far left as if it were the passing lane of a highway, they worked their way past one runner after another. Bill, Johnny, Curt, Dan, and John moved as a unit with eyes fixed on the group in white and red out in front of them.

"Where's Scott? Has anyone seen Scott?" I shouted to the J.V. runners around me with a hint of panic in my voice.

"Yeah," someone answered. "He's way up there. He's right behind the Manitowoc guys."

Sprinting wildly up a steep toboggan hill, I wondered how I'd missed him and if he'd still be there when the race came back into view. Cresting the hill on the edge of a field, I stopped and hunched forward with hands braced on sweaty knees waiting for the leaders to appear as the race turned uphill from the lake. With the sound of my heartbeat pounding in my ears, I trained my vision on the corner of a fenced parking area filled with olive drab National Guard trucks. Who would be first to emerge from the thicket behind the chain link fence I wondered as I checked my watch.

Soon I would have a clearer picture of how the race was shaping up. Some who'd gone out too fast would begin to fade at this point while the more cautious starters made their move. Once past the cheering crowd some would lose their enthusiasm for the race as more determined runners filed past. Cross country is seldom won, but often lost in the first mile.

"YEAH! MIKE!" shouted someone behind me, setting off a cascade of cheers from our group.

"That's it! Keep on it! Come on Mike…stay with it!" we begged as he drove himself forward a full twenty meters ahead of the next runner, a scowl etched on his face.

"Come on, C.J.!" someone screeched as he rounded the corner two strides behind the third place runner.

"We need that place," I yelled as if the meet depended on it. "Gotta have it, C.J., gotta have it!"

As the colorful procession of runners came into view, I did my best to evaluate our chances. In a small group, not far behind C.J., two Manitowoc runners ran side by side looking anxious to move up. Where was our next man, I wondered, ignoring the line of runners clad in green, blue, purple, and red as they streamed past. I was only interested in black and white jerseys now.

"LOOK! It's the Animal!"

"An-ah-mal, An-ah-mal, An-ah-mal," the chant began as his long bounding stride brought him in our direction with three Manitowoc runners on his heels.

The fast pace of the first mile was beginning to take a toll as Scott labored along. Willing himself forward, responding to every word of our encouragement, he held his position.

"Hang on, Scott!" I pleaded. "Eye of the Tiger, Animal. EYE…OF…THE…TIGER!"

He was in trouble and we all knew it. With more than a mile to go his form was breaking down. His arms were flailing and he leaned steeply forward, swiveling his head side to side as he sensed the Manitowoc guys closing in.

"Go help your teammate!" I shouted to Johnny, Bill, and Curt, motioning them forward. "Right there," I said, pointing ahead to the three runners in white. "That's where you need to be."

Weaving my way through the spectators scattered about the course, I dashed from point to point with a line of young runners trailing behind, shouting encouragement as we went.

"You can do it! Be tough! Get one more, get that next guy! Eye of the Tiger Animal, Eye of the Tiger. You can do it!"

Stationed just before the final turn, I watched with pride as

Mike launched his kick to the finish.

"Great race...finish it!" I screamed, leaning close as I clapped my hands together.

C. J. entered the final stretch safely in second place.

"Keep that spot! FINISH! Gotta have it!" we shouted at him hoarsely.

Two Manitowoc runners passed next as we turned our attention up the course. Other runners streamed by as we counted, totaling points in our heads. Two strides behind Manitowoc's third man, Scott fought bravely as their fourth and fifth runners closed the gap.

"AN-A-MAL, AN-A-MAL, AN-A-MAL," we pleaded, trying to help as if throwing a life jacket to a drowning man, watching as Scott attempted to stay ahead of the Manitowoc runners.

"ANIMAL! Come on, Animal!" we shouted frantically as the Manitowoc runners pulled to his shoulder and moved quickly past. With a worried look over his shoulder, Scott checked to see how many others might catch him before he could stagger across the line.

"Hang on, Scott, hang on, just hang on," I whispered softly to myself as emotion filled my throat. Surrounded by J.V. runners, I watched in silence, hoping he had just a few more strides left in him as Johnny sprinted past on his right.

"Wow!" said someone as Scott collapsed across the line.

"Yeah...Wow!" said another as we all quietly processed what we'd just seen.

A runner, apparently powered by the cheers of his teammates, had willed himself to the point of exhaustion. Undeterred by his lack of experience, he simply ran, instinctively, and like an animal running for survival, pushed himself to his absolute limit.

"That's how you run a race!" I announced to the young men around me. "That kid just ran his heart out. That was incredible!"

After collecting their finish cards, Mike and C.J. quickly exited the chute and raced back up the course to cheer on their teammates as they charged to the finish. We'd given some ground at the fifth spot, but Bill had run well and Curt was just a few seconds back. John and Dan struggled, but I knew as I raced to the end of the finish chute that we'd given the top ranked team in the state a pretty good scare. Surrounded closely by a group of admiring teammates, Scott jammed a sweaty arm into his letter jacket.

"ANIMAL!" they shouted. "Great race, Animal! That was awesome."

"Yeah, Animal," I said, using his nickname for the first time as I put an arm around him. "You were unbelievable. How do you feel?

"Coach, look," he announced, holding up his finish card. "I was fifteenth. Do I get a medal?"

"Yeah! You get a medal. Heck, after a race like that we should build a statue of you!"

"A statue? Coach, are ya kidding me?"

"Yes, I'm kidding," I said, placing a hand on each of his shoulders as my voice took on a more serious tone. "Scott, what you did out there was amazing. I am so proud of you. Look around, every person standing here is proud of you. What you did today was something very special, something you should be proud of. Remember that okay?"

"Thanks, Coach. One question...can I wear the medal on my letter jacket?"

"Sure, wear it as an earring if you want. Just don't lose it."

With the last of our place cards recorded and tucked in the manila scoring envelope, I trotted off to turn it in, leaving the guys to root through a pile of sweats in our team area. Fifty-three was an excellent total in a meet like this, and while I knew we hadn't won, I was proud of the effort. We'd run well and we were going to get better, I thought to myself as I proudly set the envelope on the scorer's table.

"I think we won," Mike said confidently as his teammates worked to replace race shoes with their trainers. "It's gonna be close, but I think we got 'em...and if we didn't..."

"MIKE!" I shouted with a stop-it-right-now tone perfected by years in the classroom. "We'll talk about it on the bus. Get your shoes on. We're going for a short cool down. Hustle up."

As the top twenty-five runners were called up for their medals, I calculated the team scores. Manitowoc had beaten us by four and Sheboygan North was surprisingly just seven points back.

"Great day, guys! You guys were great," I announced as we dragged ourselves like a retreating army toward our bus.

"Coach, look," said Scott as he pointed to the fifteenth place medal he'd pinned to the left side of his faded letter jacket. "Another medal."

"One of many if you keep running like that," I said, reaching out to shake his hand.

"Yeah, Coach and maybe even a statue," he said with a loud laugh. "Hey…a statue in a white tuxedo!"

Looking his way I smiled as I nodded my head. "On top of a limousine?"

"Yeah, on a limousine!" Scott said as he reached my way for a high-five.

A hat full of spare change once again earned Scott a fast food feast. Hair tousled and clad in his letter jacket with sleeves oddly rolled up, he turned from the counter clutching a tray mounded with wax paper wrapped treats and craned his neck in search of a place to sit.

"Over here, Animal," someone called. Dan had saved him a place at the table, the varsity table. Grinning like a lottery winner, he bolted for the spot, afraid someone would get there ahead of him. No longer exiled to the kids table, he could eat with the big boys now. Talking loudly, laughing, and gobbling his lunch, he enjoyed one of life's great moments: a day's worth of calories in a single sitting, a celebration after a hard effort, and time spent with friends.

Seated a few tables away, I listened as they analyzed the race in great detail, breaking it down mile by mile. Studying the lone mimeographed result sheet they sought out the places we could have gained points as they arrived at the conclusion that it could be done. With more hard work, we could catch the team from Manitowoc.

TWELVE

OCTOBER 1, 1985

O pen your book to page 134," I announced, pacing nervously across the front of the classroom. "I want you to read the short story about…"

"You mean the page with the picture of the old dude wearin' a bed sheet?" a student blurted out from the far corner of the room.

"Yes Andy," I replied patiently. "His name is Socrates. You might remember we talked about him last week. Socrates was known as the greatest teacher of the ancient world."

"Oh yeah, he was the dude that asked all those questions."

"Yes, it's a technique we call the Socratic Method."

"And people thought he was really annoying?"

"Yes Andy, often, when people ask a lot of questions, we tend to think of them as annoying. I'm sure we can all think of someone like that," I said, looking out at a room filled with smiling faces.

"You mean someone like me?"

"Well, it could be a child that asks why the sky is blue, the teenager who questions the value of going to church, or the kid who interrupts his teacher and calls everyone dude."

"Hey, I was wonderin' why you don't wear a toga when you teach. Oh…you want me to shut up and read, don't you?"

"Yes Andy, the story is called "The Death of Socrates."

With my wife Cheryl at home in the early stages of labor, I couldn't help wondering what my son might be like. Would he be the smart, likeable class clown like Andy or the rebellious kid with spiked, tri colored hair. Maybe he'd be popular and athletic or a nerdy bookworm, but right now I just hoped he'd be born healthy. Leaning against my gray steel teacher desk, I viewed the random collection of 29 students, quietly concentrating on their reading assignment. Each was so different, each a unique collection of good and bad qualities. How could this be, I wondered as I studied each of them individually. Were they a reflection of the parenting they'd received or were they just born this way? As I waited nervously for a knock at the door and the note that would send me scrambling for home, I was struck by the reality that soon I'd be given the chance to find out.

Everything was in place, secretaries were on alert, a substitute was on call, and I could be home in five minutes, four if I made the one stop light between school and our house. Experiencing the kind of nervousness usually reserved for race day, I slipped quietly between the rows of desks, making sure my students were on task, trying to concentrate on the lesson of the day.

Bolting from the classroom at the end of first hour, I wove my way through the maze of noisy students obstructing my path. With Cheryl already a week past her due date, I was worried and growing more impatient by the minute as I reached the office and dialed the telephone.

"Hello," Cheryl answered calmly.

"Are you okay, do you need me, is it time?" I rambled.

"No, everything's fine. The contractions are no closer than they were when you left. So calm down, I'm fine. This is going to take some time. It could be hours, it might not even happen today," she said, sending me back to class somewhat disappointed.

Really, I thought as I walked the now empty hallway...hours? What about all the news stories I'd seen about women going into labor and delivering babies in the back of cabs a few minutes later? As a guy with visions of running red lights on a mad dash to the hospital, this wasn't what I expected.

Each of my phone calls was met with the same level of calm reassurance as Cheryl did her best to convince me there was no need to panic. "Go to practice, just go," she said to my surprise. "I talked to the doctor a few minutes ago, and he thinks it isn't going to happen until late tonight or early tomorrow."

"Okay, if you're sure. I'll shorten practice and be home as soon as I can," I said, knowing it would be a hard promise to keep.

Of all the days of the season, I thought as I unlocked the door to the coaches' office, why would our child pick this one to come into the world? Today was set to be the longest, hardest, workout of the entire season. Our second big ladder would be run at a quicker pace with shorter recoveries as I encouraged our guys to attack each interval as if it were a race. Placed directly in the middle of our season, this was the workout designed to push each of us to our breaking point. With the near miss at Manitowoc still fresh in their minds, I planned to ask our guys to test their limits as we attempted to narrow the gap on the top ranked team in the state. It was going to be tough on all of us.

Mike, as always, was the first to arrive in the field house.

"This is going to be awesome!" he shouted as he pumped a fist in the air.

Positioning himself a few feet from the locker room door, he handed out high-fives as runners entered the field house. "Big Ladder today!" he yelled. "Are you ready for this? The big… nasty…ladder. Get ready. Eye of the Tiger today man, Eye of the Tiger."

Pacing nervously, I pretended to check the attendance sheet as I worried about Cheryl waiting for me at home. Studying Scott as he stood happily in a small group nearby, I thought about his parents. Why had Scott been taken from them? What had they done to him, and how had it affected him? After years of taking care of other people's kids, I was about to have one of my own. There was no way of knowing what kind of parent I would turn out to be; I only knew I was looking forward to the challenge and that I would always be there for my son, no matter what.

"Okay, guys, bring it in," I announced. "We're going to skip the stretching today. This is a long, hard work out and we need to get it started. For those of you who don't already know, I'm going to become a father sometime in the next couple of hours, so we need to get moving."

"A baby? Coach, you're going to have a BABY?" Scott groaned, throwing his hands up in disbelief.

"Scott, I've only been talking about it all season. How did you not know that?"

"Hey, nobody told me, but Coach, I'm really good with babies. If ya ever need a babysitter, I'm your man. So, what are you going to name it?"

"We haven't picked a name yet, but our doctor thinks it's going to be a boy."

"Coach, ya just gotta name him Hulk, The Hulk, The Hulkster!"

Suddenly a barrage of suggestions flew from all directions: Bert, Ernie, Scott, Thor, Zeus, Lenny, and Soapdish. "Hey, I'm not naming a goldfish here," I reminded them. "This is my son, and I'd rather he didn't get beat up every day of his life."

"Coach, think about it. Who's going to mess with a kid named The Hulk," Scott said with clearly well-reasoned logic.

"Yeah, well I appreciate the thought, but I don't think my wife's going to go for it. Hulk Behnke just doesn't seem to work."

An odd sort of quiet fell over our group as we began our jog to the park. Everyone knew the importance of this workout. This was serious business and it wasn't going to be easy. In the charged atmosphere of the bus ride home from Manitowoc, there had been talk of working harder, closing the gap, and winning a state title. These were the kinds of things often said on busses, at lunch tables, and in locker rooms. Words spoken to impress, words that sounded good, but words that are all too often just words. Talk is cheap, especially among teen age boys, and I wasn't sure if they had said these things for my benefit or if they really meant them. Today I was going to find out. Flanked by Mike and C.J. at the entrance to Bukholt Park, I asked each member of our team to give an all-out effort.

"This is meant to be the toughest workout of the season," I said as they stared at me in absolute silence. "It's the same workout we ran last week, 400, 800, 1200, mile and then back down the ladder. Take your opening mile time from Saturday, subtract ten seconds, and that's your pace. No way around it, this is going to be tough, but it can't be much harder than running in the storm last week. Okay, up to the line."

"Let's go guys! Run till you drop, come on!" Mike added in his usual style.

Running this much faster than race pace was something we seldom did and many of our young guys had never done anything quite like it. Mike and C.J. led us to the line, ready and anxious to show their teammates how it should be done. The math is simple, seven intervals at seventy to seventy-five second pace; the workout, we all knew, would not be.

Scott had a quiet focus that I had never seen from him before. Like so many other runners with attention deficit disorder, this was good for him. The combination of movement and the on task behavior of those around him seemed to help his concentration. A different person was emerging as he learned to combine the physical and mental aspects of our sport. The long, fast tempo runs were still a challenge for him, but he had certainly learned to run intervals.

Like all good runners, our leaders could dial in their pace and hit their splits precisely. Scott positioned himself directly behind Mike and C.J., with me just off his left shoulder. He ran aggressively, his long stride reaching out, his feet punishing the ground. Our once awkward puppy was slowly taking on the look of a greyhound as we moved in unison along the bank of the Wisconsin River on a beautiful fall day. Did he know how fast we were going or how far we had to go? Did he even care, I

Scott "The Animal" Longley in his beloved letter jacket.

Scott and teammate Johnny Hyland in action at the Wausau East Invitational.

Scott with Johnny Hyland waiting for his medal at the Manitowoc Invitational.

Wisconsin Valley Conference Champions 1985.
Scott with All-Conference certificate and medal.

Coach Behnke gives the team some final words of advice
before sending them to the State Meet starting line.

The start of the State Championship race.

Scott in his blue face mask hanging onto John Ceplina at the
mid way point of the State Championship race.

ACE	TEAM	NAME	YEAR	SCHOOL	TIME
1		LEE ZUBROD	11	BURLINGTON	17:29.0
2		BRYAN DEMERATH	11	GRAFTON	17:30.9
3	1	BRIAN MASSHARDT	12	MONROE	17:32.1
4	2	* C.J. HANSON	12	STEVENS POINT	17:33.2
5	3	PAT DITTMAN	11	LA CROSSE CENTRAL	17:40.2
6	4	ALBERT STEWART	12	MILWAUKEE SOUTH	17:42.5
7		GREG RITZENTHALER	11	WEST BEND EAST	17:43.3
8	5	* MIKE MONK	20	STEVENS POINT	17:46.7
9		JOHN NIELSEN	12	RACINE PARK	17:48.3
10		DAVE COLUMBUS	10	MARINETTE	17:51.0
11	6	DAVE TREMPE	12	SHEBOYGAN NORTH	17:53.0
12	7	TROY SCHMITT	12	MANITOWOC *	17:53.6
13		ERIC STABB	12	JANESVILLE PARKER	17:54.6
14		RANDY HAINES	12	LAKELAND	17:55.3
15		SHAUN ELVIGTON	12	FRANKLIN	17:56.8
16	8	RALPH VROOMAN	12	WAUKESHA SOUTH	17:59.0
17	9	DARRIN OTT	11	JANESVILLE CRAIG	18:03.4
18	10	BRUCE COLLET	11	MADISON MEMORIAL	18:04.9
19	11	JAY BAER	11	GREEN BAY WEST	18:06.2
20		BOYD JANTO	12	WEST BEND WEST	18:06.8
21	12	PETER DVORAK	12	HOMESTEAD	18:07.3
22	13	DAVE KIRCHEN	12	MANITOWOC *	18:07.9
23		MARC BUECHEL	11	BROOKFIELD EAST	18:08.3
	14	* JOHN CEPLINA	11	STEVENS POINT	18:09.8
		JEFF SHAW	11	NEW LONDON	18:10.8
26		DEAN RHODE	12	NEW HOLSTEIN	18:11.4
27	15	JOHN ROBINSON	12	MANITOWOC *	18:12.5
28	16	TODD WECH	11	MANITOWOC *	18:13.2
29	17	* SCOTT LONGLEY	12	STEVENS POINT	18:13.6
30	18	BEN FLORES	9	MILWAUKEE SOUTH	18:16.2
31	19	KEVIN HAGEN	11	CHIPPEWA FALLS	18:17.4
32	20	STEVE HOLTHAUS	11	JANESVILLE CRAIG	18:17.9
33	21	BART UMENTUM	12	GREEN BAY PREBLE	18:18.6
34	22	SCOTT GRINDE	12	MANITOWOC *	18:19.1
35	23	MATT NUNKE	12	CHIPPEWA FALLS	18:19.9
36	24	CHRIS WALLACE	11	MANITOWOC *	18:20.9
37	25	NORB LATZ	12	BROOKFIELD CENTRAL	18:21.3
38		BRIAN RESLER	12	WHITEFISH BAY	18:21.7
39		DOUG KEMPF	12	WAUSAU EAST	18:22.0
40	26	TIM EARLING	12	GREEN BAY WEST	18:22.3
41	27	GREG JOHNSON	11	LA CROSSE CENTRAL	18:22.7
42	28	BRIAN KUGEL	10	GREEN BAY PREBLE	18:23.1
43	29	PAUL BERWALD	12	MILWAUKEE SOUTH	18:25.6
44	30	RON BLAHA	11	RACINE HORLICK	18:27.0
45	31	MARK KORNMANN	10	MENOMINEE FALLS	18:28.0
46		JEFF PROBST	11	CUDAHY	18:28.4
47	32	* JOHN HYLAND	9	STEVENS POINT	18:29.2
48		PAUL JAGIELSKI	10	NEW BERLIN EISENHOWE	18:30.6
49	33	GREG SCHMIDT	10	SHEBOYGAN NORTH	18:31.0
	34	BOB FRUEHWIRTH	11	BROOKFIELD CENTRAL	18:31.4
		PETE PIERCE	12	MADISON EAST	18:31.8
52		LUKE BODENSTEINER	10	WEST BEND WEST	18:32.4
53		MIKE WATSON	12	MARSHFIELD	18:32.7

Page one of official results from the 1985 State meet. The conditions
resulted in some of the slowest times ever run at a Wisconsin State meet.

Scott clutching our State trophy.

Coach Behnke and Scott at the Manitowoc Invitational in 1985.

Donn and Scott, July 2015.

wondered as I watched him out of the corner of my eye. Wedged in the middle of the lead pack, he pushed those ahead of him as he pulled the rest of us along. Just a few weeks ago I had dragged him through his first interval session and now, in an amazing transformation, he was dragging me.

Our first three intervals, completed at goal pace, were suddenly behind us. Short recovery jogs were filled with words of encouragement as we slowly shuffled along the outfield fence of the baseball diamond in the center of the park. The apprehension we'd felt earlier had been replaced by confidence. We were all in this together, and together we knew we could do it. Our group was nearly silent as we reached our starting point and edged our way into position to start the next interval.

"Eye of The Tiger, Coach, I know you can do this," Scott said confidently as his large bony hand patted the middle of my back.

Nervous laughter shot through the group as I cleared my watch and announced, "This is it, the hardest part. It's all downhill after this."

"Don't back down! Nobody backs down!" Mike screamed.

"Do your best…set and GO!"

As we fled the starting line I began to focus on what Scott had just done. With a few words of encouragement and a pat on the back, he had inspired me and his teammates as well. I didn't need to run this hard. As the coach I was allowed to stand on the sidelines and yell times or run comfortably with the mid pack kids. I wasn't a young college kid anymore and after a full day of teaching, with a long night ahead of me, I didn't need to do it. But, somehow, here I was, charging through the park late on a Monday afternoon at an insanely hard pace, simply because this is what distance runners do. We thrive on the challenge of exploring our limits, supporting, encouraging, and pushing each other as we pursue our goals. Scott's well-placed words had set a trap for me, having told me I could do it I could not let him down. There was no way out. I'd asked him to run his hardest and now I'd have to do the same.

Rounding the final turn we charged toward the crack in the pavement near the bus garage that served as our mile marker. Mike flew across the line at a near sprint before turning abruptly up the course to loudly demand we all give our best effort. The passion in his voice rang throughout the otherwise quiet park as he ran back in our direction. C.J. stood, shouting times as John, Johnny, Scott, Bill, and Curt crossed in a tight group with Dan and I a few strides behind.

"Outstanding!" I yelled, expending what little strength I had left. I knew as I watched the final members of our group straggle across the line that many of them had just run the fastest mile of their lives.

More than a third of the workout lay ahead, but it seemed as if a great weight had been lifted. Our mood grew less serious as we began our recovery jog around the ball diamond, and there was a noticeable increase in chatter within the group as the end seemed to be in sight. Coming down the ladder, we all knew, was far easier than going up.

"Great workout!" I said, clapping my hands loudly as the final runner crossed the line to bring the workout to an end. A line of tired, sweaty young men formed at the drinking fountain as I offered handshakes and my assessment of what they'd just done.

"Hey, we've had some pretty good teams here over the last few years, but you guys ran that workout about as well as any of them. A lot of kids your age went home to plant their butt on a couch and stuff their faces with Twinkies while you were out here doing this. You made yourself a stronger, tougher person while your classmates just got fatter and lazier. Remember this — remember what we did here today. We didn't climb Everest, cure cancer, or cross the Atlantic in a bathtub, but we had an adventure, right here in our own backyard. I can't tell you what other teams might have done today but I know this, no team in Wisconsin worked harder than we did. I think the gap between us and Manitowoc just got a little narrower. We may not see it Saturday, but this workout will pay off later, believe that. Just keep working and keep believing in what we do. Now, let's get moving."

Some athletes require stadiums full of fans and million dollar contracts to perform while others need only a few gulps of cool water and a sweaty handshake. It made me proud, not just proud of our team but proud of our sport as I imagined scenes like this repeated by cross country teams across our country. Skinny young men and dedicated coaches working together, trying desperately to find a way to shave a few seconds from their 5,000 meter time. Anyone watching today would have been impressed by the effort. The fact that no one had been watching made it even more impressive

Surrounded by loud, happy young runners and carried along by the excitement of what had just happened, I felt surprisingly good on the jog back to school.

"Eat a good meal and get to bed early," I shouted as I slammed the coaches' office door and headed for my car and the race home, late, as usual.

For someone about to deliver a child for the first time, Cheryl was amazingly calm as she met me at the kitchen door. Women must be programmed this way, I thought to myself, as I tried to conceal my nervousness by rambling on about the workout we'd just run.

"Oh, Scott thinks Hulk would be a good name for our son."

"Well, that sounds about right. Did the guys have any other bright ideas?"

"Sure, but only if you like the sound of Soapdish Behnke," I joked.

It was going to be a long night, I realized as I watched Cheryl carefully avoid the ground beef portion of the Hamburger Helper I'd just thrown together. The effect of the big ladder was beginning to take hold as I cleared the table and washed the dishes. Staggering to the living room, I threw myself onto the couch next to Cheryl and checked my watch as "we" awaited the next contraction. It looked like our trip to the hospital wasn't going to happen anytime soon. Exhausted, I did my best to strike a balance between Cheryl's needs and a Monday night football game. Why, I wondered, as I struggled to stay awake, was this taking so long? Why was our kid being so stubborn? Had I known this was going to happen, I might have excused myself from the workout. Like a marathon runner, I had just hit the wall.

The first sign of morning light crept across the sky as we rolled through the flashing red light on Division Street without coming to a full stop. Like a couple of desperate criminals on a crime spree, we dared the police to do something about it as we exceeded the speed limit by several miles per hour as we finally headed to the hospital. Six hours later, an emergency C-section surgery finally brought Cheryl's lengthy labor to an abrupt end as I stood nauseous with worry outside the operating room door. The low heart rate I was usually so proud of was suddenly becoming a problem as I felt blood rushing from my head and my vision began to blur.

"You look like you need to sit down," said a nurse, grabbing my arm after noticing my ashen face.

"No, I'm okay, this happens all the time," I answered, slumping forward and placing my hands on my knees as if I'd just finished a race. Sweat rolled from my chin and hit the floor as the doctor stepped into the hallway.

"Congratulations, dad!" he said as he patted the back of my sweaty shoulder. "Nothing to worry about, it all went well. Mother and child are doing fine…but I think we need to get you to a chair."

"No, really, this happens to me a lot. I'm okay," I protested as a nurse emerged with a screaming, purple baby in her arms.

"A boy?" I asked loudly as she peeled back the blanket.

"No," she said with a chuckle, "that's the umbilical cord. It's a girl."

"She's beautiful! Is she….?"

"Yes, ten little fingers and ten little toes. She's perfect."

Spellbound, I watched as they weighed, measured, and

fingerprinted her like a miniature criminal. Suddenly, as I reached out and touched her tiny hand with my finger, I felt the connection that only a parent can fully understand. It was love at first sight. I was a father.

With our daughter tightly wrapped and safely tucked inside a clear plastic hospital cradle, I made a quick check on Cheryl in the recovery room before placing calls to family, friends, and Ray, my replacement coach for the day. Ray was a perfect fit for the job. As one of my former runners and the best team captain our program had ever seen, he would know what to do. Just two years removed from a good collegiate running career, he was lean, fit, and currently working as a county social worker. The fact that he'd worked with Scott as a group home counselor and was Cheryl's younger brother were both bonuses, and I was fortunate to have him available.

Like most coaches, I hate to miss a practice. It's not a control thing, it's more about dedication. Good coaches, like good runners, hate to take a day off. At 3:00 pm, no matter what, we go to practice.

As I hung up the phone in the nurse's station I felt completely at ease. Ray knew the routine, and he had Mike, C.J. and Curt to help him. It was an easy practice, a nine mile recovery run at a sensible pace. As long as they didn't have an encounter with "crazy shovel lady" and they kept track of Scott, nothing could go wrong. Ray had my complete trust.

Equipped with a Polaroid picture of a tired, proud father awkwardly holding his newborn daughter, I entered the field house a few minutes late for Wednesday's practice. A loud round of applause erupted from the group as I approached.

"Coach, how's the little Hulkster?" Scott yelled as guys crowded in to see the small proto I held in their direction.

"Good, but HER name is Elizabeth, NOT Hulk and she's just perfect. So, tell me, how was practice yesterday, Scott?"

"Fast Coach, you wouldn't believe how fast we ran."

"Fast? It was supposed to be a recovery day," I said, looking in C.J.'s direction.

"It wasn't that fast," he stated somewhat defensively.

"Coach! We were passing bikes and cars and trucks. We coulda got a speeding ticket!"

"How fast was it?" I asked, looking for a better answer.

"Well, it was fast, but it wasn't THAT fast," C.J. replied.

"So where was Ray during all this?"

"He was there for a while, till we dropped the hammer. Then he was gone," said Mike with a smile.

"I really can't leave you knuckle-heads alone for a second, can I?

THIRTEEN

FOND DU LAC

The Fond du Lac Relays had a reputation for attracting many of the strongest programs from the southeast corner of the state. Short of the state meet, it was the biggest race on our schedule and best of all, it would give us a second look at top ranked Manitowoc. The "relay" format meant that scoring was done on a total time basis instead of the usual total points. Four varsity races were held with teams allowed two runners in each. The five fastest times from each team were then added together to determine the final outcome. This arrangement guaranteed four race winners instead of just one, and it allowed less accomplished runners to race against those closer to their ability. It was the only race of the season in which times were more important than places, and it had me somewhat worried. Our guys were good pack runners and had learned to key off of one another. Today they would be kicked out of the flock to fly on their own. It would be a big learning experience.

With three runners in the top six and a convincing team victory, our J.V. runners got us off to a very good start. Times were not fast, but I didn't expect them to be on the hilly, challenging course. Our young guys had raced well after a very hard week of practice which gave us all a feeling of great optimism as our first two varsity runners headed to the line.

I was certain that John and Dan would start things off well for us. Our third and fourth runners just two weeks ago, there was no doubt they were the best runners in the first varsity race of the day.

"Green light," I told them. "Just go to the front and crush these guys! Let's give the Manitowoc guys something to think about and take some of the pressure off of Scott and Johnny. Get after it!"

Taking their job seriously, they bolted from the line, building a lead almost instantly. Side by side they stretched their lead with each step. After running poorly a week earlier, they were determined to make amends as they pulled far ahead of the third place runner. Followed by a gang of excited J.V. runners, I raced in zigzag fashion up and down the hill that ran the length of the course, energized by what I was seeing.

"Coach! That's not right, is it?" someone shouted, pointing to the top of the hill.

"No! John, NO!" I screamed as I began a mad dash uphill.

Someone, an inexperienced coach, had directed John and Dan off the course. They should have known better, but the coach was insistent so they obeyed. Responding to my orders, they reversed course and pressed bravely on, but the damage was done. It was a huge mistake, one from which they could not possibly recover. Our excitement came to an abrupt end and the momentum I had hoped to build was gone. It was the worst possible way to start a meet and as it turned out, something we could not recover from.

In the second race of the day, Bill and Curt ran with the leaders for two miles before struggling to the finish. Scott and Johnny suffered a similar fate in the third race. Looking good early, they made a brave attempt at a break away but it was too much to ask. The hilly course took its toll as both gave up valuable seconds in the final mile.

Manitowoc held an insurmountable lead as Mike and C.J. toed the line for the final race. As proud seniors determined to save the day, they made the kind of bold move that almost always turns out badly. Anxious to erase our deficit, they went out fast and built a large lead before being swallowed up by the pack of runners who'd shown greater patience. Impressed by their courage, I stood by and did nothing. I could have reined them in, but as our team leaders they deserved a chance to try. They had earned the right to crash and burn, and they would never go down without a fight.

It was an ugly way to end what had been an otherwise great week. Having offered little competition to the team we had nearly beaten just one week earlier, we stood in stunned silence as the final scores were read. Finishing more than a minute behind them in total time was a bitter pill for us to swallow. Maybe we'd trained too hard, or perhaps it was the many distractions of the week or the wrong turn in the first race. It was possible that last week was an anomaly and Manitowoc was just a better team. All were options worthy of consideration, and things we would talk about on the ride home. Was I pushing this young team too hard? Were we flying too close to the sun, I wondered as we slowly gathered our equipment and dragged ourselves solemnly in the direction of our bus. Few words were spoken as we threw our travel bags to the floor and dropped into our seats. C.J. placed his boom box on the floor of the bus; there would be no music, at least not for some time. It was going to take a while for the disappointment of the day to dissipate.

"Coach," said Scott quietly as the bus crept slowly out of the golf course parking lot, "are you mad at us?"

"No, I'm not mad. Why would you think I'm mad?"

"'Cause you're not talkin' and Coach, you're NEVER not talkin.'"

"Scott, listen for a second. Do you hear that? That silence, that's the sound of disappointment. It's not that we lost a meet, it's the fact that we didn't run well. Last week we were excited to be second because we ran a great race, but today, well, there's not much to be excited about. Today was like a big kick in the gut. I know that everyone gave their best effort and that's all I can ask, but they crushed us."

"Those hills, Coach. I just couldn't get away from the Manitowoc guys."

"I know, Scott, I know you did your best and I'm proud of

you. Here, look," I said, pointing to his time on the result sheet. "Of all of our guys, you were the closest to your time from last week. You had the least bad race of all of us."

"Least bad?"

"Yeah, you were our one bright spot. If I had a white tuxedo, I'd give it to you right now."

"Really, you'd let me wear a white tuxedo?"

"Sure, if I had one, but since I don't maybe we'll just buy you some lunch."

"Okay Coach. You know, if I wore a white tux, I'd just get ketchup on it anyway."

FOURTEEN

ALL CONFERENCE

On a hot summer day in 1963, I watched with great interest as a kid we called Beans stuffed piece after piece of bubblegum into his oversized mouth. Unlikely to eclipse the Babe's 714 homers or Peter Snell's 3:54.4 mile, Beans had set his sights on the neighborhood gum chewing record. So there we sat, a half-dozen of us planted on the curb in front of a small corner store on Lisbon Avenue in Milwaukee, tearing open packs of Topps Baseball Cards and passing the stale, brittle pink gum to the waiting hands of our chunky, freckle faced friend. Slimy spit escaped from the corners of his mouth and gathered at the base of his chin before dripping to the pavement between his feet as we did our best to make him laugh in hopes that he'd choke and launch the whole mess into the street. It was something a group of ten year olds would remember for the rest of their lives: the day Beans somehow managed to jam 50 thin slabs of gum into his mouth at one time. Why did he do it? Simply because we'd picked an arbitrary number, declared it to be a record, and challenged him to break it.

People are competitive by nature. We enjoy challenges and we love to set records. Whether it's something as stupid as gum chewing or as complex as racing the Soviets to put a man on the moon, if someone declares themselves to be "the best" at something, others will almost certainly step forward to prove them wrong. From an early age we're taught to enjoy the "look what I did" feeling. Young children earn applause for taking their first step, cleaning their plate, or learning to use the toilet. Life, it seems, is a never ending series of challenges as we look for ways to improve ourselves and gauge how well we stack up against those around us. Each day we have countless opportunities to succeed or fail and if we ever run out, we simply make up something new. The Ancient Greeks had the Olympic Games, Romans raced chariots, and two guys from Canada invented Trivial Pursuit all because people need to compete.

For some reason we're not content to say that a person is good at something; we feel the need to rank, classify, and label the accomplishment. Every year someone earns the grandiose title Mr. Universe or the slightly less presumptuous Miss America. People we presume to be smart get appointed as Supreme Court Justices, Senators, or Chief Executive Officers of big corporations. Skilled military leaders earn the title General which to me never seemed specific enough, and if you're exceptionally pious you might get a chance to become Pope or the Dali Lama. The list of titles and honors people can accumulate is practically limitless, especially in the field of athletics.

At the high school level good athletes make the Varsity while the less skilled are labeled bench warmers, scrubs, or the much kinder, Junior Varsity. At the top of the heap are the starters, the first string, the stars, and in some cases All-Stars. For some reason, putting the word all in front of the title makes it all the more impressive. Words like area, region, conference, state, or American sound pretty blah until you slap the word all in front of them. Suddenly these words have a powerful new meaning, being chosen all something sounds like a big deal, and often it is.

Titles and awards are a powerful source of motivation for athletes. They can inspire dedication, provide a reason to work hard, and ultimately reward success and improvement. But awards can be tricky. By rewarding only the first place finisher we run the risk of discouraging the less talented, and if we reward everyone we diminish the value of the prize. There's a fine line between too few and too many when it comes to awards. As badly as I want my runners to win awards, I don't want them to come too easily. Ribbons and medals that end up on the floor of the bus or forgotten at the bottom of a drawer are not treasured reminders of a hard effort but merely objects handed out at the end of the chute.

Competing seemed to come naturally to Scott, but like a lot of people he had trouble setting goals. The concept of working hard today for something that may or may not happen in the future was difficult for him. He lived his life day to day, simply following the house rules: do as you're told, peel some potatoes, and try not to lose your precious T.V. time. For someone in Scott's situation, long range plans seemed rather pointless. While others pondered what they might do post-high school, Scott could look no further ahead than tomorrow or possibly our next cross country meet. Life for group home residents was anything but predictable and with little control over their situation, they knew it could change in an instant.

Cross country was an ideal outlet for Scott's boundless energy, but best of all it added stability to his life and gave him a predictable daily routine. Our rotating mixture of hard and easy days, long runs and intervals, and the weekly feedback of race day was good for him. Surrounded by guys who constantly set and reset goals for practically every aspect of their lives, Scott was learning to do the same as he worked to mimic their behavior. Goal setting is a way of life for distance runners. We time our long runs, our intervals, and our races, commit the times to memory, and often write them down. We learn to set goals for each run, each day, week, season, and year. Some of us even set time goals for everyday activities like taking a shower or mowing the lawn. Like pit crews who know how long it should take to change a tire, we know our "personal record," a term almost certainly coined by a distance runner. As runners we talk about our goals, telling our coaches, teammates, families, and friends, if we think they care. We write our goals on calendars, pieces of tape stuck to mirrors, the back of a locker, or across the face of a clock radio, places where we'll see them every day. These small signs hold us accountable and give us direction. Like road maps, they guide us on our way. As the Cheshire Cat told Alice in Wonderland, "If you don't know where you want to get to, it doesn't matter which way you go." Goals show us where we want to go.

And so today, as our team stood tightly packed in the parking lot just outside the locker room door engulfed by the dark chill of a damp October morning, we prepared to chase one of our season's goals. Today we had the opportunity to win our ninth consecutive conference title. This is what we'd trained for, planned for, and set our sights on months ago. Our nine team conference meet on a Saturday morning was unlikely to draw a large crowd or much media attention, but that made little difference to any of us. This was our chance to carry on the tradition of our program and chase another championship, a chance to run a personal record, and a chance to make the all-conference team.

"Alright guys grab your gear and load up!" I shouted loudly as our bus rolled to a squeaky halt a few feet away. "Let's go win another conference title."

"Coach, one question," Scott asked quietly as we waited our turn to climb aboard. "Do I have a chance?"

"A chance?"

"Yeah, a chance at makin' All-Conference?"

"Scott," I said confidently as I draped an arm around his shoulders, "you WILL make the All-Conference team today. Just don't get too excited early, be patient, key on John, Bill, and Johnny and you'll be fine."

"Okay, got it Coach, don't worry about me."

"Oh sure, like at Manitowoc and every other week when I tell you to go out slow and you get excited and sprint out with the leaders."

"Coach, ya know… it's the eye of the tiger…The Animal's just gotta run."

"Yeah," I said as the bus door folded shut behind me. "I know, but let's put a leash on the tiger today, alright?"

"No problem, Coach, you don't need a leash. I'll be good, I promise."

With the sun struggling to find a way out of the thick cloud cover, seventy-two varsity runners headed nervously in the direction of the starting line.

"You saw what or J.V. guys just did," I pointed out as our guys shed their sweats. "Every one of them just ran 15 to 30 seconds faster than they did on this course four weeks ago, so you know it's a good day to run fast!"

After distributing a few last minute handshakes and reminders to run smart and be patient, I jogged quickly onto the course with Rob at my side. After a month as a college runner, Rob had decided to follow his heart home and help me out with the team, and Scott.

"I'm pretty sure C.J.'s too sick to be out there, but I have to let him try," I explained to Rob. "But the rest of them are ready, especially Scott. I just wish you could have seen him last week at Wisconsin Rapids. I finally got him to go out a little slower, and he ends up being our third man, sixth overall with a big P.R. It was amazing."

A small puff of white smoke followed by the faint pop of the starter's pistol signaled the start of the race. Scott burst from the line and almost instantly built a ten meter lead on the field.

"EASY SCOTT! TAKE IT EASY!" I shouted from up the course.

"ANIMAL! Get behind me, NOW!" Mike ordered to little effect.

Rob quickly joined the chorus of people demanding that Scott settle into a sensible pace.

Bolting past at a speed he couldn't possibly sustain, Scott pushed eagerly forward as our J.V. runners egged him on.

"That's it, Animal!"

"Stay with Mike, Animal!"

"You can do it, Animal!"

"Eye of the tiger, Animal, Eye…Of...The…Tiger!"

Like a force of nature, my best efforts to control Scott had no effect. It wasn't that he disagreed with me, and he wasn't being disrespectful; he just couldn't hold back. While his teammates started cautiously and worked their way to the front, Scott had chosen to jump on the tiger's back and hold on for dear life. Unlike most of us, Scott had no fear of discomfort. His harsh upbringing had given him a toughness most of us lacked, allowing him to endure what many of us could not. Hanging on came naturally to Scott, he'd been doing it all his life.

"All-Conference, Scott, ALL-CONFERENCE. You can do it!" I shouted as he clung stubbornly to second place, now fifty meters behind Mike just past the mile mark.

"Don't look back, Animal! Look up, keep your head up, look at the guy ahead of you," added Rob, noticing Scott's tendency to hunch his shoulders forward and look at his shoe tops.

Watching carefully as he passed, I was reminded of the legendary Czech runner Emil Zatopek whose running form made him look, in the words of one sports reporter, "as if he'd just been stabbed through the heart." Like Zatopek, Scott ran "as if his next step would be his last," and yet somehow, it wasn't.

Excitedly we did our best to urge him on as a pack of runners slowly closed in over the course of the final mile. Arms reaching forward, flailing left and right, Scott willed himself ahead, hanging onto the small group that had just caught him.

"That kid's done," I overheard someone say as Scott labored past.

"Eye of the Tiger, Scott!" John said as he pulled even and prepared to launch a kick to the finish. "Go with me!"

"All-Conference…right there!" I shouted, stabbing the air with my hand as I pointed to the runners a few steps ahead.

Now a kicker's race, the slight downhill gave the finishers a chance to show their speed and toughness. Johnny, with a burst of speed seldom seen at cross country meets, left the group behind to claim third place with John a few steps back in fifth. Responding to the desperate cries of his teammates, Scott, staggering the last twenty meters, secured his All-Conference goal with a seventh place finish. Helped through the finish chute by concerned meet officials, the intense discomfort of his effort was quickly replaced by the joy of being surrounded by happy teammates offering their congratulations. With hands far above his head, he high-fived everyone in his general vicinity, and while others headed quietly to retrieve their sweats, Scott made the most of this great moment. Today he'd earned the prestigious title of first team All-Conference. On this dark, cloudy fall morning in front of a modest crowd of a few hundred people, Scott had done something none of us would have guessed possible at the start of the season. Today he'd earned a label he could carry with him for the rest of his life, another medal to pin to his jacket, and the right to claim the trophy for our championship team.

With four runners in the top seven, our 29 point total was one of the best we'd posted all season and virtually all of our guys had run well. Mike, like a man on a mission, had dominated the race, running 26 seconds faster than he had on this course a few weeks earlier. Johnny, John, and Scott had run extremely well as Lee, running in only his second varsity race, locked up the meet for us with Bill and Dan finishing close behind. It was a testament to how hard our guys had worked and how far we'd progressed over the course of the season. Except for two of our senior captains, C.J. and Curt, who had struggled with illness, it had been a great day for us.

Gathered in a field near the finish line, we waited patiently for awards to be presented as a cool breeze did its best to dampen our spirits. With my hand planted firmly on the back of his neck, I pulled Scott close.

"You did it...All-Conference, and just wait till you see the medal. It's gonna look really good right here," I said, pointing to the left side of his slightly faded letter jacket.

"That makes five!" he said with a smile as he studied his small collection. "Do you think I can get one next week, too?"

"That's gonna be tough. Next week we face sixteen teams and they only give six medals. I'm not saying you can't, but you'll have to run a really smart race, maybe listen to my advice. Or maybe I should just put you on that leash?"

"NO! Coach, not a leash. Next week I'll listen, I promise."

With a beautifully engraved seventh place medal held just beneath his chin, Scott stood happily on a makeshift awards platform as proud parents crowded forward with cameras in hand. In keeping with our recently established tradition, he once again collected the team trophy as teammates circled around to watch. After pretending to shine the golden figurine with a few bursts of warm breath and a quick brush of his sleeve, he thrust it high above his head as the small crowd around him cheered. Beaming with pride, Scott clutched the trophy as we posed for team photos before carrying it to our bus as carefully as if it were a newborn child.

The golden runner attached to a thick walnut pedestal sat safely on the bus seat next to him as Scott carefully studied the medal he clutched in his left hand.

"Rob," I said quietly as I bumped him on the arm and pointed in Scott's direction.

"Animal…nice medal, isn't it?" Rob asked.

"Yeah! It's the best one I ever got, and look, it even has something on the back! It says Wisconsin Valley Conference, 1985, seventh place."

"Scott," I said, holding the result sheet and pointing to his name near the top of the page. "What you did today was amazing. I'm really proud of you. You know that, right?"

"Yeah Coach, thanks."

"Just be careful with that medal. Maybe I should hold onto it for you."

"No! I won't lose it! I'm never going to let it out of my sight. I'm gonna pin it to my letter jacket right now, as soon as I find a safety pin."

"A safety pin is okay for now, but that's a pretty heavy medal. You should really sew it on," I added.

"Yeah Coach good idea. I'll do it as soon as I get home."

With his huge hands wrapped around our new trophy and a small collection of medals clinking together on his chest, Scott strode happily across the parking lot of the fast food restaurant. Teammates stepped aside to clear a space for him at the counter as Rob, once again, gathered donations to pay for Scott's lunch. With my crumpled result sheet in hand, I made an effort to talk to each team member individually. Since this was the last race of the season for all but varsity runners, it was important that I thank them for their efforts and encourage them to continue supporting their varsity teammates.

In a small booth in the far corner of the room, Curt and C.J. sat in what seemed to be a self-imposed quarantine. Surrounded by illness and disappointment, Curt knew his season was over. What had seemed like a simple chest cold had developed into bronchitis and he just couldn't shake it. His career wasn't supposed to end this way. He'd put in a great summer of training, he was supposed to be first team All-Conference and run in another state meet. It was his senior season, his time to shine. Crushed, he sat staring at the empty table in front of him as teammates celebrated loudly a few feet away. For a national caliber athlete and an aspiring Olympic race walker, finishing third in the junior varsity race was hard to accept.

Across from Curt, C.J. sat motionless with his forehead pressed against the table. As the number two returner in the conference and the younger brother of a two-time conference champion, his twenty-first place finish was more than disappointing, it was demoralizing. C.J. was good at letting most things roll off his back, but this one hurt and there was little I could say to make it better. Emotionally and physically drained, he appeared feverish as he slowly lifted his head from the table and stared blankly in my direction.

"You look awful!" I said, stating the obvious as I patted him gently in the middle of his back. "We need to get you home, and we need to get you healthy. Two weeks till state, so take care of yourself, okay?"

Loud voices and laughter filled the small restaurant as guys and girls packed around tables pulled together in the center of the room. There, in the middle of it all, amid the delicious aroma of greasy fast food and across from the golden trophy obscured by crumpled burger wrappers, Scott sat like a king surrounded by his subjects.

"Who would have guessed?" I said to Rob with a smile as I shook my head slightly.

"Yeah, well, I'll tell you what it is," stated Rob, "hanging around with normal kids is good for him. Remember what he was like the first day of track? And now look at him. He's almost...well...normal."

Could it be, I wondered as I studied Scott from a distance, that the expectations we'd placed on him somehow played a part in this remarkable transformation? Like the sculptor from Greek mythology who brought his ivory statue to life with his expectations, was this the Pygmalion effect at work? Rob's statement, while not politically correct, was pretty accurate. Scott, of course, still had some problems, but for the most part he was becoming a "normal" teenage boy, right before our eyes. Maybe in the beginning we were all just pretending to be nice to him, I can't say for sure. But as Kurt Vonnegut once wrote, "we are what we pretend to be." We'd invited Scott onto our team, treated him with respect, pretended to be nice, and in the end it had made us all nicer people.

Our bus rocked with music on the short ride home and finished with the now traditional loud playing of 'Eye of the Tiger" as we rolled into the parking lot. Standing at the bus door, I handed out handshakes and high-fives as I sent the guys home as I always hoped to: tired, happy, and filled with a sense of pride in what we'd just accomplished. With his trademark toothy grin on his face and our latest team trophy under his arm, Scott leapt from the bus steps to slap my extended hand with all the power he could muster.

"Conference champions, Coach!" he shouted excitedly. "Nine in a row, Coach, NINE IN A ROW!"

"Scott, remember this. You set a goal, you worked hard and you made this happen...you earned this!" I said, pointing to the shiny new medal pinned to his letter jacket. "And you helped us earn another one of these," I added, referencing the trophy he held firmly against his hip. "This is a day to remember, enjoy it, and...try not to lose your medal."

"Yeah, Coach, no problem," he said as he reached down, grabbed the strap of his travel bag and flipped it forcefully over his shoulder.

"Coach, do you think we can do it?"

"Do what, Scott?"

"Win state, Coach. Think we can do it?"

"Well, if we run like we did today and if we ever get C.J. healthy, it might be interesting, but let's hold off on the white tuxes for a while. Okay?"

"HA! Okay, Coach, see ya Monday."

"Okay Mr. All-Conference," I said with a smile as Scott turned in the direction of the group home van. "See ya Monday."

FIFTEEN

LUCK

S omeone's in trouble," a voice called out from the back of
the classroom as I pulled the door shut and slowly turned
to face my students. Few things can inspire more curiosity than a
note from the office, especially a green one, from the assistant
principal.

"Who is it?" they demanded as I removed a staple and slowly
unfolded the quarter sheet of paper. Pausing, like a presenter at
the Academy Awards, I let the suspense build.

"I'll bet it's Andy," someone blurted out.

"Shhhhh!" several others said in unison.

"Andy it's....not for you. Sorry, nobody's in trouble. Well, at
least not yet," I announced as I jammed the note into my shirt
pocket. "just a note for me, nothing about any of you."

What could it mean, I wondered as I placed a timeline of
Roman history on my overhead projector. "Call Scott's group
home" is all it had said. This had to be bad, I thought. Something
had to be wrong and I had to wait until the end of the hour to
find out.

Following my students out of the room as the bell sounded, I
flew down the hall in search of the nearest phone and dialed the
group home.

"We're having a little trouble with Scott," explained one of the
counselors.

"What kind of trouble are we talking about?"

"Well, it looks like we caught him in a lie, so we're probably going to have to suspend him from practice for a while."

"What was the lie? Was it something about cross country?"

"Yeah, it was. Saturday he came home with a big trophy."

"Right, we sent it with him so he could take it to the office this morning."

"Yeah, well...that's not the problem. He told us that he'd made first team All-Conference, and that he'd won this huge medal. But when we asked to see it he told us he'd lost it. We think it's another one of his tall tales, but we wanted to check with you before we took action."

"Wow, I'm really glad you called because he's actually telling you the truth. He did make the All-Conference team and that medal, he had it pinned to his letter jacket, now maybe he lost it between school and home, but he had it with him on the bus."

"Okay, but you do realize we have to check these things out."

"I'm sure you do, but it's not something I'd lie about. Check the newspaper, it'll be in there tonight. It might even be on the front page," I said in conclusion.

On the way back to my classroom, I wondered if I had won the case. Truth was on my side of course, but that wasn't always enough. And what if the paper didn't run the article today. Would they keep Scott from practice? With a little luck this whole thing would blow over by the end of the school day, I hoped as I hurried down the hall. Just a little luck, that's all I needed.

Coaches talk a lot about discipline, dedication and hard work, but luck, unless preceded by the word bad, is seldom mentioned. We may hate to admit it, but luck is a part of sports. Whether it's the 60 foot bank shot at the buzzer, the "seeing eye single" that finds its way through the infield, or the tee-shot off a tree that lands in the middle of the fairway, luck is always a factor. Some will be good, some bad, and we can only hope the ratio leans in our favor.

Our season had not been without adversity. We had

experienced our share of injuries, bad breaks, and illnesses, but to this point good luck had far outweighed bad. In what was supposed to be a rebuilding year, we had somehow formed a very competitive team. As many of the top programs in the state struggled with problems of their own, we had emerged as the second ranked team and perhaps the only one capable of challenging top-ranked Manitowoc. Our discipline, dedication, and hard work were paying off, but what about luck? Call it luck, fate, or divine intervention, but thousands, maybe millions, of things had fallen into place for us. Somehow, despite our inexperience, we'd formed a successful team and luck had definitely been part of the equation. We were lucky to have this team, lucky to have each other, and most of all lucky to have crossed paths with Scott, the key to our success.

As a scorer, Scott's contribution to the team was obvious, but his real value ran far deeper. He brought a level of enthusiasm to the team that energized all of us. The effort he gave at practice and on race day inspired us, or at least guilted us into giving our best. At the start of the season, I feared he would be a distraction or require too much supervision, but I'd been dead wrong. As it turned out, he had given far more to our team than he had taken. Most importantly, he was a constant reminder that we should appreciate the things we have.

For Scott, a fast food meal was every bit as good as any offered at a five-star restaurant, our conference title was his Super Bowl, and an Olympic medal could hold no higher value than any he'd won. His level of appreciation caused us all to reevaluate the things around us and in some cases caused his teammates to view the world differently. They began thanking their parents for coming to meets, and for simple things like doing the laundry or making chocolate chip pancakes on race day. And sometimes, they said thanks for no reason at all.

Nervously awaiting news about Scott's situation, I paced the corner of the field house as a steady stream of guys poured from the locker room. Most raced past, tennis balls in hand, anxious to play some new game they'd invented while Mike, excited to hear about the day's workout, stopped to talk. C.J. did his best to assure me he was feeling better, but the sound of his voice gave me reason to doubt it.

"Right here, Coach, I GOT IT! This is what you've been waiting for," Scott announced proudly as he ran at me with a rolled up newspaper held above his head like an Olympic torch.

"Coach, I get to run. They saw me in the paper. I'm on the front page! Here, look."

Unrolling it quickly, I showed the headline to those standing nearby. "Here Scott, this part's about you," I said as I began to read:

"Scott gave us the gutsy race we have come to expect from him. He ran himself into third place and stayed there until the last quarter mile. His aggressive style of racing earned him a spot on the All-Valley team which is a great accomplishment."

Below the article were pictures of four smiling members of the All-Conference team: Mike, Johnny, John, and Scott. It was proof that Scott had told the truth. He had no reason to lie, exaggerate, or tear off his t-shirt and dance around. He'd accomplished his goal, earned a title, a medal, and a story to tell at the group home. A story so good it sounded like a lie.

To the casual reader of our local paper, Scott was just another of the many guys we had placed on the All-Conference team over the years, but we knew it was so much more than that. This was the story of a young man without a family, working to overcome his disabilities and in the process helping his team to a conference championship and the chance to compete for a state title. Only those close to Scott knew what a special story it was.

In the final weeks of the season our workouts change. We run fewer miles, shorten our interval sessions, and let easy days become easier as we taper our training. I also talk more…a lot more. Knowing the flea-like attention span of teenage boys, I generally limit my pre-run comments to about five minutes in length. This changes at the end of the year as I give more advice, become more philosophical, and tell more stories. Some are humorous, others motivational or inspirational, but most of the stories I pull from my vast collection fall into the category of "don't do anything stupid."

Every coach has these stories. Tales of guys, or teams, poised for greatness only to be struck by disaster, often of their own making. Stories of young men who didn't eat properly, were too fashion conscious to wear a coat in cold weather, or stayed out all night at a homecoming party and became seriously ill or found trouble. The list includes accounts of athletes injured while showing off for girls or attempting to be the gym-class hero, crashing their bike or pulling a prank that went terribly wrong. Like the high school edition of the Darwin Awards, I had an endless collection of stories, and for some reason the guys never seemed to tire of these tales of stupidity. Like Greek tragedies, the central character must suffer some great misfortune in order to teach us a lesson.

As a coach with eight years of experience, I'd learned that at some point as the season wears on I must resign myself to the fact that most of these things are beyond my control. I can spend hours worrying about injuries, illness, false starts, missed flags, and bad weather, but in the end all I can do is prepare my team, get them to the starting line, and hope for the best. Bad things can happen but more often than not things turn out okay. At least that's what I'd learned to tell myself.

C.J.'s health was about the only thing I had to worry about as we boarded the bus for the three hour trip to Menomonee. As the top ranked team in our sectional, there was little doubt that we would claim one of the two state qualifying spots that would be awarded today. I'd never say it to the team, but the threat of a bus break down was greater than any posed by the 15 teams we were about to face.

"Just get the job done, no false starts, no missed flags, and don't go out too hard," I said, making eye contact with Scott. "The first mile of this course is really narrow, and I'm sure a lot of teams feel like they have to get out fast and establish their position, but it doesn't matter. After the long, winding uphill stretch, the course widens and that's where our race starts. Just be patient and don't get frustrated if we look bad early. Just run smart and stick with the plan."

As predicted, the field of 112 runners bolted from the line at the sound of the gun and sprinted wildly for the narrow gap in the thick grove of red pines that guarded the entrance to what seemed to be an old logging trail. Buried near the back of the pack, our guys were forced to pick their way carefully through the tangle of runners ahead of them, much as they would have to do at the state meet. This was our style; we had the confidence to run from behind.

Rocky, uneven footing added to the challenge as our guys gradually worked their way into better position. Mike, unable to hold himself back, had angrily forced his way into the lead pack as the racers wound their way up the big hill. Determined to win the race convincingly, he could only hold back so long.

Scott, planted a short step behind John in the center of our tightly knit pack, was listening closely to his teammates' instructions.

"Relax, Animal," they shouted.

"Not yet, Animal."

"Settle down."

"Be patient, wait, wait, wait!"

"Save it for next week, Animal."

With little emotion and a fairly controlled effort, our guys moved steadily toward the front as many in the field began to fade. Taking the lead in the last mile, Mike pounded out an impressive win with a time only one second off his lifetime best.

C.J., looking far better than he had a week ago, moved up to eighth place late in the race, while John, Johnny, and Scott crossed the line comfortably within seconds of each other in 12th, 13th, and 14th. With Lee and Bill close behind in 18th and 19th we had performed well. While it wasn't our best race of the season, we took care of business and finished seventy points ahead of the second place team without having run all out.

Happy chants of "Animal...Animal...Animal" filled the crisp, clear Wisconsin fall air as Scott accepted the championship plaque and held it, with both hands, high above his head. Gathering around him for a group picture as other teams retreated to their busses, we lingered to enjoy the moment. We were in no hurry, and as always our bus would be the last to leave the meet site. Standing like a statue at the bus door, Scott took on the look of Moses clutching the Ten Commandments as he cradled our newly won plaque. Smiling proudly, he offered each of us a high-five and words of encouragement as we filed aboard.

"Great job guys. Sectional champs! Watch out Manitowoc! Madison, here we come! Eye of the Tiger, guys, Eye of the Tiger!" he added with each hand slap.

Laughter and broad smiles filled the bus as we tumbled happily into our seats with another sectional title to our credit and a trip to the state meet in our future. Discipline, dedication, and hard work brought us to this point and with a little luck we just might have a chance to compete for a state title. As ridiculous as it may have seemed at the start of our season, it was now something to be considered. Huddled around the mimeographed result sheet, we studied our times and enjoyed the freedom of a Saturday morning road trip with friends and a first place finish. For a bunch of high school cross country runners, life doesn't get much better.

Treated to a gourmet meal wrapped in yellow wax paper, Scott carried our new plaque in one hand while balancing his tray tenuously in the other. Guarding the slab of walnut as the Swiss Guard would protect a relic at the Vatican, he made his way to a crowded table.

"Here, I'll watch the plaque," Rob said. "Now go wash your hands."

This new treasure left his sight for only a few minutes as he obeyed our team rule and headed to the bathroom with his gold

State Qualifier medal securely attached to the front of his jacket. Returning with his hands still dripping, Scott claimed the spot Dan had saved for him and with the plaque propped carefully against his chest, began devouring his lunch.

Young voices sang along with the thumping bass of the boom box as we shook and rattled along in the slow lane of the interstate. Mike quickly lead a rebellion against C.J.'s Run DMC and Suzy's B-52's in favor of the more popular sounds of Van Halen, Huey Lewis, and Scott's new favorite, Springsteen. As "Born in the USA" bounced against the gray steel walls of the bus, I couldn't help focusing on the sad line that reminded me so much of Scott's life: "you end up like a dog that's been beat too much, till you spend half your life just covering up." Had he ever listened to it and wondered about it, or like so many people had the seemingly patriotic chorus of "born in the U.S.A., I was born in the U.S.A." obscured the true meaning of the song. Maybe it's true that young people don't really listen to the lyrics, I thought, as C.J. cranked the volume for the start of the highly appropriate "Glory Days." How could they miss Springsteen's clear warning that glory days, like this, "will pass you by...in the wink of a young girl's eye."

Perhaps, I reminded myself as I scanned the bus full of bright, happy faces, it's best not to think too deeply. These moments pass much too quickly, so maybe you should enjoy them while you can because all too soon you may be the guy on the bar stool "with nothing, mister, but boring stories of glory days."

As we reached the last few miles of our long road trip, C.J. squeezed the final bit of current from the 8 D-cell batteries in his boom box in order to play a long standing team favorite, "Happy Trails" by Van Halen, and the now traditional "Eye of the Tiger" in tribute to Scott.

"Easy five tomorrow," I shouted as the bus jerked to a halt in the parking lot a few yards from the locker room door. "Get a good night's sleep and don't do anything stupid over the weekend. We might have a shot at a state title next week. Let's try not to screw it up!"

Delivered to the group home by Rob, Scott proudly displayed his latest awards for all to see before heading for a workbench located in a corner of the basement. Equipped with a scrap of plywood, an assortment of felt tipped markers, and a small collection of dull, rusty woodworking tools, he set out to create a duplicate of the Sectional plaque that he'd been tasked with delivering to school on Monday morning. The fact that his finished product bore little resemblance to the original didn't matter to Scott as he hung it proudly among a small cluster of items on the stark white wall next to his bed. In the small room he shared with three other group home residents, he'd created a shrine to our team, to our season, and most of all to himself. Newspaper clippings, photographs, and result sheets documented his accomplishments, his glory days. For Scott, the significance of these few objects was greatly magnified. While his teammates saw our season as just one of the many good things they expected to experience during their lifetimes, for Scott our season was the luckiest thing that ever happened to him—and for all he knew it might be the luckiest thing that ever would.

SIXTEEN

BAD NEWS, COACH

Who in the world would call at this late hour, I wondered as I dashed towards the kitchen to snag the loudly ringing telephone. Sunday night at 7:30 isn't late, unless you're the parent of a finicky newborn who had finally given up the fight and drifted off to sleep.

"Hello," I said softly as I stepped quietly into the back hallway.

"Bad news, Coach," a familiar voice responded. "Really bad news!"

"Scott?"

"Yeah Coach, it's me, The Animal, and I got some bad news."

"Don't tell me, you lost your sectional medal," I said, hoping it was as simple as that.

"No Coach, this is real bad news. Coach, I won't be running in the state meet on Saturday," he said softly as his voice cracked with emotion.

"Why? What's going on? Are you in trouble?"

"No Coach, I'm not in trouble. They're shutting the group home down and they're gonna send me to Oconomowaukee."

"I think you mean Oconomowoc. It's near Milwaukee."

"Yeah, that's it, Oconomowoc."

"Is this just you or are they moving the other guys, too?"

"Everyone Coach, they're movin' all of us. Wednesday's gonna be my last day here."

"That's just crazy!" I said in disbelief. "They can't do that to you, there's no way they can do that! You earned the right to run at state and you're going to run. I know this seems really bad, but we're going to find a way to fix this. I don't know how, but we're going to find a way. I'll drive to Oconomowoc and kidnap you if I have to, but you will run, I promise you that. Okay? Now, go get one of the staff members and put him on the phone and don't worry, this is all going to work out. I'll see you at practice tomorrow, okay?"

"Okay Coach, I'll see you tomorrow."

How could they do this on such short notice, I wondered while waiting for a counselor to pick up the phone. Maybe the situation wasn't as serious as it seemed, maybe Scott had gotten it wrong. At least that's what I hoped.

"No, it's true," the counselor confirmed. "These kids get shuffled around way too often, it's just a numbers game," he explained. "They have room at other facilities so they shut this one down. They told us last week and we told the residents this morning at breakfast. It's a bad deal for the kids, but it happens all the time. Bottom line, sometimes it's just too expensive for the state to keep a small facility like this up and running."

Aware of Scott's unusual situation, he suggested, with a slightly pessimistic tone, that I call one of the county social workers in the morning and try to find a way to keep him around for a few days.

Monday morning after a fitful night's sleep I arrived at school in the pre-dawn darkness to begin working on the problem. Planted at one of the long lunch tables near the entrance to the school's office complex, I paged through my lesson plan book as I waited impatiently for the arrival of Mr. Anderson. Andy would know what to do, I was sure of it, and if he didn't I knew he would point me in the right direction.

"I've got a problem," I announced abruptly, without bothering to say hello or good morning. "It's about Scott."

Andy unlocked the door to his office, hit the light switch, and peeled off his coat as he listened intently to my hurried explanation.

"We can fix this," he said calmly as he reached up to pat my shoulder with a hand the size of a catcher's mitt. "We'll find a way. Now let's go see if Ramone is in yet."

As the person in charge of our at-risk and special needs students, Mr. Stade was the logical place to start. Experienced and analytical, he would be a great resource in our search for a way out of our dilemma. Maybe, I thought as we worked our way through the office, this can be fixed with a couple of quick phone calls. Perhaps common sense would prevail.

Unfortunately, what seemed obvious to me was not so simple for the tangle of Wisconsin state agencies we were dealing with. Scott was their ward and as such he needed to be in the direct care of a person, or persons, certified by the state. This was not going to be easy, Ramone discovered during a day-long game of phone tag with a wide range of social workers and state officials. Working his way up the chain of command, he ran head on into the bureaucratic web of a large state agency where apparently nobody had the authority or courage to grant an exception to one of their many rules. Apparently we were asking the impossible. Having patiently worked his way through the maze of county and state employees, Ramone was nearing the top of the food chain when the school day came to an end.

"I'm getting close," he said, looking up with a most serious gaze as I stood in the doorway of his office. "I can feel it. I'll get this thing figured out if I have to drive to Madison and push my way into the Governor's office. I'll get you an answer tomorrow. I'm on a mission."

"Thanks," I said, reaching out to shake Ramone's hand. "We have to find a way. He earned the right to run—there just has to be a way to fix this. Let me know as soon as you get an answer."

What if it can't be done, I wondered as I jogged quickly down the main hallway. What if Ramone never locates the mysterious "man behind the curtain," the one and seemingly only person with the power to grant our wish? Is it possible that we would be running the state meet without Scott, I worried as I pulled open the field house door.

"I don't have an answer," I shouted loudly in the direction of the team as they stood huddled together in our usual spot near the locker room door. "Hey, we've got a workout to do, let's get movin'. Mr. Stade will get an answer in the morning. It's all gonna work out," I stated confidently. "So let's go! Come on guys, time to stretch."

A strange quiet surrounded us as we formed a small circle. Suzy, just a few days away from a chance to win her fourth consecutive state title, sat stretching with her teammates a few yards away. Happy and carefree, they went about their daily routine completely unaware of the problem we faced. Consumed by worry, Scott and his teammates quietly stared up at me with blank expressions as they waited for further instruction.

"Hey!" I shouted harshly. "Nobody died. We have a problem, but it's not the end of the world. We have a workout to do. Yeah, I'm worried too but we'll find a way to work this out." With a hand firmly planted on the top of Scott's head, I added, "This guy needs to run in the state meet, and he will run in the state meet, trust me, and we will come home with a trophy. I don't know if it'll be silver or gold, but we will come home with a trophy, so let's just focus on that."

Taking someone away from their home is wrong. The guys knew it and it made them angry. Losing a teammate to illness or injury is one thing, but this was almost beyond comprehension. Some arbitrary pencil pusher, in the interest of saving the state of Wisconsin a few bucks, was about to take something important from Scott and in the process ruin our chances to chase a state title. We could quietly accept it, call it "bad luck" and move on, or we could dig in our heels and fight back.

"Let's boycott," someone shouted loudly as we exited the school and began our run across the student parking lot. "If Scott can't run, nobody does!"

"Yeah! Boycott! Let's do it!" another responded excitedly.

"Sure," Mike added angrily, "but who really cares if we don't show up? Who's gonna notice? If a football team did that it would be front page news, but if we did it…well I guess it would make the Manitowoc guys happy."

A teenage brainstorming session erupted as we passed the soccer fields on our way to the park.

"Let's hide him! Put him in the attic like Anne Frank. They can't take him if they can't find him!"

"Call the newspaper, the radio station, Channel 9 and Channel 7!"

"Handcuffs — we'll handcuff all of us together."

"Egg their houses!"

"Limburger cheese on their engine blocks!"

"Sugar in their gas tanks!" they shouted eagerly.

Someone was to blame. Someone had to be punished. But who? Who should be the target of their anger?

This was supposed to be a fun week filled with short, easy workouts, a small pep rally, and a spaghetti dinner on Friday night. We were supposed to be thinking about the race, not this. As creatures of habit, we thrive on routine and the comfort of keeping things as close to our normal pattern as possible. A distraction like this was the last thing we needed, but then again nothing about this season had been routine.

Scott ran silently a few feet to my left with his eyes cast to the ground. Positioned in the middle of the group, he found himself closely surrounded by his team. Shoulder to shoulder, stride for stride, we entered the tall stand of white pines near the park's entrance. Like a herd protecting its most vulnerable member, we drew in close, shielding Scott, ready to defend him in any way we could as we prepared to start our interval session. It was a simple workout, four half-miles at slightly faster than race pace. Run relaxed, run smooth, keep an even pace and feel good were my instructions. With a quiet focus we shuffled to the starting line as an unusual level of seriousness took hold. Paused motionless, they waited for my command, anxious to be turned loose. Filled with emotion we vented our frustration as runners often do...by running hard, too hard.

I could have stopped it, but I loved the passion and energy as we shot from the line in unison, attacking the half mile interval as if we wanted to hurt someone. We ran with a sense of purpose, like a finely tuned machine or a team of horses working together to pull a heavy load. Full of frustration and lacking anyone to punish, we had to settle for inflicting discomfort on ourselves by running fast.

Adversity can drive people apart or bring them together. Today we ran with a unity that seemed almost religious and as we did, I began to realize that Scott's problem might, in some strange way, work to our advantage. This was no abstract concept. This was clearly unjust. Someone, for whatever reason, was trying to ruin our team. "They" were not just taking away a team member, they were trying to take away our dream, and we were determined to stop them.

"Great workout, guys!" I shouted as I worked my way through the group, shaking hands along the way. "We're ready! Remember, get to bed early, eat smart, and don't do anything stupid," I warned while pulling a sweatshirt over my head in preparation for the mile and a half cool down jog back to school. "We need to stay healthy for five more days. And don't worry about The Animal, it's all going to work out," I assured the guys in my most confident tone of voice as we shuffled along Maria Drive. "We should have an answer by tomorrow."

By Tuesday afternoon, Ramone's telephone quest had, at long last, reached a conclusion. After countless phone calls, emotional pleas, angry demands, and a little well placed profanity, he'd managed to reach the top of the bureaucratic mountain and the one and seemingly only person in the state capable of doing the right thing and granting our wish. The Secretary of the Wisconsin Department of Health and Family Services had been reached, understood the seriousness of the situation, and with the wisdom of King Solomon solved our dilemma. Having promised to meet any and all of the state's conditions, Ramone was granted permission to keep our "ward of the state" until Saturday afternoon, after the state meet. Suddenly we had a chance to chase the goal we'd been working toward all season. Our team could stay intact for four more days; all we had to do was feed, house, and supervise Scott until someone from Oconomowoc came to collect him after the race in Madison. The fact that he wouldn't be on the bus for the trip home was somehow lost in our excitement. Scott was allowed to run and that was all that really mattered.

Delivered by a group home official to Mr. Anderson's office on Wednesday morning with all his worldly possessions jammed into two tattered cardboard boxes, one large duffel bag, and the small blue and white travel bag he carried on meet days, Scott was now in our care. After practice Rob and I loaded Scott's belongings into my Buick Skylark for the short trip to my house where Cheryl and I would serve him supper before turning him over to the Morgan brothers.

"Coach, do I get to hold the baby?" he asked as I slammed the trunk closed. "You said I could hold the baby."

"Yes, but you have to be really, really careful, okay?"

"Sure Coach, no problem. I'm good with babies."

Scott rocked anxiously in his seat next to me as we turned onto Meadow Street. I could tell he was excited. Released from the rigid, highly structured environment of the group home for the first time in years, he was enjoying his new found freedom. Home cooked meals prepared in small quantities by someone other than a bunch of teenage boys on K.P. would be something new. For nearly three days he was going to experience what many of his teammates took for granted, a real home and a family.

With Beth cradled gently in her arms, Cheryl met us as we came through the back door and stepped into the kitchen.

"Hi Scott, welcome to our home," she said warmly. "This is Beth. Supper's almost ready, so set your stuff over there, hang up your letter jacket, and wash your hands."

Polite and well-mannered, Scott was a near perfect guest. He folded his hands to say grace as we sat down, talked practically non-stop about school, running, and his teammates as we ate, and sprang quickly from his seat to clear the dishes immediately after.

"I'll get it, Coach," he said happily as he pushed his shirt sleeves up to his elbows in his trademark style. "I'll bus, you can wash, and then I'll dry, okay?"

Amazing, I thought to myself as I rose from the table and cast a smile in Cheryl's direction. Half an hour into his stay and he'd already adjusted to his new surroundings. Evidently moving from place to place had taught him to adapt, like a chameleon. With our kitchen clean-up complete, Scott retrieved his large duffel bag from near the back door and extracted what looked suspiciously like the cardboard lid of a pizza box.

"You brought me a pizza?" I joked.

"No Coach, these are my meds, see?" he said as he held it proudly in my direction. "I put 'em on here so I don't forget. See, Wednesday, Thursday, Friday, and Saturday—morning, noon, and bed time."

"You use scotch tape?"

"Yeah, clear tape so I can see through it and tell what color the pills are."

"That's the system they use at the group home?" I asked in amazement as Cheryl, clearly amused by our strange conversation, looked on with a smile.

"No, Coach, they lock up our meds at the group home. This is just till I get to Oconomowoc."

"Well, just make sure you don't lose track of your little system 'cause I have no idea how we'd replace them. Lose you meds and we're all in trouble."

"No problem, Coach, I got it! Hey, now can I hold the baby? You said I could hold the baby."

"Yes," I said sternly as I finished drying my hands with a dish towel, "but you have to be very, very careful. You have to support her head, you know that, right?"

"Coach! No problem, I've held lots of babies. I love babies! I'll be careful. I'm good with babies."

Cheryl looked in my direction, casting the kind of nervous, protective gaze only the mother of a newborn could produce as I prepared to transfer our month old daughter into Scott's large, outstretched hands. Bending slightly at the knees, he cradled her gently, as if handling a bundle of high explosives. Twisting slightly at the waist he rocked her side to side for just a few seconds.

"Okay, I think she wants her mom now," he announced, suddenly pushing Beth in the direction of Cheryl's eager arms.

"Now Coach, what about those pictures? You said we could look at pictures. Can we do that now, Coach?"

"Yeah, good idea. Kick off your shoes and go into the living room. I'll go get 'em."

With two large photo albums in hand, I returned to find Scott seated comfortably on the couch studying Beth as she downed a bottle of formula while rocking in her mother's loving arms.

"This is it," I announced proudly, "the history of our program...all eight seasons."

Watching intently while I flipped from page to page, Scott pressed me for details on virtually every picture. Fascinated by our many successful teams and individuals, he was especially interested in our 1984 state meet.

"Tell me again," he pleaded like a small child at bed time, "how you lost the meet by one point to those guys from Green Bay in the white tuxedoes. I gotta hear that story one more time, Coach!"

For someone with a learning disability, Scott showed an amazing capacity to acquire and retain information. Like so many of our guys, he wanted to learn the history of our program and feel a part of something bigger than just this one year. He wanted to help add another page to our history and just maybe, as his teammates kept telling him, he'd get the chance to wear that white tuxedo he'd been fixated on all season.

The sound of the doorbell brought our little history lesson to an abrupt end as the Morgan brothers arrived to gather their teammate, something Scott had been looking forward to all day. For the next two days and three nights, Dan and Michael would serve as the Animal keepers. Socially adept, comfortable in any situation, and fun to be around, they were perfect for the job. The fact that their mother had a degree in social work was an added bonus. With duffel bags slung over both shoulders, Scott said goodbye to Cheryl and Beth, politely thanked us for supper, and headed happily out the door and down the front walk with his new "family."

"SHOTGUN! I got shotgun!" he called out.

"No way, Scott. Animals ride in the back," ordered Michael as he quickly grabbed the handle of the front passenger-side door.

Watching in amusement from the front porch, I could only hope that we would send him off to Oconomowoc with that same happy, excited look.

Seventeen

Rain

Awakened in the early morning darkness by the sound of rain against the nearby windowpane, my mind began to race. How bad is it, I wondered, listening carefully to the faint drumbeat while waiting eagerly for my alarm clock to announce the start of the day. Everything needed to be analyzed as we drew nearer to the big race. Every change in the weather, every sneeze or sniffle, and every bag of ice carried from the training room was a possible reason for concern. Rain had been forecast, lots of it, all day and through the night into Saturday morning. Calmly, I reminded myself that our best workout of the season had been run in a driving rainstorm. Maybe this would work in our favor, I thought, as I envisioned runners and spectators slogging through standing water on the course at Yahara Hills in Madison. Or perhaps conditions would tilt the table in the direction of a senior heavy team like Manitowoc or some unexpected team of "mudders" who would rise up and surprise us all. Soggy footing was now added to the list of variables that might factor into the outcome of the meet. What part the rain would play couldn't be determined at this early hour, but it was certainly something to think about or, in my case, to worry about.

Bad weather gave me an opportunity to drag out a few time tested clichés, things like "This is why we train in bad weather" or "Let's not let the weather beat us." Coaches, it seems, have a saying for just about every situation as we attempt to put things in perspective and instill confidence in our athletes. Heart-warming "win one for the Gipper" speeches, philosophical observations like "we control our own destiny" and the always ridiculous "they put their pants on one leg at a time" (as if that fact is in any way relevant to the outcome) are all part of every coach's arsenal. Pointing out the obvious "Everyone has to deal with the same conditions" may be the clearest and most helpful of the weather related sayings, until you consider the other half of the equation. Conditions may be the same for every runner, but since runners are not all exactly the same, each will be affected somewhat differently and each will respond in his own way. Some will thrive in the wet and cold, some in heat and humidity, on steep hills, winding uneven trails, or deep snow. Each runner's unique combination of physical and psychological attributes will provide an advantage in some cases and a hindrance in others. Yes, we would all run in the same conditions, but just how our guys would react to them could not be determined as I lay studying raindrops on the window pane in the first light of morning. That would have to wait until tomorrow.

Today was set to be a fun and exciting one for our guys. The school had organized a "send-off" at the end of the day, a local T.V. station was coming to do a story on us, and a spaghetti dinner was planned for after practice. This, I'd reminded them, should be a day to remember, a special day, and a celebration of a special season. Mike had declared that a shirt and tie along with a nice pair of pants was the appropriate attire for the final day of our season. A neck tie, they all knew, would definitely draw attention as they walked the halls of school. People know in an instant that anyone in a tie is either an athlete on game day, a troubled kid headed for a court appearance, or a new transfer from some sort of overly strict private school. Normally our guys didn't feel the need to draw attention to themselves, but this year was somehow different. Against all odds we had built a highly competitive team, and we'd built it around this kid from the group home who through a weird twist of fate was attending his final day of school in our town. It was a great story, the kind that needed to be told, and one that few around school knew. Maybe this would be a good day to share this remarkable tale, maybe today, if someone asked "What are you dressed up for?" our guys could tell the story.

As my students worked to complete the last section of the unit test on Roman history, I gazed out my classroom window, studying the cadence of the windshield wipers on passing cars and attempting to gauge the volume of rainfall on this miserable gray Friday afternoon. It wasn't exactly a downpour, but it was heavy and steady, the kind of soaking rain that looked as if it would never end. Clearly we were going to get wet at practice today, and tomorrow didn't look much better. There was no way around it, it was going to be a very wet state meet and for the first time all season our guys might need to wear more than just shorts and a jersey on race day. Thinking of Scott while studying the ugly conditions, I made a mental note to check the lost and found before practice to see what the "window people" had left for him to wear in this foul weather.

"There will be a short send-off today," Principal Von Feldt stated as his end of the day P.A. announcement interrupted eighth-hour class, "beginning in five minutes for those who wish to attend. We'd like to honor the hard working members of our boys cross country team and our very own Suzy Favor as they prepare for tomorrow's state meet. I hope to see you there."

Students bolted from the room at the sound of the bell. "Good luck tomorrow, Mr. Behnke," one of them called out, "Yeah, good luck Coach!" said another.

A "send-off" is not nearly as big a deal as a pep rally, but in many ways it's better. It's smaller, more personal, and since students attend voluntarily, it's clear that those in attendance have come to show sincere support for their classmates being honored. With the school pepband rocking to the sound of "Louie, Louie" and cheerleaders doing what cheerleaders do, we marched into the part of school known as "north commons." Several hundred packed the noisy room as Mr. Von Feldt organized our small group against the east wall.

"Listen, everyone," he shouted into the microphone as he worked to gain the crowd's attention before launching into a few well planned compliments about Suzy as she stood next to him smiling brightly. As the most famous athlete ever to come out of our school and arguably the best young female runner in America, everyone knew Suzy Favor and they listened with interest as Mr. Von Feldt rattled off a list of her many accomplishments.

Dressed neatly in shirts and ties, our team stood straight and tall, lined up behind Suzy, as we waited for our turn to be introduced. For someone barely five feet tall, she cast a pretty big shadow over us, but we didn't mind. We respected her discipline, dedication, and toughness. If you took away her natural talent, speed, and good looks, I sometimes jokingly told the guys, she would be a good fit on our team.

Scott stood smiling broadly directly in the center of our row. His hair was a mess and mysteriously his tie had disappeared, but it didn't matter. With his letter jacket sleeves pushed as far up his arms as they could possibly go, he stood proud and happy as Mr. Von Feldt concluded his remarks and handed the microphone to me while the band struck up the school's fight song for the rather large turnout of appreciative students.

Walking nervously to the center of the commons, I asked each team member to step forward and join me as I introduced him to the tightly packed crowd. With the room strangely quiet, I proudly summarized our season and told of our hopes to add another state trophy to the three we'd collected in the previous five years. Staring out at the many attentive faces in the crowd as I spoke, I could feel the sincere support of those in attendance and a sense of community. Is it possible they knew about Scott's situation, I wondered, as I finished up, thanked them for attending the send-off, and handed the microphone back to Mr.

Von Feldt.

"Listen up," he said as he reached over to take Scott by the arm and walk him to the front and center of our group. "I have something to tell you and this is important. As Coach Behnke told you, this young man is Scott Longley. But what he didn't tell you is that this is Scott's last day as a SPASH student."

Several hundred students and teachers listened carefully as they learned about the kid we called Animal and his unusual situation. Two of his biggest fans, Andy and Ramone, stood nearby as the crowd leaned in and learned that Scott would be sent to a new group home immediately after the state meet. Sad, puzzled faces filled the room as the audience strained to get a look at the main character in Mr. Von Feldt's tragic tale. Standing calmly in front of his collection of new found fans, Scott basked proudly in the attention. For possibly the first time in his life, he was being recognized, like Hulk Hogan after a match, in front of a large group.

"Animal! Animal! Animal!" came a chant from somewhere in the middle of the group, no doubt the work of some of his J.V. teammates. Tomorrow he would deal with the reassignment to Oconomowoc, but for now, he simply enjoyed his moment in the spotlight as his teammates stood smiling in the background, proud of the fact that they had helped put him there. Like all good teammates, they understood that recognition for one is recognition for all.

As another round of the always popular "Louie, Louie" sounded to announce the end of the program, many in the crowd pushed forward to wish us good luck. Scott, surrounded by curious students, did his best to answer questions about his living situation as we shook the hands of well-wishers and thanked them for their support.

Many, if not most, in the group had never seen Scott before today. In a school of 2,700 students, it's pretty easy to get lost in the crowd, especially if you spend most of your day with the special education students in a far off corner of the building, behind the Driver's Ed. classroom. After going unnoticed for a year and a half, Scott had now been exposed. Suddenly he'd gained a small measure of what, for many, high school is all about…popularity. The big, scruffy looking kid with the odd nickname had, in a matter of minutes, become new, interesting, and exotic. Students who knew nothing of him a few minutes ago were now his fans. Caught up in this strange human interest story, many in the crowd suddenly wanted us to win a state title for the Animal. For them this story didn't just need a happy ending, it seemed destined to have one.

As the diehard horn section of the band continued to play on, the final bell of the school day sounded, and the crowd began to slowly filter away.

"Thanks everyone!" I shouted to those still milling about. "Now break it up…time for practice…let's get moving!"

Approaching the large hallway windows on our way to the locker room, I could see two television news vans parked at the curb in the now pouring rain.

"Yeah! Rain! I love it!" Mike shouted excitedly from a few feet behind me. It was definitely going to be a wet run, but to him it didn't matter. It was Friday and Friday runs, as Mike knew very well, are always fun, even in the rain.

"Where's Scott?" I asked, looking around as I entered the field house with a sweatshirt from the lost and found in one hand and my clipboard in the other.

"Over there," C.J. answered, pointing to the far corner of the expansive room and smiling. "He's watching Suzy get interviewed."

Surrounded by television crews with lights and cameras mounted on towering tripods, Suzy fielded questions about the meet and her quest for an unprecedented fourth state title. With her teammates and Scott looking on, she handled the interview as easily as she did opponents on race day. For Suzy this kind of attention had become pretty routine, something she'd learned to deal with, just a normal part of her day. For our guys, finding themselves suddenly in the spotlight was anything but normal. Standing patiently at the edge of the crowd, I couldn't help noticing the excited look on Scott's face as I waited for the camera crews to finish with Suzy.

As much as all this commotion disrupted our routine, there was little I could do about it, and after all, I reminded myself, our guys deserved to be recognized.

"Got time for a few questions, Coach?" one of the sports guys asked as he headed quickly in my direction with a camera crew in tow.

"Sure," I answered as I reached out to shake his hand.

"So Coach, it looks like you have a pretty good team again this year," he began while working to untangle his microphone cord before starting the interview. "And I hear you have a kid on your team with a very interesting story. His name is Scott… something…."

"Right, Scott Longley."

"Yeah, it sounds like a great human interest story, so if you don't mind I'd like to ask a few questions about him as soon as we get set up here."

"Sure, the story's a bit complicated, but I'll do my best," I responded while noticing one of our main office secretaries walking quickly in my direction.

"It's canceled!" she called out, sounding somewhat out of breath. "They just called. The state meet's been canceled… postponed till next Saturday!"

"No, that can't be," I said with disbelief, turning my attention away from the lights and cameras, "We never cancel cross country meets. This has to be some sort of mistake."

"They said the course is under water. Evidently Madison got three inches of rain and they said they're not letting anyone on the golf course until it dries out."

"Are you sure? This sounds like a practical joke. Like some kids in a motel room in Madison trying to get us to miss the meet."

"No, it's the real thing! I've taken calls from the WIAA office before, and I know the person who called. I recognized the voice."

"Well, okay then I guess it's true, but still…it just seems so strange. Did they tell you anything else?"

"No, all they said is same time schedule, same course, Yahara Hills, next Saturday."

As the T.V. guys shook their heads and packed up their equipment, I did my best to comprehend what I'd just been told and then, suddenly, it hit me. SCOTT. What were we going to do about Scott?

"Mike!" I shouted with a somewhat panicked voice, heading for the field house door. "Get practice started. I've got to find Mr. Anderson!"

Dashing down the hallway, I processed the disastrous news. The bus order could be changed, practices could be adjusted, but how, at 3:40 on a Friday afternoon, would we ever get permission to keep Scott for another entire week?"

"Relax," Andy said calmly as I burst into his office. "Ramone's on the phone right now. We'll get this worked out."

"I don't know, Andy. They barely agreed to three days, and now a whole week. I don't know how we fix this. This is trouble."

"Look," he said as he stood up from his desk and looked me squarely in the eyes, "we'll get this all worked out. I promise. Now go to practice, just go take care of your team and I'll see you after."

With our school's two "elder statesmen" working on the problem, I felt a little better as I headed quickly back to the field house. Both were now emotionally involved in Scott's dilemma, so I knew they'd give it their best shot.

"Here's the deal, guys," I announced to the collection of worried faces huddled right where I'd left them a few minutes earlier. "Mr. Anderson and Mr. Stade are working on the problem right now. We have 16 hours till the Oconomowoc people come looking for Scott, so that should be enough time to get something worked out. They gave us permission to keep Scott this week, so I'm sure they'll let us keep him next week, too," I explained confidently. "It'll all work out, and if it doesn't, well, we go to plan B," I continued.

"And what's plan B?" asked Mike seriously.

"Well, I thought we could put one of our J.V. guys in Scott's letter jacket, mess up his hair a little bit, and send him off to Oconomowoc for a week. Once the race is over, we explain that we've made a terrible mistake. It's foolproof. So who wants to volunteer?"

Hands shot into the air in an instant. Everyone, including our only runner of Asian descent, Wei Hong Wang, wanted to be a part of our little ruse.

"Wei Hong," I said with a smile, "I don't think you can quite pull it off."

Of course there was no such thing as plan B, but that didn't stop a half dozen guys from jumping up and auditioning for the part of the "fake Animal." With their hair tousled and their shirt sleeves pushed well above their elbows, they did their best to mimic Scott's loud raspy voice. "Coach Behnke, one question" they shouted in my direction as Scott sat on the floor, laughing and clapping his hands in approval.

"Okay guys, we have a workout to do. Put on another layer, it's cold and wet out there," I reminded them. "Let's move!"

Finally able to focus our attention on running, we sprang from the side door of school and begin a quick five mile run in the rain, wind, and forty-five degree temperatures. Splashing across the parking lot, we said little as we settled into a pace very near to what many of our guys ran on race day.

Runners are by nature collectors of information. We pay close attention to things like times, distances, point totals, and personal records. We like numbers because they're logical; you can add, subtract, multiply, and divide them. They help us measure our pace, effort, and progress. Numbers make sense to us. The decision to delay the race for a week just didn't. We were ready to race, ready to compete in any conditions, and this delay was hugely disappointing. Had we known the true condition of the course in Madison, we might have understood the logic behind the decision, but from our point of view the verdict seemed like a bad one, one that could end up costing us a runner and a chance to chase our dream. Fear of the unknown hung over us again as we charged through the steady cold rain on this gray, miserable day, a couple miles into the loop we called "in town." Standing happily alongside the band and cheerleaders just a short while ago, life had abruptly thrown us a curve that we were now forced to deal with. Suddenly the mood had soured for all of us. All, except Scott. Wedged, as always, in the center of our group, he seemed to take it all in stride. He ran quietly, as if nothing was wrong. In the unstable world of Scott "The Animal" Longley, things like this happened all the time and he, as it turned out, was better prepared than any of us to deal with the situation.

"Hold up, guys," I ordered as we reached the edge of the parking lot by the back door of the school. Steam rose from our shoulders as we stood trying to stomp the mud and sand from our soggy shoes onto the glossy black asphalt. This was, in my opinion, the ideal time and place to talk for a few minutes while the body heat generated from the hard run kept us warm in spite of the cold soaking rain.

"Tomorrow, rain, snow, or volcano we practice at 8:00."

"Volcano?" Scott said with a laugh.

"Yeah...volcano! They can cancel the state meet but we NEVER cancel practice. Hard intervals at the park tomorrow, so be ready. Dress for the weather...rain, snow, volcano or whatever, okay? I know this delay is annoying," I continued. "You don't like it and I definitely don't like it, but this could actually work in our favor. Think about it. Right now there are a bunch of teams sitting in motel rooms down in Madison. So, do they check out and go home or stay at the motel and screw around all night? Did they run a hard workout today, did they run at all, and what will they do tomorrow? Do you think these other teams will be ready to race eight days from now? My guess is a lot of them won't be.

I don't know and I don't care, that's their problem. But I'm sure of this, Manitowoc will be ready to race next week, and I expect us to be ready, too," I said, pointing a wet finger in the direction of my silent collection of soggy runners.

"What about Scott?" Mike asked, sensing I was near the end of my short pep talk.

"Nothing's changed. We got permission last week and we'll get permission this week, too. Scott's going to be there with us— count on it. So let's just do what we always do, have a good week of practice, give our best effort on race day, and come home with a trophy. Bring it in....white tuxedo on three. One, two, three...

"WHITE TUXEDO!" we shouted in unison.

"Okay, now let's get out of this rain. I have to go find Mr. Anderson."

Andy stood waiting at the far end of the field house as I jogged, dripping wet, in his direction. With his trademark Popeye-like forearms folded across his chest, his stoic look gave nothing away.

"Good news, Coach!" he announced as a smile erupted across his face. "Ramone just got off the phone with Madison. We've been given permission to keep Scott for one more week."

"That's great! That's just great. Wow, you guys are amazing. Thanks, thanks for everything!" I said, reaching out to shake his huge, powerful hand. "Now we just need to figure out where he's going to stay."

"All taken care of," he said proudly. "Scott will stay with me this week. I think it's better if he doesn't have to bounce from place to place, and since he and Eric are friends it's a good fit."

"Really?" I said in disbelief. "That's really nice of you, Andy. You have no idea how much I appreciate this. I can't thank you enough for all your help. Scott!" I shouted excitedly, motioning him in my direction. "Good news, Scott. We have permission for you to stay and you're going to spend the week with Mr. Anderson and Eric."

"Really!" he said with a look of happy surprise.

"Yeah! And I expect you to be on your very best behavior, alright?"

"Coach, no problem. Remember how well behaved I was at your house?"

"Yes, you were a perfect gentleman. But remember, Mr. Anderson was in the military, so if you step out of line at his house it's K.P. for the whole week, okay?"

"Okay, Coach, you don't have to worry about me, I got it."

"Dan and Michael will help you gather up your stuff and drop you at Mr. Anderson's. Oh! What about your meds?"

"Well, I got enough for tomorrow, but that's all so maybe we should call my doctor."

"It's 4:30," Andy said, glancing at his watch, "I'll take care of it, Coach. Come on, Scott, let's go make the call."

Once again, the Animal had a new keeper, I thought as I watched them walk away. Again Scott would transition, without hesitation, into a new living arrangement. For a week he would find himself in a stable home environment with the chance to watch a devoted, loving father care for a son affected by many of the same developmental issues he had. Scott and Eric knew each other well. They spent most of the school day together in the classroom for students with physical and cognitive disabilities. Both were tall, muscular, solidly built kids with smiles that could light up a room. Similar in so many ways, they both loved to be around people, they loved to talk and laugh, but most of all they shared a passion for sports, any sports, making it a perfect match.

Watching carefully as the two of them neared the doors at the end of the long hallway, I saw Andy reach up and place his meaty hand on Scott's broad shoulder with the same gentle touch he used on his own son. I had a good feeling as I turned to walk away. I knew it would be a good week for Scott, a week with the Andersons, a week with his team and another week at a school where people now knew and supported him.

EIGHTEEN

SNOW

Normally adding another week to the cross country season would be a good thing, but not this year. Having a newborn in the house was much harder than I'd ever imagined as night time feedings, diaper changes, and trips to the laundromat kept Cheryl and I busy around the clock. Teaching, coaching, parenting, and keeping track of Scott was turning out to be a tough balancing act, and I was ready for the 1985 campaign to reach its conclusion.

As difficult as the extra week was for me, the inverse was proving to be true for Scott. Living with Andy and Eric seemed like a dream to him. He had his own room, good, healthy, home cooked meals, and people who treated him with kindness and generosity. After seeing Scott's tattered wardrobe, Andy, without hesitation, threw most of it in the trash and took him to the nearest K-Mart store. A shopping spree of sorts netted a duffel bag full of jeans, shirts, sweaters, socks without holes, and underwear with elastic that actually stretched. For Scott, Christmas had come early this year complements of the Stevens Point High School Athletic Department's equipment account.

Wearing a fresh, clean, new outfit each day was something new for Scott and like a thousand dollar suit on a businessman, it made him feel good. Teachers, classmates, and teammates could hardly help noticing, and if they didn't Scott was sure to point out whatever new attire he was sporting in combination with his beloved letter jacket. For one entire week he lived what, for him, was the lavish lifestyle of the rich and famous and all he had to do in return was remember to say please and thank you. Time spent with the Andersons had been good for Scott, but as all good things do, it passed far too quickly.

Andy Anderson was a good man, but like far too many athletic directors he never really understood or appreciated the sport of cross county. Much as he tried, he couldn't see why anyone would want to run further than the length of a football field. As a fan of the traditional team sports of football, basketball, and baseball, in his mind there were true sports for the real athletes and other activities for kids who couldn't quite make the cut. Now, forced by Scott's unique situation, Andy began to take a new look at our "minor" sport and in the process developed a newfound appreciation for our program. Recognizing the dedication, commitment, and passion shown by our runners, he was, much to my surprise, becoming a cross country fan. In a sport he'd always thought of as "individual," he now saw teamwork, and not the fake kind coaches try to force on selfish players, but the type John Wooden talked about. The kind of teamwork where people work together and "no one cares who gets the credit." Through us he'd seen a team where it didn't seem to matter how much talent you had, what you looked like, or your family's income. On our team no one got cut, everyone was given a fair chance, and the best runners received little, if any, special treatment. The old school "star system" Andy had grown accustomed to throughout his long career in athletics was slowly dying, a new era was dawning, and he found it appealing. After spending a few weeks closely attached to our team, he had come to see that cross country running was far more than "a sport where you run 10 miles just to throw up" as Bill Cosby had so famously observed. Now, in his final year as our Athletic Director, Andy was beginning to see why some of us love to run. Having taken a very personal interest in our team, he planned to do anything he could to help us.

Somehow, despite the many distractions of the week, our team managed to stay focused. Workouts had gone well, the guys seemed to be healthy, and the state of Wisconsin had made no further changes to Scott's living situation. Recapturing the excitement of the previous week proved difficult. There was no send-off, no speeches, fewer wishes of "good luck" in the hallways, and our local television stations, it seemed, had forgotten all about us. In a strange way it felt like the state meet had already happened as we headed into the final practice of the season…for the second time. Getting ready this time around would definitely be a challenge, especially for teams lacking a clear goal upon which to focus.

"You need to have a reason to race tomorrow," I reminded the guys as they sat quietly on the field house floor in front of me. "Think about your goals, think about our goals, the things we've talked about and worked for all season. Adding a week to the season has been a big distraction and most high school athletes don't do well with distractions. But I think it can help us. C.J. had another week to get healthy, and we ran a couple of great workouts on days when I'm pretty sure a lot of other teams just sat on their butts. Teams are going to have trouble tomorrow, especially teams that don't really have a good reason to run their hearts out in the last mile. So don't think about failure, don't think about excuses, just focus on our goal: a state trophy…and maybe, just maybe, a white tuxedo. Mental toughness, gentlemen, that's what it's going to come down to tomorrow, mental toughness!" I said, finishing with all the passion of a television evangelist as I studied the serious faces staring up at me.

"One question, Coach," Scott called out, shooting his hand high in the air like an excited first grader.

"What is it, Scott?"

"Is it true what Mr. Anderson said? He said he's gonna get us one of those big fancy busses, is that true?"

"Yeah, Scott. It's true. Mr. Anderson chartered a coach bus for us. I don't know why, but for some reason he seems to like you guys," I said with a smile. "And, don't spread this around, but he picked up the costs out of his budget. It's his last year as AD and he wanted to do something nice for you. He just thought it would be better, especially because someone has to bring all his new clothes and medals and everything he owns along with us," I said, nodding in Scott's direction.

"Oh yeah, one last thing guys. Check the weather tonight. It's going to be cold tomorrow, probably upper thirties but maybe colder. Be sure you have a hat, gloves, and long sleeve t-shirt for under your jersey," I said, issuing my standard late season warning. "I don't think it's gonna snow, but it might…and I've been told the course still has some standing water on it so conditions are not likely to be very good. All I can tell you for sure is the temperature will be somewhere between 100 degrees and minus 20 with about 50 percent chance of rain, snow, sleet or volcano. So prepare for the worst. Remember, whatever happens tomorrow, we need to be ready. We might end up second, third, or tenth but let's not let the weather beat us. Okay? Now let's go run."

Happy and carefree, the guys spent much of our short run chattering about the charter bus we would ride in the morning, boom box music for the ride home, and their plan to head to Bill's Pizza after practice for a spaghetti dinner. As always, it didn't take much to get them excited, especially if there was food involved.

"We're leaving for Bill's in twenty minutes, so hustle up!" Mike shouted as we finished up our easy five mile run and shuffled to a halt near the back door of the field house. "Meet in the back lot, guys. Animal, you're riding with me so no time for screwin' around. Go get changed and don't forget to comb your hair, okay? You do have a comb, don't you?"

Spaghetti was by far Scott's favorite meal. Cheap and easy to make, it was a staple at every group home he'd lived in and something he never seemed to tire of. Excitedly he changed into his brand new jeans, shirt, and sweater before working on the tangled tumbleweed of hair atop his head and rushing out to wait by Mike's truck.

At the restaurant, greeted by a young hostess in a maroon apron, the guys followed, single file, as she guided them to the long table near the lunch counter.

"MIDDLE! I CALLED IT!" Scott shouted loudly, starting a battle for the preferred seats at the table's center. Like a hotly-contested game of musical chairs, they rushed to grab a spot and avoid being stuck at the far end, away from the fun and conversation. With Scott positioned directly in the center of the group, the scene took on a bit of a Last Supper quality as friends sat down to enjoy their final hours together.

"Animal, you don't have to shout," Dan reminded him. "There's other people in here you know, so act normal, okay."

"Yeah, and take your jacket off, you're not at McDonalds," added C.J. "This is a real restaurant."

The concept of a "sit-down" restaurant was new to Scott. For possibly the first time in his life he was about to order from a menu that wasn't attached to a wall behind a counter.

"Try not to get spaghetti sauce on your new sweater."

"Use your napkin."

"Don't talk with food in your mouth…it's gross."

"Animal, not so loud! Animal, keep it down!"

Advice flew at him from all directions, delivered simply, directly, and unfiltered as only an older brother can do. Laughter rang through the crowded restaurant as Scott answered questions about his now famous pizza delivery job and the mythical "six foot pizza." Mounds of spaghetti disappeared from white plastic plates as if by magic, and garlic bread and pitchers of lemonade were devoured quickly as the tiny young waitress did her best to keep up with the demand.

Finally, as the flurry of consumption ground to a halt, Scott watched in amazement as C.J. studied the bill, calculated the tip, collected money, and made his way to the cash register to settle up. The simple idea of eating a meal before paying for it, or in this case, before his teammates paid for it, was an entirely new concept.

"Thanks guys! That was some great spaghetti," he said politely as the group stood to leave.

"Come on, Animal, let's get you home," Mike announced. "You do know where you live...don't you?"

"Well," Scott said taking a long pause as those standing over him awaited his response.

"I know it's somewhere in that direction," he said motioning a thumb over his right shoulder. "At least I'm pretty sure."

"ANIMAL! How can you NOT know where you live?" Mike demanded.

"Well, I only lived there for a week, ya know! It's a big brown house and it has a big garage on the one side and, oh yeah, it's on that really long straight street we ran on a couple weeks ago."

"Yeah, well, you just described a thousand houses in town," Mike explained sarcastically while everyone within earshot smiled and shook their head in disbelief. "Okay, let's go, there's a gas station down the block. Let's go find a phone book and figure out where Mr. Anderson lives."

Looking up from the copy of the *Stevens Point Daily Journal* stretched across the counter in front of him, the large, round faced gas station attendant studied the rusty Toyota pickup truck as it screeched to a halt in the parking lot in front of him.

"Can I help you guys?" he asked, setting down a half-eaten sandwich as Mike and Scott pushed their way through the door.

"Yeah, do you have a phone book? We have to figure out where this guy lives."

"Yeah, sure, right over there...HEY! You're that kid! The kid on the front page," he said, flipping pages to find the headline story on page one. "Here it is, right here. LONGLEY GETS TO RUN LAST RACE AS A PANTHER," he read as Mike and Scott studied the picture of Scott's smiling face above the four column article.

"Kid, that's one great story. You're practically famous," he said with a smile. "Now, how can I help you guys?"

With the assistance of the friendly "sandwich man," Scott was delivered safely to the big brown house with the big garage on Green Avenue for a final comfortable night with the Andersons. As teams from around the state sought sleep under thin, sometimes nasty bed coverings at motels near the meet site, we enjoyed the comfort of our own beds, gladly passing up the fun of an overnight trip for the chance at a better night's sleep. Accustomed to long bus trips, the two hours to Madison would be a minor inconvenience, especially in the quiet comfort of a charter bus.

Planted comfortably on our living room couch, I studied Cheryl's gentle, loving touch as she fed Beth her last bottle before bedtime and reflected with great satisfaction on the season that was finally about to end. Somehow, in slightly more than two months, we'd built a team from a most unusual collection of individuals and tomorrow, against all odds, we would have the chance to compete for another state title. Content with the knowledge that I'd done all I could for "my guys," it was now time to relax and put my worries aside. All we had to do now was get a little sleep, take a bus ride, step to the line, and give our best effort. My work was, for the most part, finished. As Cheryl carried our sleeping "little monster" carefully off to bed, I picked up the remote control and I flipped on the recently added Weather Channel to make one final check on our local conditions.

"It's snowing in Wisconsin," the cheerful meteorologist in a bright blue blazer announced as he pointed at the large pink and white blob covering the distinctive mitten shape of our state.

Leaping from the couch, I pulled back the curtains on our picture window and watched in horror as large, wet flakes dove from the sky past the glow of a corner street light. Snow turned to slush upon hitting paved surfaces, and grass, shrubs, and trees were already covered in white.

"You could see accumulation of 4 to 7 inches of sleet, snow, and freezing rain by morning," the weatherman continued as if delivering some kind of happy news.

"Cheryl, you have to see this!" I called out softly, being careful not to wake our lightly sleeping child. "Can you believe it? Look at this."

"Look at what?" she asked tip-toeing into the room.

"SNOW! It's snowing, it's not supposed to snow! Look at that," I said holding the curtain back to let her see for herself.

"So it's snowing, it'll probably melt by morning," she stated calmly. "Relax, you know weathermen always exaggerate."

"Yeah, well, I'm not worried about our guys running in it, I'm worried about the course. A couple inches on top of an already wet course, what if Yahara won't let us on the course, then what?"

"Really?" Cheryl asked with a smile while gently patting the middle of my back. "What are the chances of having the meet canceled two weeks in a row? Think about that?"

"Yeah, you're right, but still, it's been that kind of season."

As large blobs of wet, wind driven snow splattered against our bedroom windowpanes I lay perfectly still, counting backwards from one hundred by threes, hoping to keep my mind occupied long enough to drift off to sleep. Putting my worries aside was next to impossible and sleep was hard to come by. Good, deep, restful sleep would have to wait until tomorrow.

The digital alarm clock on the nightstand read 4:37 when I finally gave up and quietly climbed out of bed. Carefully gathering up the large pile of running clothes from the floor, I snuck slowly into the living room to dress in the glow of the television screen and study the latest weather forecast. Standing in silence with the volume barely audible, I watched, spellbound, as a weather bulletin scrolled across the bottom of the screen. A WINTER STORM WATCH IS IN EFFECT FOR WISCONSIN AND PARTS OF ILLINOIS, IOWA, AND MINNESOTA. A huge band of snow and freezing rain, indicated by a pink and white blob on the radar map, had parked itself over our portion of the world and was expected to stick around for most of the day. With the temperature at 24 degrees and wind gusting to 30 miles an hour, the already bad road conditions were getting worse by the minute, and the travel advisory in effect for much of the state gave me more to worry about than just the course conditions at Yahara Hills. I had no way of knowing what things were like 100 miles to our south, but from what I could tell as I gazed out the window to study the accumulation of snow on my front lawn, the situation didn't look good. Gathering up the last of my gear I packed my travel bag with very little care and considered the possibility that our state athletic association might postpone the meet again or that road conditions might prevent us from getting out of town.

Pellets of sleet bounced from the shoulders of my new Sub 4 Gore-Tex jacket as I quietly pulled the back door shut and stepped out into the driveway. Several inches of heavy, wet snow had accumulated on my car overnight with more on the way. Icy slush flowed over my shoe tops, instantly soaking my socks as I worked to uncover the windows of my trusty Buick Skylark. An uneasy feeling gripped the pit of my stomach as I backed out of the driveway to begin the short trip to school in the pre-dawn darkness. Pushing my way down an unplowed street, I listened carefully to the sound of my tires as they tossed the sloppy mixture in all directions and tried my best to assess the road conditions.

Rounding the final corner of my journey, I entered the faculty parking lot and slid to a stop next to Mr. Anderson's car. Comforted by the sight of half a dozen cars parked randomly at this early hour, I knew I wasn't alone in my concern about the conditions. Vaulting from the car with only my keys in hand, I trotted toward the locker room door, entered the school, and headed quickly down the long dark hallway on my way to the main office complex.

"Good morning, Scott," I called out loudly, using the most cheerful voice I could muster.

Sitting with his head down and a blue duffel bag across his lap, Scott waited quietly on the floor, his back against the outer wall of Andy's office.

"What a great day! Think about it, we get to run a state meet in the snow. Are you ready for that?"

"I'm ready, Coach. I'm always ready, but are they gonna cancel it AGAIN? Mr. Anderson said they might. He's on the phone right now," he said, looking up at me with a look of deep concern.

"Scott," I said taking a knee directly in front of him, "it's all going to work out. Trust me, this is going to be a great day, let me do the worrying. All you have to do is think about the race. Eye of the Tiger, young man. Eye of the Tiger!"

"Yeah Coach, Eye of the Tiger," he answered, flashing only half of his normally bright smile.

Leaning through the office door I saw Andy at his desk with a phone to his ear. Coach K., our girls volleyball coach, was seated across from him, and Mike Olson, Suzy's coach, paced nervously just inside the doorway.

"Any news yet, Ole?" I asked quietly.

"Yeah, the meet's on, state volleyball too, if we can get there. He's checking with the bus garage right now."

"No busses!" Andy exclaimed, shaking his head as he hung up the phone. "No district busses will be allowed out. Conditions are just too bad."

"WHAT?" Coach K. screamed, vaulting from her chair as if challenging a bad call. "I can't believe it. What are we supposed to do now? These girls have earned the right to go, they've worked too hard, there's no way we're staying home. We're going! What if I get their parents to drive them? Would that work?"

"Yes," Andy responded calmly, "have them sign a release form and they can drive their own child."

"DONE!" she said angrily. In an instant she was gone, leaving Ole and I to figure out our particular situation.

"Where does that leave us?" asked Ole.

"Well, that's up to the charter bus company. It's their bus so it's their call. We'll have to see what the driver thinks when he gets here," Andy explained.

"I'll go see if he's here yet," I said as I charged out the door and flew past Scott at a near sprint on my way back to the snowy parking lot.

Our fate was now in the hands of Tom Rath who, as luck would have it, just happened to be a good friend of mine. Rath, as I always called him, was a fellow social studies teacher who supplemented his income by driving buses on the weekends. Tall and athletic with jet black hair and a thick mustache, his physique had changed little since his days as an outstanding colligate track man at UW-Oshkosh. With years of driving experience, he knew his vehicle's capabilities well, but more importantly, as a former track and cross country coach, he understood the importance of this trip. He knew how much time and effort our young men had invested in this day, how badly we wanted the chance to chase a state title, and what was at stake for Suzy. Had this been a group of old ladies on a trip to the casino, he would have almost certainly turned the bus around, but this was different and he knew it. This was more than a simple road trip. Today we were on a mission.

Standing in the lot studying the falling snow as it passed the orange glow of a lone sodium vapor streetlight, I strained my ears anxiously for the sound of an approaching bus, confident that I could count on Rath to get us safely to Madison.

Suddenly, the roar of a four-cylinder Toyota engine broke the silence. It was Mike, flying into the lot at an absurd rate of speed. Cranking the wheel hard right, he executed two beautiful full donuts and skidded to a halt right in front of me. Jumping excitedly from the cab he slammed the driver's side door, threw both hands in the air, and shouted at the top of his lungs, "YEAH! THIS IS GONNA BE GREAT! I LOVE IT!!"

I knew very well that I should talk to him about driving too fast, about parking lot donuts, and the general concept of being a stupid teenager, but I just couldn't. Not now anyway. I loved his enthusiasm, his passion, and his confidence. As a mature, responsible man of thirty-two, I was envious of his carefree exuberance. The kid had a love of life I wished everyone could experience, and I just couldn't bring myself to deliver a lecture.

With concerns about Mike's driving habits on hold, I turned my attention to the low pitched growl of the charter bus entering the lot at a very cautious speed. Standing motionless in the near blizzard conditions, I watched hopefully as it rolled to a stop and settled onto the snow a few yards away.

"Don't look so worried, Coach," Rath called out, looking down at me with a friendly smile as he forced the bus door into the full open position. "I'll get you there. It might take a while, but I'll get you there! I've been on the radio and it seems like the roads should get a little better the farther south we go."

"That's great!" I said while quickly climbing aboard to offer Rath a thankful handshake.

Amid the small crowd of curious runners and parents assembled in the flying snow near the bus door, Andy stood with Scott at his side.

"Well Tom, how does it look?" he asked in a serious tone.

"I think we'll be okay. If it gets really bad we might have to turn around, but I think we'll be okay. We'll just take it slow."

"Alright, just be careful out there," he said, reaching out to shake Tom's hand. "Okay Coach," Andy said, turning in my direction. "Let's get you guys on the road! Come on, Scott, we need to get your stuff on the bus."

"LOAD UP GUYS, WE'RE MOVIN'!" I shouted, my voice filled with emotion. People suddenly began scurrying in all directions. J.V. runners brought their snowball throwing contest to a quick end and with Rob's guidance, pitched in to transfer Scott's collection of boxes and duffel bags from Andy's car to the bus's huge cargo compartment. Car doors slammed and trunks flew open as runners rushed to retrieve their gear. Parents quickly hugged their sons goodbye as they lined up to push their way aboard the warm, dry bus.

"Scott," I asked as he said goodbye to Mr. Anderson, "do you have the hat I gave you last week?"

"Ahhh…I don't know, Coach. I think I lost it."

"Well, you're definitely going to need one today," I reminded him impatiently. "Rob, get 'em loaded up. I've got to go check the lost and found."

Anxious to get moving and just a little annoyed that Scott had somehow managed to lose yet another hat, I raced to the South Office, threw open the door, and dove into the musty, nicotine laced pile of items beneath the office counter. With a nappy, royal blue stocking cap firmly in hand, I jumped to my feet and hurried back to the bus. Old and well worn, it wasn't much but it would have to do. I had no time to search any further.

"Here," I said as I bounded up the bus stairs and tossed it in Scott's direction, "compliments of the window people…just don't smell it."

For the first time in my coaching career I slipped into the comfortable, high back seat of a coach bus. Reaching forward, I tapped Rath on the shoulder and yelled, "LET'S ROLL!"

The bus lurched forward as I turned in my seat to take a quick head count.

"Do we have everyone, Rob?"

"Yeah, I think so," he answered, sounding fairly confident.

With that we were moving, moving slowly, but we were moving. Slush flew from under our tires as we made our way to the interstate and begin our trip south. Leaning from my seat to check the speedometer, I realized that thirty miles an hour was about all the speed we could muster under the conditions.

"We should make it," I said to Rob, seated across the aisle. "Suzy might not have much warm-up time, but if the roads don't get any worse I think we'll be okay. Good thing we built an extra hour into our schedule."

Truckers chattered on the C.B. radio about road conditions as wind driven snow continued to fall heavily, reducing visibility to well under a quarter mile. From my study of the cars in the oncoming lanes, I tried to convince myself that based on their speed and the snow accumulation on their hoods conditions were no worse to the south of us. Confident that conditions couldn't possibly deteriorate quickly enough to prevent us from getting to the meet, I took a deep, relaxing breath and turned my attention, for the first time, to the guys scattered about the bus behind me. Seated in no particular order, most of the guys looked pretty relaxed. Some occupied themselves by reading, some seemed to be sleeping, and a few sat staring straight ahead with the nervous look of soldiers in a landing craft headed for a beach head. Each handled the stress of race day in his own way as our plush, comfortable ride motored quietly along at an agonizingly slow thirty-two miles an hour.

"Scott, what are you doing?" I asked as I peered around the seatback to find him hunched over his letter jacket, working feverishly.

"Writing, Coach. I'm writin' some stuff."

"On your letter jacket?"

"Yeah Coach, here look. On this sleeve I wrote 1985 Wisconsin Valley Conference Champs with all the guys' names listed under it. And on the other sleeve I put 1985 Sectional Champions. And right here," he said pointing to the empty space below, "I saved a place for today, ya know, 1985 State Champions."

"That's nice, Scott, but you might want to hold off on that one. First we have to get there, then we have to run the race, and then...in case you didn't know, there's this team from Manitowoc. You might have heard about them. They're the number one ranked team in the state, they beat us twice this season and they're pretty darn good."

"Yeah Coach, heard all about 'em. But ya know, Coach, it's like you always tell us. Ya gotta set your goals. Ya gotta believe, Coach. Ya gotta believe!"

Nineteen

State

From the highway off-ramp, through the shroud of falling snow, we could see the course at Yahara Hills. Thousands of spectators trudged slowly through the snow in long, ragged columns reminiscent of Napoleon's retreat from Moscow in the bitter winter of 1812. It was exciting to see so many people out in this foul weather. From all across our state people had braved the treacherous conditions for the chance to watch their sons and daughters, friends and neighbors, in this the final meet of the cross country season. Dressed in heavy boots and parkas, some with umbrellas to ward off the wet snow, they lined the course in anticipation of the first race of the day. Ready to cheer on their favorite team, the leaders, the stragglers, and everyone in between, today they would appreciate the effort of every last competitor as they rushed from point to point. These hearty fans had no interest in bleacher sitting; they were here to be part of the event in a way unknown to other sports.

In the warm, dry comfort of our bus we attempted to evaluate the course conditions as meet workers directed us to the parking area. The horizon vanished into the thick, gray distant haze, concealing the fact that it was mid-morning. Heavy snow collected on trees, cars, busses, and the hats and shoulders of those already out on the course. For some, it was a perfect day to stay home, curl up with a good book, and a cup of hot chocolate, but for those brave enough to venture out this would definitely be a day to remember.

Standing in the center aisle as the bus slowed to a halt, Suzy and Coach Olson waited impatiently for the door to swing open. With less than half an hour till race time, she needed to start her warm-up, view the course, and test the conditions. Shouts of "Good luck, Suzy!" filled the bus as she leaped from the bottom step into the thick, wet snow. Watching quietly as she and Ole slowly disappeared, we wondered how the conditions of the day might affect her. Unstoppable at any distance for the last four years, could this be her downfall? Suzy was the greatest female runner in Wisconsin history, and thousands were here to watch her cruise to another easy victory and claim a record fourth consecutive state title. Later, we planned to join the cheering mob out in the snow, but for now we sat tight, passing the time and staying warm and dry.

"This was where they held the NCAA national meet in '78," I announced, breaking the uncomfortable silence. "It was a cold, gray, windy day, kind of like today minus the snow," my story began as I did my best to fill the time with what I hoped would prove to be an interesting and perhaps even valuable story. "Henry Rono from Washington State was the guy everyone wanted to see. He was the two-time defending champ and he'd set four world records over the summer. He was the greatest distance runner in the world, maybe the greatest ever. And I was standing right there," I said, pointing to the top of a small rise a few hundred yards away. "I watched him go by in the lead looking like it was a jog in the park and then… somehow he ends up in 237th place, last, dead last," I continued dramatically, as if lecturing one of my history classes. "People were screaming 'Where's Henry? Where's Rono?' To this day I don't know how it happened, but somehow he got off the course. Some said he sprained his ankle, I don't know, but there were a lot of really disappointed people on this course that day," I explained to my attentive audience. "Alberto Salazar won the individual title that day and a really strong Oregon team, that everyone thought would win, got beat by a team of newly recruited Africans from Texas El Paso. Most of them had never seen cold weather like this, and I heard their coach took them to K-Mart the night before and bought 'em long underwear and blaze orange stocking caps to race in. Oh, and it was deer hunting season so these guys fresh off the plane from Africa are wondering why people in Wisconsin drive around with dead animals strapped to their cars. I heard they were a little confused by that."

My story may have seemed like a bit of ancient history, but it held the guys' interest, got a few laughs, and had a couple of obvious lessons built in. Lessons like know the course, dress for the weather, and sometimes the unexpected happens. Sometimes the favorite gets beat.

"Alright guys, bundle up! Time to go see the course," I shouted, clapping my hands together as I jumped to my feet.

Anxiously the members of our small group pulled on sweatshirts, jackets, hats, and gloves as we prepared to abandon the safe refuge of our warm bus and plunge our feet into the icy slush hidden beneath the fresh white snow. Jogging out onto the course as Suzy and the rest of the Division I field assembled at the line, we quickly resigned ourselves to the fact that our feet would be cold, incredibly cold, for the next few hours. Running on tip toes or jumping and dancing around low spots was of little help. In the end, we had to accept the discomfort, deal with it, and above all, keep moving.

"Just follow the brown trail," I shouted, referring to the mixture of mud and slush left in the wake of previous races. With course markings hard to find in the snow and low light conditions, we would follow the tracks of countless footprints on the three long narrow out and back loops. Getting lost today was not a concern. "Even Henry Rono couldn't get lost today," I joked as the faint "pop" of a distant starter's pistol signaled the start of the race.

Joining the thousands lining both sides of the brown stripe

that now designated the center of the race course, we cheered loudly as Suzy and the rest of the field charged past us.

"Let's jog," I shouted as the already struggling back of the pack runners made their way to the crest of the first hill and disappeared from view. "We'll look at the first section of the course and then jog over to see Suzy finish. Oh, and I have two reminders for you. One, know the course, and two, run your butt off. That's it, that's all you have to do today. Think you can remember all that?" I asked with a smile.

Suzy had won 40 of her 42 high school cross country races, so few in our little group had ever seen Suzy lose. Standing somewhere just short of the two-mile mark, we waited for her to appear on the horizon on her way to another easy victory.

"There they are!" someone shouted as eyes strained to determine who dared challenge Suzy this late in the race.

"It's Hartzheim, the girl from Lakeland," C.J. announced to those around him as Suzy pressed the pace and worked desperately to break away from her rival. With barely a two stride lead, she struggled to make it three and then four as she surged from slightly more than a thousand meters out.

Among chants of "SUZY, SUZY, SUZY" we cheered her on as she entered the final section of the course, a sweeping turn that lead to a long, slightly downhill home stretch. Pulling her frozen feet from the icy slush, she drove her knees high and applied her superior turnover on her way to a six-second victory. Having expected to see Suzy cruise to another easy win, the crowd had been treated to a memorable display of toughness and will power as Suzy and Mary, having poured heart and soul into the race, staggered across the line just a short distance apart.

As runners and spectators engulfed the finish chute, we turned away, left the commotion behind and headed off to finish our warm-up. Conditions were less than ideal for Suzy today, but somehow, as great athletes do, she found a way to win.

Bundled in our sweats, warm from the jog, and away from the crowd, I stopped our group to deliver a few last words of advice.

"Take a good look at this spot," I said, ignoring the tiny ice pellets that bounced from my face. "This is where the meet will be decided, RIGHT HERE in the last mile. I can't tell you how things will turn out today, but on days like this you better have a good reason to be out here. There will be guys in this race who can't find that reason. They had their fun at the motel last night, or last week, and they'd rather be back on that nice warm bus. Yeah, they'll run well for a while, but only the guys who are really committed to their goals will continue to fight in the final mile. Look at this," I said, pointing out at the vast winter storm that engulfed us. "It's terrible out here. This is the worst weather I've ever seen at a cross country meet. No one expects you to run well in this, no one will blame you if you pack it in, and no one will know if you did—no one but you. Look at the guy standing next to you, right there, that's your reason to keep fighting. Do you think Mike and C.J. will give anything less than their best? Remember that day at the park? The big ladder we ran in the wind and rain? I tried to send you home and you looked at me like I was nuts. That was something special, that's what I'll always remember about this team and that's the kind of team we want to be today. I don't expect you to run fast times, and I don't expect to beat Manitowoc. I just expect your best effort, so focus on that. This is our last day together, the last time we'll ever be together just like this. It's been a great season, a season to remember, so let's make this a day to remember and let's do something we can all be proud of."

Pausing for a moment to let my words sink in, I wondered if I'd overstated the case. After all, it's not as if I was preparing soldiers to climb from the trenches and rush across no man's land nor was I sending firemen into a burning orphanage. Could a high school athletic contest really be as important as I'd just made it sound? For those in our tightly huddled group, the answer was, of course, a resounding yes. In a day, a week, or a year, the importance of today would fade, but for right now, at this moment, this five thousand meter run in the snow was, as it should be, the most important thing in the world.

Looking into the eyes of "my guys" as they stared silently in my direction, I continued.

"Get out a little harder today," I said in a most serious tone. "I think we need to get in the top half of the field right away. We can't afford to get stuck too far back, I just think that running in this slop will make it too tough to move up later in the race."

"Yeah," Rob added, "don't sit behind people. Don't get stuck behind guys that are giving up. Keep your head up, keep chasing guys down."

In my nine years of coaching I'd never sent a team out fast. It wasn't our style, it wasn't my style. We always ran patiently, from the back, relaxed and under control. Always, that is, until today. Today we would be aggressive, go out hard, and make other teams run us down. I knew very well that the state meet is no place to try something new, but under these conditions I felt it was the best choice. For runners short on talent and long on desire, bad weather can be a great equalizer, and today we would turn the race into a battle of attrition.

"We might crash and burn," I said quietly to Rob on the jog back towards our bus, "but if this comes down to a battle of willpower, it just might work."

Returning to the parking area we found our bus packed with Suzy's excited fans, friends, and teammates.

"Twenty minutes till race time," I shouted as we pushed our way up the steps and down the center aisle. "I want you at the line in ten, so get moving. Spikes on, numbers on, hats, gloves, and long sleeves. Hustle up!"

The bus grew silent as many on board left to stand in the snow while others slid quietly into seats away from those getting ready to race.

"Animal! You pinned your number on upside down," barked Rob.

"No I didn't. Look, number 402," Scott said, pulling his jersey away from his chest as he peered down to read it.

"It's not there for you to read, it's for the officials! Here, let me fix that."

Like so many conversations between Scott and Rob, it brought smiles to our faces and helped ease the tension as I pulled a damp, crumpled list from my pocket and checked to see that each of our guys wore the correct number and had it right side up.

"On the line in two minutes, double knots. You don't want to have a shoe come untied today," I warned.

"Triple knot 'em, guys, let's go!" Mike shouted, his voice full of energy and raw emotion.

Dry, spike clad feet once again met ice-cold slush as we exited the bus and rushed off in the direction of our assigned position on the starting line. Without hesitation the guys left our warm shelter behind, looks of grim determination on their young faces. Thoughts of retreat were not allowed. They had a job to do. They were ready.

"We can do this!" I shouted from my position a short distance out from the start line.

"Hurry back!"

"Work hard!"

"Every point counts!"

"Give your best effort!"

"Make us proud!" I continued as guys lined up for one last hand shake and a solid slap on the back.

Equipped with cotton gloves, a long-sleeve t-shirt under his jersey, and the nappy, nicotine laced, lost and found hat I'd given him, Scott was excited, happy, and ready to go. Reaching out as he jogged in my direction, I hooked his arm, pulled him to a stop, and placed my hands firmly on his shoulders to give him my final instructions.

"Scott, I want you to latch onto John, okay? He'll get you out in good position. Just don't get too excited, okay? When I said get out fast, I didn't mean you should sprint out like a madman. Just be patient and stick with John. That's all you have to do, got it?"

"I got it, Coach, don't worry, I got it," he said, flashing a toothy grin as he raised his hand for a final, powerful high-five. "White tuxedo time, Coach!" he said as he turned to sprint off. "Ya gotta believe, Coach!"

Fighting back a smile, I turned my face to the sky and studied the fast moving dark clouds as a knot formed in my throat and tears began to well.

"What are you looking at?" Rob asked, as he stood beside me.

"Just thinking, Rob," I said, clearing my throat as I pointed to the sky. "If there's someone up there…well, I just hope he's watching this. The kid from the group home, in his first cross country season, and here he is, about to run a state meet, in a blizzard, on his last day with us. And because of him, we have a chance at a state title. What a story! What an unbelievable story. Rob, somebody oughta write a book about this." Turning to jog up the course we made our way from the starting line with a mob of J.V. runners, alternates, and alumni trailing close behind.

The moment we'd worked for was, at long last, about to get under way. With heightened senses we waited, ready to cheer our guys on and sprint all-out from point to point. Finally, after so much doubt and delay, the race was at hand and the fastest 20 minutes of our season was about to begin. All too soon we would be back on the bus, struggling to reconstruct and comprehend the events we were about to witness.

Thick, heavy snow began to fall right on cue as a sudden wave of motion from the starting line followed a half-second later by the faint report of a .32 caliber cartridge signaled the start of the race. Runners vaulted from the line eager to establish position, churning the snow as they sprinted in our direction. Seldom, with the possible exception of a presidential assassination, does a single gunshot create such frenzy. The roar of the crowd rolled across the long open spaces of Yahara Hills as the field of 136 runners funneled down to a single column six, eight, or ten bodies wide. With spectators bolting in all directions, we held firmly to our place atop the crest of a slight hill, ready to assess the position of our runners as they passed.

Clad in blaze orange hats, Mike and C.J. were easy to find. Positioned well within the top twenty, they'd gotten out cleanly, just as we'd hoped. Seconds later John, Johnny, Lee, and Bill filed passed in close formation. All, as instructed, were in the top half of the field and they looked good.

"Where's Scott?" I yelled frantically. "Did anyone see The Animal?"

Somehow he'd slipped past us, all of us, without being noticed. Glancing in Rob's direction with a look of panic, I shouted again, "Where's the Animal? Somebody must have seen him!"

Sprinting wildly to the next spot on the course, I waited for an answer as the wind picked up and snowflakes grew in size and number.

"Where is he?" "Where's the Animal!" "Find him," screamed others around me.

"Donn!" someone called out through the now thick curtain of snow. "Donn, he's way up there. He's way the hell up there!" came the excited report from twin alumni Lance and Louis Wasniewski. "Yeah, really, he's right behind the leaders."

Lining the course, we strained to see the front runners as they turned to come our way just beyond the half-mile mark.

"There! There he is!" someone called out, pointing to the chase pack a few yards behind the leaders.

In the middle of a tightly formed group of runners, Scott ran with confidence, looking as if he belonged among the top runners in the state. Having at some point discovered a face mask in the hat I'd given him earlier that morning, he'd donned his disguise just before the gun. With the look of a bank robber, a super hero, or one of the professional wrestlers he so admired, he'd taken on an alter ego determined to save the day with his super power—the ability to tolerate pain.

"Relax, Scott, just relax!" I shouted in an effort to calm him down as he loped past, his long stride chewing up the snow covered ground. "Oh God!" I said, placing my gloved hand atop my head. "What's he doing?"

"Easy, Animal! Take it easy," I heard Rob scream as I turned my attention back up the course to find C.J. and Mike now just a few yards behind Scott.

"Animal!" Mike demanded angrily. "Get behind me! NOW!"

"Relax, Animal. Stay with us," added C.J. calmly.

With three runners on the back end of the chase pack and three more not very far behind as the race turned toward the mile mark, we'd thrown down the gauntlet. For a team used to going out slowly, these were uncharted waters, but there was no turning back now.

"Great position!" I yelled confidently. "That's it... keep on it!"

At this point in the race it was far too early to get excited, I reminded myself, while secretly hoping I hadn't sent my guys on a suicide mission. Frozen in place, I nervously scanned the mass of runners as they passed, looking for the white and red uniforms of the Manitowoc runners, knowing that their pack would not be far behind ours. Somehow, with his high knee lift and awkward arm swing providing some strange mechanical advantage, C.J. had managed to join the three runners in the lead group as they approached the mid-point of the race. With Mike clinging stubbornly to the front of the chase pack and Scott still ahead of Manitowoc's first runner, we cheered excitedly.

"Come on, guys! You can do it, guys!"

"Come on, Animal!" we screamed as we watched him slide further and further behind Mike with each stride. "You can do it, Animal! Hang on, Animal! We need you, Scott, we need you!"

The determined runners clad in white and red now focused their attention on our masked mystery runner, and with John stuck in the center of their pack, they began to hunt him down.

"Eye of the Tiger, Animal, Eye of the Tiger," John said softly as the group pulled even with Scott. "Risin' up, Animal! Come on, Animal, come on!" he added, knowing all the right words to inspire his fading teammate.

Now locked in an epic two team battle in the final mile, with a state title hanging in the balance, we desperately needed him to stick with John and the Manitowoc runners. Eye of the Tiger became our war cry as we cupped our hands to our mouths and leaned in close to urge him on. Each time he dropped a step behind, he heard the chant "Eye of the Tiger, Animal! Come on, Animal, Eye of the Tiger! You can do it, Animal! EYE…OF…THE…TIGER!"

Responding to each cheer, our masked hero tilted his face to the sky, gulped air, flailed his arms, and pushed his way back to John's side. How many times could he do this I wondered as we urged him on? How much could we ask of him? How much did he have left to give?

With the race nearing the final half mile, John and Scott worked to stay in contact with the group of three Manitowoc runners while Johnny and Lee, running side by side, struggled to hold their position. As runners in white and red moved steadily forward, our once comfortable lead began to evaporate. The meet would be decided in the final few hundred meters where every stride, every icy step, was crucial. Well aware of the situation, we lined the course, shouting at the top of our lungs before sprinting, leap frog style, to the next vantage point.

"We can do it!" "Hang on!" "Every point counts!" "Get one more, just one more!" we pleaded with every ounce of our strength.

Unbelievably, inexplicably, C.J. was still attached to the back of the lead pack as they entered the final stretch, a slight downhill about 400 meters from the finish line.

"Start it, C.J.! Go now, C.J.! Kick, C.J.!" we shouted as the leaders launched their furious kicks, leaving him behind almost instantly.

"Hang on! Hang on!" we demanded, hoping he could get to the line without surrendering another point. We watched just long enough to see him fall across the line in fourth place.

Quickly turning our attention up the course, we watched as Mike suffered a similar fate. Caught by two late kickers, he staggered bravely toward the line and stumbled into the chute a few places behind C.J. and just slightly ahead of the first Manitowoc runner.

"Three Manitowoc guys!" I heard someone shout. "Right there, look! THREE OF THEM!"

Separated by only a few seconds, the Manitowoc runners worked together to pull away from John and Scott.

"Go now! Start now! Don't wait…gotta go now!" we shouted excitedly.

"Three guys, right there," I said, punching holes in the air with my index finger as I pointed towards our opponents. "GET 'EM!"

"Come on, Animal," John shouted over his shoulder, leaving his exhausted teammate behind. "Eye of the Tiger… let's go!" he pleaded as he applied his quarter miler speed and flawless running form to the task at hand—chasing down white jerseys.

Bent dramatically forward at the waist with head down and arms flailing side to side, Scott labored mightily to extract his feet from the heavy slush as a picket line of runners closed in, anxious to overtake him. It was over. His great strength was slipping away and along with it our hopes for victory.

"KICK SCOTT!" I screamed in desperation, dropping to my knees as if praying for a miracle. Frozen like a statue, I could now only watch as the long line of snow covered runners sprinted toward the finish, knowing there was nothing more I could do but admire the effort and watch Scott drop one place and then another.

"Animal, Animal, Animal," the call went up from somewhere down the line. Started by our J.V. guys, it grew in volume and intensity as others joined in.

"AN-AH-MAL…AN-AH-MAL…AN-AH-MAL," they chanted in unison to the rhythm of their clapping hands as he labored along.

More than just words of encouragement, it was their tribute to Scott, a tribute to effort and to courage. It was their way of saying thanks for all he'd given us. We knew he'd given his all and done his best, he didn't need to do more…but somehow he did.

Our blue-masked superhero somehow, amazingly, found one last surge. With his head raised and eyes now focused on the finish line, he straightened his posture, quickened his arm swing, drove his knees upward, and launched a furious kick. Clumps of packed snow flew from his heals as he streaked past several runners who had passed him just moments earlier and fell just one stride short of catching Manitowoc's fourth runner at the line. In an amazing confluence of events, John, Scott, and three Manitowoc runners had crossed the line in a jumble of exhausted bodies, separated by only a matter of yards. Now, as so often happens in close meets like this one, the outcome would be decided by the fifth runners.

"That's their fifth…and sixth," I heard someone shout as I turned my attention back up the course to see two Manitowoc runners sprinting side by side.

"Where's Johnny…and Lee…and Bill?" Rob called out impatiently as we trained our vision to examine the approaching runners.

Bill, I knew, would not be a factor today. After looking good early he'd lost contact with our group and was slowly swallowed up by the back half of the field as he labored along. Lee started cautiously and had steadily worked his way further and further toward the front. Almost unnoticed for the first half of the race, he'd suddenly appeared at Johnny's side in the last mile. Together they struggled to sustain the pace. Well aware that they could give up no more places, they worked together, pushing each other as the Manitowoc runners continued to lengthen their lead.

"That's it! Right there! Two Manitowoc guys!" we shouted, hoping they could somehow close the gap, hoping they had something more to give.

Just an average J.V. runner a year earlier, Lee was running the race of his life and we all knew it. Charging through the storm with his awkward "toy soldier" running style, he stayed, stride for stride, at the side of his freshman teammate.

"Come on, Lee! Come on, Hack! You can do it, Hacker!" we screamed, amazed by what we were seeing.

And then, in an instant, he was down. Stepping on an unseen sprinkler connection hidden in a slush-filled depression, he lurched forward and landed hard, face first, in the icy mix. Arms flailing as he slid to a stop, Lee sprang quickly to his feet and with a blood curdling scream attempted to regain his position. But it was no use. Try as he might, the weight of his sodden clothing made recovery impossible. The fate of our team now rested on Johnny's tiny shoulders and for him, the finish couldn't appear soon enough. As he crested the final small hill, we could see him in the midst of a large group of runners—struggling.

"Johnny! Get those guys!" we demanded as he passed our group, laboring to hold on.

"Go now, Johnny! Start now!"

The harsh conditions had taken their toll. This was not a day for young, slightly built runners and our fast start had done him no favors.

"Get your knees up, get your knees up, come on," I said quietly to myself as if sending some sort of telepathic message to him, hoping he could hold on just a little longer.

"Look!" Rob called out excitedly. "He's kickin'. Look at that!"

With the finish line now clearly in sight, Johnny suddenly broke from his labored, plodding stride and began to sprint. Blessed with an exceptional stride length and tremendous turnover, he appeared to have been shot from a gun as he flew toward the line, passing one clump of runners with his sights set on others still ahead.

"Come on, come on, one more, get one more," I mumbled excitedly, watching him lean and lunge at the line before disappearing into the mass of bodies around the chute.

From the small knoll overlooking the home stretch, I stood motionless, squinting through the snow, attempting to comprehend the incredible performance I'd just witnessed. Ignoring the commotion around me I paused to collect my thoughts. What would I say to my team? How could I possibly make them know how proud I was?

"Did we do it, Donn?" Dan asked loudly while a group of "my guys" began forming around me. "I think we did it," he added with some degree of confidence.

"It's going to be really close, but I think we got it," Curt said cautiously.

As if by some magnetic force we were drawn together, each of us anxious to share our thoughts.

"I don't know," I said, shaking my head as our little circle pulled in tighter. "But I hope you guys realize what you just saw. This race, this day, if you live to be a hundred you'll never see anything quite like this again. Yeah, I hope we won, but even if we didn't it's okay because today WE, all of us, were part of something special. Could you feel it? That energy! That passion! You guys were absolutely nuts out there. And that Animal chant, man, I thought I was gonna cry. What a story, what a great, great story. We made a wonderful memory today and that, gentlemen, is what life is about, memories of days like this when a bunch of crazy people met on a golf course to run around in the snow and scream like the world's about to end. What could be better than this?" I asked, throwing my arms up at the sky. "Remember this moment, remember this day! And if, somehow, we pull this off, remember that every one of you owns a little part of it. There's just no way this happens without you guys out there. You're enthusiasm carried those guys. Because of you guys, we have a chance. Now, let's get to the bus."

Sprinting excitedly to the parking lot, we soon found ourselves amid a crowd of nervous parents and fans assembled near the bus door.

"Great job, guys! Great effort! That was amazing!" I shouted while climbing aboard to find C.J. standing on the top step, smiling happily, next to his brother Keith. Now a senior at Marquette University, Keith was among the best collegiate runners in America and he knew just how well his sibling had run. Like all of us, he could barely believe what he'd just seen.

"Almost! Almost!" C.J. repeated emphatically. "I was that close!" he said, holding his thumb and index finger a few inches apart. Normally one of the quietest guys on the team, he chattered excitedly, full of energy, looking as if he'd just taken a casual morning jog.

Slumped in their seats, our other runners sat quietly, looking frozen and exhausted. Lee struggled to peel off his cold, soaking wet uniform, John curled forward in "crash landing" position, hugging his dry sweats, and Mike, unhappy with his race, tore his spikes from his feet and launched them at the floor.

Excited parents, alumni, and J.V. runners clambered aboard to offer their congratulations as speculation about the meet's outcome ran rampant.

"We gained a bunch at one and two," I heard someone say.

"Yeah, but they picked up a lot at number five and that hurt us."

"But some of those guys had to be individuals so maybe it wasn't as bad as it looked."

"There's no way they beat us, no way. I think we got it!"

Walking the center aisle, Rob began the process of collecting wet finish numbers from runners trained to hold them tightly. With the bus now almost silent, Rob carefully added our point total as Keith stood close, craning his neck to double check the math.

"SEVENTY!" Rob called out happily. "We have seventy!"

A wave of excitement spread from the bus, spilling out to the small group still standing near the door in the snow and wind.

"Seventy! That's good, isn't it?" Scott asked, looking up at me from his seat.

"Seventy's a great total," I announced for all to hear as Rob snuck from the bus and dashed off into the storm with our manila scoring envelope firmly in hand. To here

"Seventy could win it," I explained to my eagerly listening audience. "But remember, three years ago we scored 60 and lost by a point and last year we had 91 and came up a point short, too. It's going to be another close one, but no matter what happens, I want you to know how proud I am of what we did today, the race our guys just ran, and of everything we've done this season. Everyone on this bus contributed something that helped get us to this point. So, no matter how things turn out, keep your chin up. I'm proud of all of you. Things like this don't happen every day so appreciate it, soak it in…enjoy it," I reminded them with a smile and a nod as I reached out to pat the top of Mike's wet head.

Condensation droplets formed and trickled down the foggy bus windows as more and more people pushed their way up the steps and down the center aisle. Our once loud, excited group now spoke in hushed tones as we began our wait.

"This is killin' me, Coach. How long is this gonna take?" asked Scott.

"It's hard to say. Most years it takes 10 or 15 minutes, but when it's close like this they have to check and double check. It could take an hour. Last year it took almost two hours to find out we'd finished second."

"Two hours, Coach! How could it take two hours?"

"I don't know, Scott. They said it was a power surge, a computer problem, or something. Personally, I think the monkey hit the wrong key."

"A monkey? They let monkeys score the meet?"

"No, Scott, I was joking. But sometimes it seems like it."

While some waited impatiently, tormented by the delay, I made a conscious decision to enjoy the anticipation and soak up the excitement of our most unusual situation. As in the Schrödinger's cat paradox, the feline can be thought of as both alive and dead at the same time, until the box is opened. For a while, at least, as long as the box remained closed we were the state champions, and personally I was in no big hurry to learn of the cat's condition.

Working my way back to the front of the bus, I smiled happily while distributing handshakes and compliments. Time seemed to stand still as we waited, and then, through the cloudy bus windshield, I caught a glimpse of Rob at the far end of the snow covered parking lot. Like Phidipides striding across the plains of Marathon, he approached at a near full sprint to deliver the news. Nothing in his expression or posture gave me a clue, only his pace led me to believe that the cat was still alive. No one, I concluded, would run that fast to deliver bad news.

"Seventy-three!" he shouted from the bottom step. "They had seventy-three!"

Not quite as eloquent as "Rejoice, we conquer," but as in Athens 2,500 years earlier, it brought a wave of happiness, cries of joy, and a euphoric celebration as we comprehended the news.

Teenage boys leapt from their seats screaming at the top of their lungs, almost too excited to know what to do next. They exchanged high fives and pounded one another on the head, shoulders, and backs. Bodies flew about as the bus exploded in a mix of emotions. Proud parents hugged their sons, pulled cameras from damp coat pockets, and attempted to capture the moment. Amidst the confusion, I searched for Scott as I pressed through the crowd, shaking hands along the way. There he was, proudly standing atop a bus seat for all to see, like "The Hulk" on a turn-buckle. With arms stretched to full length, he accepted high-fives from all directions as our collection of wet, happy runners restarted the chant, "An-ah-mal, An-ah-mal, An-ah-mal."

While others shared the moment with parents and siblings Scott found himself surrounded by teammates, coaches, alumni, and fans. Stepping forward to fill in for his missing family, we offered our congratulations and helped him celebrate our team's victory. In a remarkable chain of events, Scott had risen from the obscurity of our J.V. team to our varsity before emerging as the number four runner on our state championship team. The group home kid with his collection of emotional, behavioral, physical, and learning disabilities had reached the highest level of achievement for high school athletes. Like every other runner allowed to ascend the awards podium today, Scott had earned his award fairly, through hard work, dedication, and effort, incredible effort. No one had stepped aside for him.

Surrounded by those who not long ago sought to avoid him and a coach who thought he might prove to be a distraction, Scott stood beaming triumphantly. For this one brief, shining moment he stood over us like a king surveying his loyal subjects. Forcing us to confront our prejudices, Scott had shamed us into giving him a chance. As it turned out that's all he needed. We'd done him no great favor and made no great sacrifice. We'd simply been nice to a less fortunate person with no motive other than that it was the right thing to do. Today, because of that small act of kindness, we'd been rewarded with a state title and a lesson none of us would soon forget. Whether Scott realized it or not, he had led us to this great moment and in the process he'd made us all better, more understanding people.

"Off the bus," I ordered happily. "We need a team picture. Out in the snow, one last team picture. Hustle up, let's go!"

As J.V. guys bolted excitedly for the door, cold, tired varsity runners worked to jam their still numb feet into heavy wet shoes one more time. Dressed in a variety of outfits, we ventured out into the heaviest snow of the day to secure photographic evidence of the conditions we'd just faced. Wearing his beloved well-worn letter jacket and the brand new gray corduroy pants he'd pulled on over wet running shorts, Scott anchored the center of our formation. With his long arms draped across the shoulders of C.J. and Johnny, his huge, bright, smile cut through the gray snowy gloom as a small collection of photographers struggled to keep the snow from their lenses while lining up their shots.

Some, still cold and tired from the race, struggled to produce a smile during our brief photo session, but Scott, oblivious to the foul conditions around us, enjoyed every second of our snow covered celebration. Like a small child on Christmas morning, he could barely contain his joy on this, perhaps the best day of his life.

"Alright, let's load up! We have a trophy to collect!" I shouted with a laugh. "And, I don't know why, but for some reason we're the last bus in the lot...AGAIN! So let's hustle."

With tires spinning to gain traction in the now mostly vacant parking lot, we pushed our wet gear to the bus floor and wedged ourselves into the seats.

"Hey guys," I asked loudly while firmly pounding Rath's right shoulder, "how about our driver?"

"YEAH!" they called out appreciatively, followed by a rowdy round of applause and a sincere but fairly off key attempt at "Three cheers for the bus driver!"

The guys knew, as all good teammates do, that credit is not something to be hoarded. It needs to be shared and evenly distributed among all who played a part in the win, no matter how large or small. They knew that without our determined driver and a charter bus, compliments of Mr. Anderson, this day may have turned out differently.

TWENTY

BUS RIDE

Filled with the voices of excited young men, our bus negotiated a left turn onto the highway and headed slowly toward Madison La Follette High School. Each of us having seen the race from a slightly different perspective, we talked simultaneously as we anxiously reported our version of the great victory. Like witnesses at a crime scene, we were anxious to give our testimony as the group worked to recreate the race in infinite detail. Heavy, wet shoes were thrown to the floor, socks were peeled away, and cold hands wrapped tightly around icy blue feet. Few things held greater value at this moment than a dry pair of socks, if you were lucky enough to have them.

Paying no attention to the condition of my own feet, I worked my way to the back of the bus with our only copy of the result sheet firmly in hand. This was my chance to pass out compliments, to say something meaningful, memorable, and perhaps even profound as I patrolled the center aisle. Every guy on the bus had played a role in our victory, and it was up to me to point that out now with their bodies still tired from the effort, as the realization of what we'd accomplished began to sink in.

I knew from past experience this feeling of euphoria, along with the attention we were about to receive, would be short lived. An awards ceremony in a packed auditorium, a brief mention on the evening news, an article in our hometown paper, and a first hour P.A. announcement was about all we could expect. Perhaps a classmate or a teacher would offer congratulations at some point on Monday, but by Tuesday morning it would be over. The half-life for a story about a state cross country title is extremely short; in less than forty-eight hours we would be old news.

"Look at this!" I announced loudly, pointing to the result sheet from my spot in the middle of the bus. "Three points…THREE POINTS! You know how close that is?" I asked rhetorically. "If Ceplina doesn't kick past two Manitowoc guys, if Monk doesn't hang on to that second pack, if Johnny doesn't find the hugest kick I've ever seen, we don't win. If C.J. doesn't run completely out of his mind, we don't win. And what if The Animal doesn't spend the summer runnin' around his back yard for an hour a day, or what if we lose him in the Dewey Swamp, or worse yet, what if he quits because people were mean to him? None of this happens. If you guys aren't out there sprinting around, screaming Eye of the Tiger every fifty feet and chanting Animal's name along the home stretch, there's no way we win this meet. Everyone on this bus contributed something that helped us win today. Remember that—we built this team. Somehow we built a state championship team out of this! This odd collection of human beings," I said smiling as I waved my arm in front of me like a priest giving a blessing.

"Enjoy this! Have fun with it! Celebrate! Now let's go collect a trophy—a gold one," I finished as a loud cheer filled the bus. Aware that they would remember these few short hours for the rest of their lives I did my best to say something to each of them as I worked my way up the aisle. Shaking hands and slapping backs like a politician on the campaign trail, I never stopped talking. "Great job today. Couldn't have done it without you. Thanks guys, you guys were great out there," I said to the tangle of cold wet J.V. runners around me. There would be time to study the result sheet in greater detail later, but right now I couldn't resist unfolding it and scanning down the first column.

"C.J., how in the world did you end up 4th?" I asked with a

laugh as he smiled up at me like a third grader on a field trip. "How does a guy finish 21st at conference, 8th at sectionals, and 4th at the state meet?"

"What? You didn't think I could do it?" C.J. asked.

"C.J., nobody thought you could do that!"

"Hey, what can I say? I like running in snow."

Across the aisle sat John, still cold and uncomfortable as he watched me with piercing blue eyes as I ran my finger down the first column of the results. "Look at this, John," I said excitedly. "You were two seconds behind their second man and here, look, you outkicked their third and fourth runners."

"Yeah, I had to. I didn't want us to come up short like last year."

"Tenth," I said moving my finger up the page. "Next year, you're the tenth returner. Not bad for a sprinter," I joked, referring to his great range as a trackman.

"Thanks, Donn," he responded as we exchanged a handshake.

"No, thank you, John. What you did with the Animal today, that was something special. I've never seen anyone help a teammate like you did today. Look, he ended up 29th, a step behind their fourth man. That's just unbelievable."

From his seat in the row ahead of us Johnny listened intently, trying his best to get a look at the result sheet.

"Here Johnny, you were 47th overall and, let's see," I said, pausing to study the list.

"Here, only one freshman ahead of you. I know you wanted to be the top freshman, but look at the conditions. Today was perfect for big, slow footed, pure distance runners like C.J., guys who could grind their way through the slop. But you, what you did today with your puny little body, that was amazing. Forget your time, today was a survival test. I don't know where you found that kick, but here, look, you got back to within ten seconds of their fifth guy and that won it for us."

Finishing with a quick handshake, I jumped to my feet and threw myself into the seat next to Lee. Shivering beneath a pile of his teammates' sweats and jackets, he didn't look at all like a guy celebrating a big win.

"I'll be okay, Donn," he said with a quivering voice. "I'm just soooo cold!"

"Lee, you were incredible out there today. Two years ago you were one of the worst guys on the team and now…if you hadn't done a face plant in the last half mile you probably end up in the top fifty," I said, jabbing my finger at the result sheet to emphasize my point. "Every runner knows how hard it is to recover from a fall, especially late in a race. What you did out there today, well, most guys would have packed it in after that. I'm really proud of you," I said, hugging him around the shoulders with one arm as I patted the top of his still cold and wet head.

Mike sat quietly one row ahead, clearly the least excited of all our guys. Like most good runners, he could be very tough on himself. Finishing 8th was not at all what he was hoping for. In his mind, he had failed. Solemnly working to untie the triple knot in his race shoe, he refused to join the celebration.

"Mike," I said as I dropped into the seat next to him, "you were only seventeen seconds off the lead and four seconds from making the podium. And look at this, you were seven seconds ahead of their first and twenty-one seconds ahead of their second man. I know you're disappointed, but look," I said, flipping to the back page and pointing at the team scores. "This is what matters. We had seventy, they had seventy-three. Remember after the Manitowoc meet? You said we could do this, and we did. We did it because of you, because you're just too stubborn and ornery to give up. You led us to this moment, and now let me give you some advice. This is not a time to pout about a bad race. If you need a little time to beat yourself up, that's okay, but remember, things like this don't happen every day. It would be a shame to miss it. So, be as quiet as you want right now, but if I see a scowl on your face when we get to the high school, I'll have to kick your butt," I said with a smile as I held up my fist playfully at eye level.

"Yeah, I got it," he said laughing a little while pulling the wet, blaze orange stocking cap from his head and stuffing it into the travel bag on his lap.

Realizing that time was running short, I shook Mike's hand and turned to look for Scott as the bus slowed to exit the highway. Standing squarely in the aisle a few feet from me, Scott had the happy look of a guy who'd won the Super Bowl, the World Series, and cured cancer all on the same day. He wore the kind of smile I'd seen so often in history books. Grinning like a sailor in Times Square on VE Day, there was no doubt that Scott was enjoying the moment as he held court, surrounded by a band of excited J.V. runners. Other conversations would have to wait; right now I needed to talk to Scott and with his attention deficit and hyperactivity in full bloom, it wasn't going to be easy. Whether it was the excitement of the moment, the fact that he'd hugged Suzy, or some malfunction with his "pizza box" pill schedule, I had no way of knowing. Somehow in the commotion and excitement of the day, I'd never thought to ask if he'd taken his meds.

With a hand on Scott's arm, I pulled him in the direction of an empty seat, sat him down, and asked for his full attention. If I was going to hand him a state championship trophy, I had to be absolutely certain he would behave appropriately. Worried that a lifetime of watching professional wrestling might influence his behavior in an auditorium full of people, I needed to make a point.

"Scott," I said sternly while lowering myself into the seat across the aisle, "did you remember to take your meds this morning?"

"Yeah Coach, I remembered."

"Good. Now, we're going over to the school to shower and clean up. Then we go to the auditorium for awards. They hand out the girls awards first and then the boys, small schools, medium schools, and then us, so you have to be patient, okay?"

"Yeah Coach, got it."

"And remember, when they call us up on stage, when they put the gold medal around your neck, shake the man's hand, look him in the eyes, and remember to say thank you. It's very important, so don't forget."

"Yeah Coach, say thank you. Got it, Coach!"

"And when they give me the big gold trophy, as soon as I finish shaking the man's hand, I'll bring it to you. You'll be the first to hold it. Just remember, you are NOT The Hulk, you are NOT The Animal, you're Scott Longley and how you behave reflects on all of us, so I need you to be on your best behavior. We ran really, really well today, but so did the Manitowoc guys, and we need to show them the respect they deserve. Remember what we talked about after the Panther Invitational?"

"Come on, Coach," he said with laugh. "Are you ever going to let me forget that? I was just a dumb kid back then. I know what to do now. I've changed."

"I know, Scott, I was just kidding. I know I can trust you. That's why you're in charge of the trophy. No one else gets to hold it until we get it back to the bus. It's your trophy because without you there's no way we go home with the gold one. So have fun. Just remember, be a good sport."

Scott had changed in so many ways, changes that were easy to see and yet impossible to measure. No longer the odd, hyper, misfit who'd danced shirtless with a trophy atop his head just a few months earlier, he was now a fun, social, confident, and, as Rob had put it, "almost normal" kid. Our sport had been good for him, our team had been good for him, and he, as it turned out, had been good for us.

With the high school just a few blocks away, there were still so many things I wanted to say to Scott. I needed to tell him how much I'd enjoyed coaching him and how important he'd been to our team. Like a father preparing to send his son off to college, I had words of advice and precious little time before "they" came to take him away. Soon we'd be forced to watch him pack up his

belongings and drive away to his new "home" and new "family."
Until this moment the reality of Scott's situation had not really
sunk in. Preoccupied with the other events of the day, I'd refused
to think about it, hoping in some strange way to prevent the
inevitable. However, like holding back a sunset, it was impossible
to stop. Terms like "relocation" and "internment" came to mind
as I imagined Scott being taken from us in a big, shiny
government owned van headed for some place in Oconomowoc.
Taking a kid from a good situation and moving him halfway
across the state could only make sense in the bureaucracy of the
child welfare system, I thought as I bent to scoop Scott's wet
jersey from the floor.

"Here Scott," I said as I handed it to him. "I want you to keep
this."

"REALLY?" He shouted launching himself into the air as a
smile lit his face. "Really, Coach, I get to keep it? I can't believe
you're letting me keep it. I'll take good care of it, Coach. I
promise I won't lose it Coach... promise. OH MAN, this is the
best day EVER!"

"Here and you better take this, too," I said, bundling his soggy
black and white sweat suit along with his school issued hooded
sweatshirt and stuffing them into his blue travel bag. "I want the
people in Oconomowoc to know where you came from."

"And what about this?" he asked, pulling his letter jacket open.
"Do I get to keep my lucky t-shirt?"

"Yeah, keep that too," I said, pausing as I pointed to the
number 70 printed on the winged foot in the center of the shirt.

"Hey! Look at that Coach...70. That's how many points we
had today. HA! I told you it was a lucky shirt."

"Scott," I said with a hand planted on the top of his head, "I
don't think it was the shirt. I think our luck came from the guy
wearing it."

"Thanks Coach! Here," he said, holding his right palm in front
of my face for a high-five. "Number four thousand, eight
hundred and sixty-seven."

The equipment I'd just given Scott didn't belong to me. It was school property and I wasn't supposed to give it away. I knew the rule, but I broke it simply because I realized how much these few items of clothing meant to him. For Scott, the black and red jersey was more than just a uniform, it was a costume, and when he pulled it on he became a different person. For a short time each Saturday morning, he could put his troubled life aside and become "The Animal." Combined with a royal blue facemask today, he was a superhero, our hero. With the power to endure hardship, laugh at pain, and run to exhaustion, Scott had rescued us from another loss to the team from Manitowoc and led us to our fourth state title in six years.

"Scott, if I don't get the chance to say it later, I just want to say thank you for everything you did for us. What you did this season," I said, pausing for a moment, "well, I've never seen anything like it. This whole story, this season, this ending—it's the kind of thing that only happens in movies."

"Yeah Coach, maybe they should make a movie about us. And you know who they should get to play me?" he asked.

"Oh, let me guess, Hulk Hogan?" I said playing along.

"You got that right, Coach!" Scott said, smiling as he raised both arms to flex his biceps. "HULKAMANIA!"

As the bus ground to a halt at the edge of the parking lot, I yelled a reminder, "We've got 20 minutes to shower, dress, and get to the auditorium, so hustle up. Let's go!"

A flurry of activity ensued as guys scrambled to gather their travel bags and began pushing and shoving one another toward the bus door.

"Come on guys, time to collect another trophy!" Mike shouted happily while flashing a huge smile in my direction. "LET'S MOVE!"

Watching suspiciously as I took the jersey from his hand and began removing the safety pins from his race number, Scott asked, "Whatcha doin' Coach?"

"Here, keep your number. Write your time and place on it and maybe you can hang it in your room in Oconomowoc," I said as I strung the pins together and attached them to the front of my maroon North Central College hooded sweatshirt.

"Why'd ya do that?" Scott asked.

"Well, now every time I wear this sweatshirt I'll look at these pins and I'll think of you."

"Really, Coach, you mean you might forget me?"

"No, Scott. NO! I will never, ever, forget you. I don't think anyone on this bus will EVER forget you!" I assured him.

"HA! Thanks Coach," he said with a smile as he jammed the wet jersey into his travel bag and sprang to his feet. "Come on, let's go."

With snow still falling lightly, we climbed from the bus and crossed the freshly plowed parking lot behind the school. Walking at Scott's side with an arm thrown over his shoulder, I had time for a few final words.

"Scott, you know, if not for you none of this would have happened. There is no way we win without you. Remember that and no matter what happens in the future, remember what happened this year. Today was not just some big happy accident. We set our goals, we worked hard, we worked together, and that's why we won. You know, all these things we do to help us become better runners, well, they help make us be better people, too," I said in a serious tone as I stopped him a few feet from the building. "I'm proud of you, young man. Proud of how hard you worked, proud of everything you did for this team. Today you were unbelievable, you were, well, an Animal out there."

"Thanks, Coach! And Coach, do I get to take the trophy to the office on Monday?"

"No, Scott. I'll have to do that this time."

"Oh! Oh yeah, I almost forgot. I'll be in Oconomowakee," he said as his usually loud, gruff voice trailed away softly. "Coach, can you do me a favor? When you see Mr. Anderson, can ya tell him thanks for takin' such good care of me? I really liked livin' there. Oh! And thank him for all my new clothes, too. That was really nice of him."

"Sure, Scott, I'll tell him."

"Thanks, Coach. Now…one question," he said with a mischievous look in his eye as a smile returned to his face. "What about those white tuxedos?"

And with that, he turned to bounce through a set of maroon doors and head off to join his excited teammates.

TWENTY ONE

GOODBYE

Wet towels littered the floor of the nearly empty La Follette High School locker room, as rows of showerheads filled the room with the haze of warm, steamy air. The smell of soap, deodorant, and body odor combined to create the unique, unmistakable smell of a locker room, a guy's locker room.

"Grab a towel, guys," I shouted, pointing to a small stack on the table near the door. "You have exactly ten minutes to shower, change, and get out in the hallway," I ordered, holding my watch at eye level while pressing start. "Get moving!"

In a flurry of activity they dropped their gear on the long narrow locker room benches and set about the assigned task. There was no time for a long, hot, relaxing soak. Now on the clock, they would attempt to break the four minute shower.

"Hustle up, guys," Mike demanded. "We're gonna look really stupid if we walk in late."

A powerful sense of happiness and excitement surrounded them as they rushed to get ready. Filled with the realization that an auditorium full of people and a gold trophy awaited them, they showered in record time and dressed at a speed known only to firefighters and young men in a hurry. Fresh socks were pulled onto still wet feet, legs were thrust violently into pants, and arms flailed about as shirts and sweaters were added to complete their outfits. The annoying roar of wall mounted hand dryers ricocheted about the tile walled room as some sought to dry their hair with the short time remaining.

"Where's Scott?" I asked, looking in Rob's direction while jamming the last of my wet running gear into my travel bag.

"Down there," Rob said, pointing to the far end of the locker room where Scott sat alone on a bench, lacing up a pair of brand new brown leather shoes.

"Animal!" Rob shouted to gain his attention. "Did you take a shower?"

"No, I didn't Rob. I showered yesterday."

"Well then, at least comb your hair, okay?"

"Already did Rob, look," he said, pulling a comb from his shirt pocket and holding it proudly in the air.

"Good work, Scott. Hey, I like the shirt!" I added in reference to his crisp blue plaid long sleeve.

"You're not wearing wet socks, are you?" Rob demanded like a mother questioning a small child, walking in Scott's direction.

"No, here look," he said, pulling up the leg of his new corduroy pants and proudly showing the red and black stripes of a fresh, clean pair of over the calf tube socks.

"Alright guys, let's go, let's go, let's go, time's up!" I barked to prod them along. "Pack up, check the floor, time to move."

Standing at the doorway like a general inspecting the troops I offered handshakes, pats on the back, and compliments as they filed past.

"Looks good, guys!" "Lookin' sharp." "Like the tie, Mike." "Nice sweater, Lee." "Hey guys, one last thing. Remember to check your fly," I added, knowing that in the rush to get ready this important detail might have been overlooked. "Rob, have the guys wait in the hall. I have to check the floor one last time."

Turning into the now quiet locker room as the door shut slowly behind me, I scanned the area for lost items, confident I'd find something. A single, lonely, wet sock sat on a bench, a pair of team issued black running shorts lay on the floor partially covered by a wet towel, and at the far end of the row of lockers, lying in plain sight, was a blue stocking cap. I knew instantly it was the one I'd borrowed from the window people, the one Scott had worn—the mask of our super hero. Scooping it up as I hurried past, I rescued it, along with the black shorts, from the janitor's mop. The dirty sock would have to fend for itself.

Pausing at the door I stuffed the two soggy items into my bag as the events of a very busy day swirled in my mind. Our great season was about to come to an abrupt end and soon our team would be torn apart by some cruel, heartless people from Oconomowoc. Gripped by a wave of profound sadness, I froze with my hand on the locker room door. Enjoy the moment, I reminded myself. There will never be another one quite like it.

"Alright guys," I shouted happily as I stepped into the hallway. "Let's move, let's go get that trophy! Hey, is anyone else hungry?"

Chattering excitedly as we made our way down the hall, food became the center of the conversation. Talking as if they hadn't eaten in days, they dreamed of steak, endless quantities of soft serve ice cream, and soda, something many of them had given up for the last few months.

"No cheap hamburgers today, Animal. Today we get real food," Mike explained.

"Spaghetti?" Scott asked.

"No, Animal, not spaghetti. Today we get steak, and I'm gonna order two, maybe three!" announced C.J., the most notorious eater on the team as we turned a corner and entered the auditorium.

"Okay guys, drop your bags over here," I ordered, pointing to the back corner of the very crowded room. Hundreds of wet, hungry people from all across the state waited as meet officials prepared to start the presentation. People who'd braved the elements to spend the morning in a blizzard, ankle deep in slush, were now anxious to see their sons and daughters receive their awards.

Escorted to the front of the auditorium, we filed into our

designated row, right next to the runners from Manitowoc. Somber looks were cast our way as we took our seats in the place reserved for the Class A Team Champions. I knew for the top ranked team in the state going home with a silver trophy would seem a bitter disappointment. Watching as we filed happily into our seats, they were left to study a crumpled copy of the result sheet and wonder. Hundreds of little, seemingly insignificant things had factored into the final outcome. Today things had gone our way. Hard work, willpower, and effort had earned us the victory, but luck had played an undeniable part. Of the sixteen teams that stepped to the line today, only two had run well. Two good teams had fought with every ounce of their strength in incredibly difficult conditions, and only one was allowed to carry home a gold trophy. I knew how they felt as I looked down the row and studied the faces of the Manitowoc runners. In a meet as close as this one, the results could easily have been reversed.

With Scott at my side, we rose to stand at attention and face the flag on the stage as the P.A. system blared our National Anthem. Happily and without a hint of self-consciousness, Scott sang along loudly with the same raspy, Springsteen-like voice we'd heard so often on our bus rides. Like a man proud to have been "Born in the U.S.A.," he sang the song as it ought to be sung, with his back straight, his chin up, and a hand placed firmly over his heart.

As we sank back into our seats the excitement of the moment was somewhat overshadowed by a strong sense of impatience as we waited for the program to begin. People wanted to see their runners rewarded, head to their warm cars, and find something to eat. With many in the room facing lengthy journeys and poor road conditions, there seemed to be no reason to make an already long day any longer. No one would dare to deliver a long winded speech under these conditions, I thought, as the first of several meet officials dressed in suits stepped to the microphone.

"How about that weather?" asked the first of a procession of speakers determined to lecture us about everything from meteorology to the sorry state of their frozen toes. They spoke in glowing terms of the greatness of our sport, the fine qualities of the athletes, coaches, and fans in attendance and the value of athletics as we strive to build character in the young people who will one day run our country. All were valid and important points, but for most of us sitting politely in the crowded, stuffy auditorium, they were words we didn't want or need to hear at the moment.

For reasons I couldn't quite comprehend, Rob and Scott sat completely still, almost spellbound as they focused attentively on every word uttered by each of the speakers. Impatiently twisting in my seat, I scanned the room and located my father and brother standing with their backs against the far wall of the auditorium. They were the reason I was here. Having pushed, prodded, and dragged me into the sport as a high school sophomore, they were the reason I'd become a runner. Through good races and bad, win or lose, they'd always been there for me. So with a smile and a nod in their direction, I acknowledged their contribution to my success and the success of my team as the first award winners were called to the stage.

Proudly watching as a parade of fit, healthy young people marched across the stage to politely accept their awards, I studied their smiling faces. Surrounded by appreciative families, fans, and coaches, dedicated and hardworking young runners climbed the stairs and stood in the spotlight for a few moments.

Called up in order, girls teams then boys, small schools first, followed by medium and then large schools, the top six individuals and top two teams in each division moved forward to receive their medals. Each had a different name, a different home town, and yet to me, they seemed so much the same, these proud, neatly dressed kids from Wisconsin. This could be any place, it occurred to me, any state. At this time of year, events just like this were taking place all across our great country. Proud to be a part of such a great occasion, I clapped loudly to show my appreciation for the award winners, knowing better than most how hard they'd worked to reach this point.

Quickly we jumped to our feet to chant "Suzy! Suzy! Suzy!" as the Class A girls stepped onto the stage. A standing room only crowd voiced its approval with a thunderous ovation. Some yelled "Badgers! Badgers! Badgers!" in hopes of influencing her college choice. Many in the crowd had come just to see her, the greatest runner in the history of our state, maybe the best in the nation. To them she was a celebrity; to us, she was just Suzy, the tiny kid we called "Bug," the one nobody could run away from, and no one could out kick. With a gold medal draped around her neck, she waved to her admirers amid hundreds of camera flashes, looking more like a Miss America contestant than a champion athlete. Shouting at the top of his lungs, Scott did his best to be heard above the din of the crowd. Among her biggest fans, I doubt he fully understood or even cared how good she was. In a school where most people ignored him and some were mean to him, Suzy said hello and called him by name. She'd always been nice to him, and that was all he needed to know.

Cheers faded and cameras were tucked away as Suzy stepped down from the stage and the Class C boys were called up.

"Pay attention, Mike," I said leaning over to tap him on the shoulder. "I need you to lead us up there."

"Yeah, got it, Donn," he said confidently while fighting back a laugh. "Hey, look at the Animal."

Motionless amid the growing anticipation, Scott's eyes were locked wide open as he carefully studied the activity in front of him. Bright stage lighting bounced from the shiny gold and silver runners attached to walnut trophies shaped like Wisconsin. Medals fixed to red, white, and blue ribbons were arranged neatly on the table in front of them. Soon it would be our turn to receive these symbols of accomplishment on the brightly lit stage and like a child on Christmas morning, Scott could hardly wait.

Scott's love of awards was well known to all of us by this point. For him medals and trophies, like religious relics, held an exaggerated value. He alone was allowed to collect our trophies, to cradle them like newborn babies safe in his arms on the bus ride home, and to proudly deliver them to the school office on Monday morning. His more experienced teammates understood that the best awards come in the form of handshakes, high-fives, and the feeling of satisfaction you get after a well-run race. They knew that medals and ribbons eventually find their way to the bottom of some forgotten drawer, but the pride of accomplishment is something that never really leaves you. Scott hadn't been around long enough to know this. To him awards were not symbolic at all; they were valued possessions. For a person who could fit all his worldly belongings into a couple of cardboard boxes and a duffel bag, almost any new object was a treasure. Medals were not something to be shoved quickly into a jacket pocket or casually tossed to the bottom of a travel bag. They needed to be worn proudly around your neck or pinned to your letter jacket, even if you hadn't yet been given a varsity letter. Now, moments away from adding the rarest medal of all to his collection, Scott sprang from his seat as our group was invited to approach the stage.

"Easy, Scott," I said as he pushed excitedly past me in the aisle. "Let Mike lead."

"Got it, Coach, but I get to hold the trophy, right?"

"Yes, Scott! As soon as they give it to me, just remember…"

"Yeah, I got it Coach, don't worry, I got it."

With a look of pure joy on his face, Scott bounced anxiously on the balls of his feet with his hands planted firmly on Mike's shoulders. Happy and excited, we stood at the base of the stage steps and watched as C.J. was awarded an individual medal for his surprising finish.

Ready to accept our fourth gold trophy in six years, this was a proud moment for our program and, of course, for me. Part of a state championship team fifteen years earlier, I knew very well that my guys would remember this moment for the rest of their lives. Proudly wedged among this collection of happy, wonderful young men, I could only hope that I had done for them, in some small measure, what my high school coach had done for me. I was a runner because of my father and brother, but I was a coach because of a little man in a white shirt with a black bowtie, thick glasses, and a comb over. His name was Leo Potochnik, and at Milwaukee Marshall High School he'd done what all good coaches do for their athletes—he inspired me. He saw something in me that I couldn't see for myself. He believed in me, he pushed me to set goals, to work hard, and to succeed. Coach Leo expected a lot of his runners. "Silver or Black," he used to tell us, in reference to the colors of factory workers' lunch boxes, should not be the biggest decision of our lives. He expected us to be good runners, but he also expected us to make something of ourselves and to do something with our lives. Pausing to reflect, I knew I could never repay this giant of a man who stood all of five-foot-five. I could only follow his example and pay it forward. Part of the Marshall Striders tradition was alive and well at Stevens Point Area Senior High and I knew, as I stood watching the second place team accept their awards, that Coach Potochnik would be proud.

Unable to contain his excitement any longer, Scott pushed his way ahead of Mike and shot up the stairs as our school name was announced. With a look of pure happiness, he rushed the surprised presenters at the awards table while the crowd cheered our victory.

"An-a-mal, An-a-mal, An-a-mal," his J.V. teammates chanted in unison as he bent forward to have a gold medal adorned with a red, white, and blue ribbon placed over his head.

"Wow," he said while shaking the presenter's hand as if pumping water from a well. "THANKS! Thank you very much!"

His smile lit the auditorium as he stood alone for a moment in the spotlight, staring down at the gold medal in his hand. This was the reaction we'd come to expect, pure and innocent, filled with child-like joy. Reaching out he offered an enthusiastic handshake as C.J. joined him at center stage.

"Congratulations C.J." he announced loudly before reaching

out for Lee who was next in line. "Great race, Hacker, way to go Johnny, we did it John, we really did it," he said while greeting each with a highly animated handshake or high-five. Steady applause continued for Mike, Bill, and Dan as they politely accepted their medals before taking a spot in line alongside their teammates. Shoulder to shoulder for one last time they stood tall and proud, smiling the type of smile reserved only for moments like this. Not the smile you try to fake for school pictures and driver's license photos, but rather the easy, natural smiles that stay in place for minutes at a time, smiles so strong they infect the people around you. Studying their happy faces from the right side of the stage, I did my best to preserve the image in my mind as I walked forward to accept our team award. Presenters offered handshakes and congratulations as they passed the last of the trophies from the awards table to my waiting arms.

Then, like a running back taking a handoff, I placed the trophy on my left hip and offered handshakes to anyone within reach as I made my way towards the prearranged meeting with Scott. Teammates stepped back to clear a path and watch as Scott rushed forward to take the trophy from my hands to a position of honor high above his head.

"An-a-mal, An-a-mal, An-a-mal!" our fans chanted proudly as Scott rotated the trophy, like The Hulk showing off a gold championship belt. C.J., Mike, John, Johnny, Lee, Bill, and Dan filled in around him as the crowd gave a loud, sustained, round of applause. "Eye of the Tiger Animal, Eye...of...the...Tiger!" someone called out as Scott lowered the trophy to exhale on the golden runner before pretending to shine it with the sleeve of his crisp new shirt. Somehow the crowd knew that they were a part of something special as Scott inched closer and closer to the edge of the stage. Bouncing like Rocky Balboa on the top step of the Philadelphia Museum of Art, he urged the crowd on, prolonging the ovation.

And so, as we stood smiling and applauding along with an auditorium full of people, I began to hope that somehow the shiny gold medal around his neck and this moment of great joy would, in small measure, balance out some of the less joyful moments in his life and the fact that he would soon be shipped off to his new "home." Thunderous applause grew to a crescendo, like the grand finale of a fireworks display, and then…slowly…sadly, faded away.

"Yeah An-a-mal!" someone shouted out one final time as he lowered the trophy to allow inspection by his teammates.

Amid the low pitched rumble as the crowd shuffled toward the exits, we worked our way toward the back of the auditorium to collect our gear and head for the bus.

"Let's go get some food!" I shouted at the group as we moved slowly down the long, rapidly emptying hallway. Pausing for a moment as families gathered to exchange hugs and take a few last photographs, we lingered. True to our long standing tradition, we would, once again, be the last team to leave. Among the guys the excitement of the awards ceremony had quickly shifted to the excitement of eating. Speaking loudly of consuming "mass quantities" and the repeal of their self-imposed prohibition on soda, they walked a few steps ahead of me as we exited the school.

"That must be it," I said to Rob, pointing to the vehicle parked next to our bus as we splashed through ankle deep slush in the dim, gloomy light of late afternoon.

"That?" Rob asked, "That's what they sent?"

"Yeah, I guess so," I answered, shaking my head as we approached the old Dodge station wagon and the two men standing next to it. This rusty, putrid green piece of junk was not at all what I had anticipated. "NO WAY!" I thought to myself as my parental instinct kicked in. "You're not putting my kid in that piece of crap!" Expecting a late model van with something cheerful printed on the side, I was shocked to see that the state of Wisconsin had sent the kind of sad old vehicle I imagined a child molester might drive. With Rob at my side, I worked to compose myself as I approached the two obviously unhappy young men standing beside the big boxy car.

"You must be the guys from Oconomowoc," I said with a hand extended in the direction of the counselors who'd been assigned to collect Scott.

"Yeah, we're here for Scott Longley," one of them said as Suzy and the guys lined up to board our warm comfortable bus.

"We were told you'd be done by 2:00," one of them stated harshly.

"Yeah well, sorry about that," I said with hands outstretched and my palms turned toward the still lightly falling snow. "The weather got us a little off schedule."

"Yeah, we noticed," he responded with a squinty nod. "Okay then, let's load up, we gotta get movin'."

"What? Wait, just wait a second," I said quickly as Rob, my father, and brother stepped in close. "Scott needs to eat. He hasn't eaten since breakfast. The school gave us meal money and we're gonna stop at the Ponderosa."

"No. We're late as it is. We'll hit a drive through on the way outta town. We need to get on the road."

"Well look, the restaurant's on the east side, it's on your way outta town."

"Yeah, I know, but we don't have time."

"Look, I'll buy you guys supper, the biggest steak on the menu, anything you want. Okay?"

"No! We were told to pick him up at 2:00 and it's already 4:00. We have to go."

"Hey! I don't know if you realize this, but we just won a state title and Scott was a big part of it. Don't you think he deserves to celebrate with his team? Can't you just help us out? Really, we'll be quick. It probably won't even take an hour."

"Sorry, we just can't do it. We're way off schedule as it is. We have to go!"

"Come on, guys!" Rob pleaded loudly. "It's only an hour and you get a free meal."

"Sorry, guys, we just can't do it."

"Really? One hour? You can't give the kid one lousy hour to

eat with his team?" added my brother Glenn as he turned away in disgust. "You selfish bastards!"

Suddenly, with negotiations at an end, the moment we'd dreaded was upon us.

"Okay Rob," I said, motioning towards the bus. "Go get Scott, and tell the guys to come out here, too."

Maybe on a bright sunny day it would have been easier or perhaps if we hadn't been so happy just minutes before this whole thing would have seemed less traumatic. Why had we agreed to this terrible arrangement, I wondered as Scott came bounding down the bus stairs, smiling happily.

"Scott, these are the guys from Oconomowoc," I said, reaching out to place a hand on his shoulder. "They need to take you, and they have to take you right now."

Scott's bright smile instantly evaporated. He knew this moment would come, but like all of us, he didn't expect it now. Shock and sadness covered his face as he looked to me for an explanation.

"We tried Scott, we really did. This isn't how it was supposed to happen, but things just ran late because of the weather," I said, pulling him towards me as I looked into his tearful eyes. "These guys will take good care of you," I said softly as I fought to control my emotions. "It'll be okay. Just remember, no matter what happens, remember this day. Remember when you work hard and follow the rules goods things happen, good things like this," I reminded him once again while pointing to the gold medal around his neck. "Don't ever forget that, okay Scott?"

"Animal, we couldn't have done it without you," John said, stepping forward to give Scott a hug.

"Yeah, Animal, thanks man," added Mike softly as the rest of the team formed a line to express their condolences as they might do at a funeral.

"See ya, Animal." "Great race, Animal." "Eye of the Tiger, man. Good luck in Oconomowoc," they said as they filed past.

"Here Animal," C.J. said with his hand held in the air. "One last high-five. What's the number?"

"Ha! Four thousand, nine hundred and seventeen," he answered with a partial smile. "I guess I'll have to start a new collection in Oconomowoc."

Sad and helpless, we stood watching as Scott's belongings were removed from the cargo compartment of our bus. Two cardboard boxes, one large duffel bag, and a white plastic K-Mart bag full of brand new socks and underwear fit easily into the back of the station wagon. Stepping away I turned, looked up at the drab gray sky and fought back tears as the line of guys, unable to watch their friend being abducted, climbed sadly aboard the bus.

"Got your meds?" I asked urgently while wiping my eyes.

"Ya Coach, right here," he said, pointing to the crumpled pizza box cover sitting on the back seat of the miserable car he was about to climb into.

"Hey, be good, young man. Make us proud, okay?" I said with a quick hug.

"Yeah," Rob said, grabbing him by the arm. "Behave yourself or I'll drive down there and set you straight. And you know I will!"

"Rob, you don't have to worry about me, I'll be okay," he said as he climbed into the back seat, pulled the doors shut, and after wiping the condensation from the inside of the window with the knit cuff of his beloved letter jacket, sadly waved goodbye.

Standing silently, we watched as the Dodge wagon lurched into gear. Sputtering, it belched out a puff of black soot and began to slowly roll forward before coming to an abrupt halt. Scott quickly rolled down the back window and looked our way.

"Hey, one question Coach. What about those white tuxedos?"

"Yeah, I looked into it. Turns out they don't make tuxes for animals."

"Ha! Good one, Coach. See ya!"

Turning quickly, I exchanged a somber goodbye with my father and brother before climbing aboard the bus filled with sad, angry young men. Not a single face was visible above the seat backs as teenage boys did their best to conceal the fact that they were crying.

"Rath," I said quietly to our bus driver as I slid carefully into the seat behind him, "we're gonna need a few minutes. Maybe we should take the long way to the restaurant."

"Sure, I'll just go check the cargo doors one more time," he said, his own tears welling.

Turning in my seat, I noticed Rob standing quietly in the aisle staring down at the gold trophy in the second row right where Scott had left it. There it was, the object we'd worked so hard to obtain, sitting by itself, alone, sad, and neglected. No one dared touch it, that was Scott's job, and with our teammate now gone the trophy was more a symbol of loss than of victory. Somehow, through a ridiculously complex series of events, our moment of euphoria had collided head on with a feeling of tremendous sadness. Angrily I grabbed my travel bag and pushed it to the bus floor, put my face in my hands, and struggled to make sense of the cruel events that had just taken place. Completely overcome by emotion, I thought of the stupid white tuxedos I knew we would never wear, the horrible car that had taken him away, and the silly blue hat he'd worn in the race. The hat with the attached face mask that he'd left on the locker room floor, the one I now held in both hands and pressed to my face in an effort to conceal the fact that I was crying, too.

"Ready, Coach?" Rath asked softly as he climbed back into the driver's seat.

"Yeah," I croaked hoarsely, without looking up.

A painful sadness hung over all of us as the bus inched forward and began to roll across the slush covered parking lot at the pace of a slow recovery jog. Once joyful and excited, we now sat stunned and crying, trying our best to regain our composure and reconcile the fact that Scott was really gone.

As a final tribute to our missing teammate I reached across the aisle and draped the soggy blue cap atop the golden runner attached to our latest trophy, the Animal's trophy. Now in the hands of his new keepers, he was gone, on his way to another group home, a new school, and perhaps a new team. Would they appreciate him the way we did, I wondered. Would they give him a chance? Would they take care of him? I had no way of knowing. I only knew that suddenly there was a gaping hole in our team, a void so big it couldn't be filled by a state title, a shiny trophy or even a steak dinner. Sitting in a silence broken only by the whine of the bus engine, we pondered the fact that we'd just won a meet and lost a friend. A friend none of us would ever forget.

"C.J.," I said, pointing to the boom box he held balanced on his lap. "A little music?"

"Got just the thing," he replied, nodding confidently as he pushed the play button without having to look down.

In an instant the silence was broken by clear, crisp music that filled the bus as we began to pick up speed. We listened sadly, spellbound by the lyrics as if truly hearing them for the very first time.

Rising up, back on the street
Did my time, took my chances
Went the distance, now I'm back on my feet
Just a man with a will to survive

So many times, it happens too fast
You trade your passion for glory
Don't lose your grip on the dreams of the past
You must fight just to keep them alive

It's the eye of the Tiger;
It's the thrill of the fight
Rising up to the challenge of our rival.
And the last known survivor
Stalks his prey in the night
And he's watching us all
With the Eye of the Tiger

EPILOGUE

Watching the grimy, old Dodge station wagon roll out of the LaFollette High School parking lot on that dreary November day so long ago I had no idea if I'd ever see Scott again. We all knew he was being dragged off to Oconomowoc but that was about it. A few months later Rob Sparhawk and Kim Lasecki managed to track him down, figured out where his new group home was located, and even paid him a visit.

In spring we crossed paths with him at a big track meet in Madison. I remember entering the stadium, walking along the back-side of the track, and hearing Scott's unmistakable loud, raspy, voice. "Coach Behnke!" he shouted, flashing his trademark toothy grin as he came bounding across the infield with the distinctive running style I would have recognized anywhere. Quickly his former teammates circled up to exchange greetings. It was odd to see him dressed in an Oconomowoc jersey and he seemed to be just a little bit bigger than the last time I'd seen him, but he looked good, clean-cut, well-kept, and happy. He had that kid on Christmas morning look that we all knew so very well and a smile that went on for hours and hours. Scott was in the slow heat of the mile that day and while I don't remember his place I do know he ran a very respectable 4:41. How I remember that, I can't tell you. There are just some things I can't seem to forget. As my brother likes to say, we distance runners are the idiot savants of the sports world.

Standing along the fence on the back straightaway our group dressed in red and black cheered wildly for the kid dressed in blue and gold as he ran along, wedged in among the tangle of bodies in the lead pack. "Come on Animal! You can do it Animal! Eye of the Tiger Animal!" we shouted as we'd done so many times before. I'm sure it looked odd to anyone who happened to be watching – our group going completely nuts for some seemingly random kid from another school running in the slow heat of the mile. But to us it was completely natural because we still considered Scott one of us. He'd been our teammate; he'd always be our teammate.

A few years after graduation Scott reunited with his brother and returned to Stevens Point for a visit. Equipped with a couple of paper grocery bags they arrived on my doorstep one summer day and announced that they were going to make lunch for Cheryl, Beth, and I. Naturally they chose to make spaghetti and as I remember it was actually pretty good. At the conclusion of the meal they jumped up from the table and proceeded to bus and wash dishes with an almost military-like precision as they shouted orders at one another. I'm not entirely sure what Cheryl was thinking as she sat quietly with four-year-old Beth on her lap, but I'm pretty sure I found the process more entertaining than she did. After a short visit they bolted for their car and headed off to the high school to admire our latest addition to the trophy case before traveling back to whatever city they happened to call home at that particular time.

I know Scott had hopes of returning to Stevens Point, finding a job, and getting a place to live but that never happened. He made a few return visits over the following weeks but eventually ended up living in Norfolk, Virginia with his sister, who I believe was in the Navy. Over the course of the next few years he called me on a pretty regular basis from the PX on the naval base. The calls were always collect and he was always anxious to hear news about his former team and teammates. He told me he was running with some of the guys from ODU (Old Dominion University), he worked for a landscaping outfit, and had earned a certificate signed by the governor because he'd helped clean up storm damage after a hurricane. He always sounded happy and up-beat with a kind of laugh in his voice as he spoke. He was especially anxious to tell me of his accomplishments at the Virginia Special Olympics where he seemed to be far and away the best of the best, especially in the mile.

One spring day in 2003 he called to announce excitedly, "Good news Coach....We're going to IRELAND!"

"Who's going to Ireland Scott?" I asked.

"You and me Coach, you and me," he answered, explaining he had earned a spot in the World Special Olympics.

I'm not quite sure what happened, but we never did make that trip to Ireland. Evidently the state of Virginia didn't have the funds to send all of their qualifiers and Scott hadn't made the cut. He sounded pretty disappointed when he called with the news a few weeks later, but he didn't seem to dwell on it. As always, he had a knack for letting bad news roll off his shoulders.

Over time the collect, person-to-person calls became less frequent and eventually Scott settled into a pattern of calling each November to see if we'd won another state title. At some point, I don't know when, he left Norfolk and moved to Texas. I remember talking with him about our state championship teams in 1994, '97, and '98, but sometime after that the calls stopped. I never really thought of calling him, I just assumed he would call me someday. Years passed, eleven, maybe twelve without a word from Scott. I thought of him often and worried about him from time to time. I hoped he was healthy, happy and not in any sort of trouble. Most of all I hoped he was in the company of good people who cared about him. If he had that, I knew he'd be alright.

As this book neared completion several friends, former runners, and family members volunteered to help find Scott, something which turned out to be a rather formidable task. Over the course of a year we located more than a few Scott Longleys before finally getting in touch with him.

"I'm speechless, Coach, SPEECHLESS!" Scott shouted

excitedly into the phone when I first called him. Nearly 30 years had passed but the sound of his voice, the tone, inflection, and definitely the volume was just as I remembered. During the course of our short conversation he told me he was doing well, he was healthy, and still "ran a little and walked a lot." He was proud to tell me that he had his own apartment, lived independently, and that he liked living in Texas which he described as "a lot different than Wisconsin." I was speaking to a man just short of his 48th birthday who sounded very much like the enthusiastic 18 year-old I'd known so well. It was good to hear the happy sound of his voice, to know that he was doing okay, and to have finally found our missing "Animal."

In July 2015 Rob Sparhawk and I made a trip to Texas to visit Scott. "Coach! You got so old!" he shouted with a laugh as he swung his apartment door open to greet us. "I think we all did Scott," I added while studying the slender, bearded man standing in front of me. Dressed in a tattered Green Bay Packer Super Bowl cap and a rather nice looking gray suit he'd picked up at a yard sale the day earlier, he'd done his best to clean himself up. "I wasn't expecting you guys so early," he said over and over as he scurried about wiping down tables in the living room of his modest, one bedroom apartment. He knew we were coming, but clearly we'd upset his routine as we stepped into the narrow confines of his world.

We spent two days together, presenting him with a plaque commemorating our state title, some newspaper clippings, and a small collection of grainy photos from long ago. We took him out to eat, bought him some fresh clothing, and of course, some new running shoes. Offers to do more were met with resistance as Scott reminded us that "I'm not greedy Coach, I'm not greedy." It was a short, but nice visit. We spent a lot of time talking about sports, his favorite teams, players, and a Cowboys v. Vikings game he'd gone to a couple of years earlier. He recognized names of his former teammates, remembered the snowy day of the state meet, and of course the big gold trophy that he'd once held aloft in joyous celebration. Other memories of our great season, however, seemed to be gradually slipping away. "That was so long ago," was a response he used more than once as we brought up the many events and stories we remembered so clearly. It appeared time had taken a toll on Scott.

A wave of sadness came over me as we left his apartment and headed towards our rental car, leaving our teammate behind, but fortunately not alone. During our short stay we'd met several kind and compassionate members of the local police force, some helpful, friendly staff in the apartment complex office, and a family next door that treated Scott like a good friend. It's good to know that there are people like them in our big, sometimes unfriendly world. They are, it seems, the newest "Animal Keepers."

Afterword

Donn Behnke retired from teaching in 2010 and continues to coach cross country at Stevens Point Area Senior High. Now in his 38th year his teams have earned state titles in 1980, 1981, 1983, 1985, 1994, 1997, 1998, 2003, 2008, and 2013 with runner-up finishes in 1982, 1984, 1990, 2001, 2006, 2007, and 2014. This record ties the program for the most state titles in the modern era of Wisconsin High School Cross Country. Donn has also coached 6 individual state champions. Two of them, Keith Hanson and Chris Solinsky, went on to become NCAA Division I national champions. Donn was named the National High School Coaches Association Coach of the Year in 2001.

Elizabeth Behnke, Donn's daughter born during the 1985 season, became a varsity track and cross country runner and valedictorian of her class at Stevens Point Area Senior High. She attended the University of Wisconsin Law School and currently lives and works in Madison, Wisconsin. Growing up listening to her father's many stories, Beth developed a particular fondness for the "Animal Story" and played an instrumental part in the writing, editing, and publishing of this book.

Mike Monk ran four seasons of track and cross country at the University of Wisconsin-Eau Claire where he earned numerous All-Conference designations, set a school record at 5,000 meters, and qualified for indoor and outdoor DIII nationals in the 5,000 and 1,500. He holds a master's degree in music education and now lives in Kenosha, Wisconsin where he is a middle school band director.

C.J. Hanson followed in his brother's footsteps and attended Marquette University where he ran one season of cross country before transferring to the University of Washington where he earned a degree in psychology. He currently lives in Yakama, Washington.

Curt Clausen became a world class race walker competing in the 1996, 2000, and 2004 Olympic Games and the 1997, 1999, 2001, and 2003 World Championships. As a high school senior he was the USA Junior national champion at 10k and went on to capture seven U.S. race walking titles at 50k and four titles at 20k. His career best finishes include earning a Bronze Medal in the 1999 World Championships for the 50k walk, and a 22nd place finish in the 50k at the 2000 Olympics. He earned a law degree from Duke University and currently lives in New York City serving as General Counsel at Tickets.com.

Rob Sparhawk attended the University of Wisconsin - Stevens Point before starting a 15 year career as a high school coach first at Stevens Point Pacelli where his teams earned four state cross country titles, and then at Amherst High School where he lead the boys track team to a state title. He currently lives in Hayward, Wisconsin where he owns a retail sunglasses business and works as an EMT for Sawyer County.

John Ceplina ran four years of cross country and track at the University of Wisconsin - Stevens Point where he earned a degree in computer science in addition to numerous All-Conference honors and Division III All-American status in the 4x400 meter relay in 1991. He currently lives in Stevens Point where he works as a software consultant and serves as an assistant track and cross country coach at his high school alma-mater. His son John is a member of the SPASH cross country team.

Johnny Hyland ran four years of track at the University of Wisconsin where he earned Division I All-American honors in the 4x800 meter relay in 1991. Graduating with a business degree, he currently works for Sentry Insurance in Stevens Point. His son, Johnny Hyland III, is now a member of the SPASH cross country team.

Lee Hacker attended the University of Wisconsin-Stevens Point. After graduation he moved to Las Vegas, Nevada where he began a career working with special needs students. He is currently employed by the Clark County School District.

Bill Kleckner attend the University of Wisconsin - Stevens Point and the University of Wisconsin - Eau Claire. He currently lives in Madison, Wisconsin where he works in construction management and still enjoys recreational running.

Kim Lasecki attended Marquette University where he ran three years of track and cross country before transferring to the University of Wisconsin - Stevens Point where he finished his running career by earning DIII All-American honors at 10,000 meters in 1990. Kim earned a Ph.D. from the University of Utah and now works as a clinical psychologist at Belin Hospital in Green Bay, Wisconsin. He is an assistant track and cross country coach at Green Bay Notre Dame Academy.

Dan Morgan attended Marquette University where he spent one season on the cross country team as a walk-on. After completing his undergraduate degree he attended law school in Chicago. He currently serves as the Chief Operating Officer of Sentinel Security Life Insurance, in Salt Lake City, Utah. Dan continues to be an avid runner, enjoys running with his children, and has run a number of marathons with a personal best of 3:05:00.

Michael Morgan earned a degree in Political Science from the University of Wisconsin - LaCrosse and currently works as a Senior Sales Representative for an insurance company in San Diego, California. He did not run in college but has completed 30 marathons, 2 ultra-marathons, and 9 Ironman triathlons, including the 2013 Ironman World Championships.

Leroy "Andy" Anderson was named the Wisconsin Athletic Director of the Year in 1986 and received the Wisconsin Athletic Directors Lifetime Memorial Award in 1987. He retired from Stevens Point Area Senior High in the spring of 1987 and passed away in May of 1993. Each year the Wisconsin Athletic Directors Association honors one of its members with the Leroy "Andy" Anderson award for outstanding service. Andy's son Eric, an active and enthusiastic participant in the Special Olympics, passed away in 2013.

Suzy Favor (Hamilton) ended her high school career as an 11 time Wisconsin state champion in cross country and track. She attended the University of Wisconsin where she won 9 NCAA Division I national titles and became a 14 time NCAA Division I All-American. As a professional runner Suzy won 4 Outdoor and 3 Indoor USATF national titles at 1,500 meters, set an American record at 1,000 meters, and went on to compete in the 1992, 1996, and 2000 Olympic Games.